# MOR_ .ING
# HAS BROKEN

With all good wishes

Rosemary Harward.

# MORNING
# HAS BROKEN

Written and illustrated by
## Rosemary Harward

*Morning Has Broken*
Rosemary Harward

Published by Aspect Design 2013
Malvern, Worcestershire, United Kingdom.

Designed, printed and bound by Aspect Design
89 Newtown Road, Malvern, Worcs. WR14 1PD
United Kingdom
Tel: 01684 561567
E-mail: allan@aspect-design.net
Website: www.aspect-design.net

Cover Design Copyright © 2013 Aspect Design
Original artwork copyright © 2013 Rosemary Harward
ISBN 978-1-908832-30-6

To Richard, without whom this would never have happened.
And, of course, Bryony, Matthew, Barnaby and Natasha.

When you can see daylight between their legs, you know that morning has come and the milking is nearly over.

A milker

# CONTENTS

# MAIN CHARACTERS

## The Lyndon Estate

Arable foreman . . . . . . . . . . . . . . . . . . . . . . . . . . . . . . . Harold
Builders . . . . . . . . . . . . . . . . . . . . . . Paul, Stuart, Stan, Walter
Calf rearers . . . . . . . . . . . . . . . . . . . . . . . . . Kevin, Malcolm
Dairyman at Owlnest . . . . . . . . . . . . . . . . . . . . . . . . . . . . Bob
" at Quincey's . . . . . . . . . . . . . . . . . . . . . . . . . David
" at Home Farm . . . . . . . . . . . . . . . . . . . . . . . Graham
Dairymen at Honeybed . . . . . . . . . . . . . . . . . . Greg, Rodney, Vic
Dairy foreman . . . . . . . . . . . . . . . . . . . . . . . . . . . . . . Philip
Farm manager . . . . . . . . . . . . . . . . . . . . . . . . . . . . John Peregrine
Foreman for young stock . . . . . . . . . . . . . . . . . . . . . . . . . . . Jim
Gamekeepers . . . . . . . . . . . . . . . . . . . . . . . . . . . Hugh, Tim
JCB driver . . . . . . . . . . . . . . . . . . . . . . . . . . . . . . . . . Alan
Office staff . . . . . . . . . . . . . . . . . . . . . . . . . . . . . Sarah, Simon
Tractor drivers . . . . . . . . . . . . . . . Bert, Colin, Fred, Geoff, Mick,
Norman, Ralph, Ron, Tom, Will


## Friends and Family

Children . . . . . . . . . . . . . . . . . . . Andrea (eighteen), Daniel (ten),
Elizabeth (nine), Roger (sixteen)
Cat . . . . . . . . . . . . . . . . . . . . . . . . . . . . . . . . . . . . . . Kilvert
Dogs . Brock (Labrador crossbreed), Jack Russell, Rufus (Red Setter)
Ex-husband . . . . . . . . . . . . . . . . . . . . . . . . . . . . . . . Edward
Friends. . . . . . . . . . . . . . . . . . . . Anne, Catherine, the Coventrys,
Julian and Clare, Linda and Tony,
Margaret and Christopher,
Ruth and Emma, Tom and Jenny
Sister . . . . . . . . . . . . . . . . . . . . . . . . . . . . . . . . . . . . Juliet
Student . . . . . . . . . . . . . . . . . . . . . . . . . . . . Susan (sixteen)

# SOME PLACE NAMES OF FARMS AND FIELDS
## MENTIONED IN THE BOOK

**Hazelwood Farm** was a mile outside the park boundary and did not have its own dairy, the nearest was at Home Farm.

**Home Farm** was situated within the Lyndon Park Estate, and included the following fields: Cathill One, Cathill Two, Deermead, Greenmoor, Golden Gate, Loxwell, and Pond Ground.

**Honeybed Farm** was four miles outside of the park boundary, and consisted of Park Field, Tower One and Wood Field.

**Owlnest** was the second farm within the boundary of the estate parkland, and was made up of these fields: Hanging Ground, Marquis Leaze, Merchant's Close, and Moat Ground.

**Quincey's** was also outside the park boundary, but was not far from Owlnest, it encompassed the fields called Eleven Acres, Lower Quincey's, Nine Acres, Poole's Night, and Twenty-Two Acres.

Other fields mentioned, such as Harvey's Ground, Shepherd's Ground, and Stump Ground, were outside of the dairy fields, but were located within the overall area of the estate.

# INTRODUCTION

*Advert in the Riverton Gazette of Thursday, 18 October 1979.*

RELIEF MILKER (MALE/FEMALE)

The Lyndon Estate has an interesting position available for a Relief Milker to cover the four herds on a large, progressive, mixed farm. A good salary is offered and excellent four-bedroomed farm house, vehicle and pension scheme.

Apply in writing to:
The Farm Manager,
Lyndon Estate Office,
Marford.

\* \* \*

Causeway House,
Riverton

Dear Sir,

I am extremely interested in the post advertised in today's *Riverton Gazette,* for a relief milker for four herds on the Lyndon Estate.

I have had four years part-time relief milking experience

with a hundred-and-twenty-cow herd in a herring bone parlour, after obtaining my Milking Proficiency certificate during my time at Riverton College of Agriculture. I took a day-release course in General Agriculture during 1974–1975 and the following year I took the Milk and Beef Production courses and passed the City and Guilds exams with credit.

I have also been running my own small-holding, have a cow, buy and sell calves at market, keep hens and rear pigs.

I have four children, the eldest of whom has just gone to university and the youngest is nine.

I am forty, very fit, capable, reliable and hard-working. Due to the fact that I am separated from my husband, and we are having to sell our property here, I am looking for a permanent, full-time job, and I very much hope to get a job in farming as, in spite of my original teachers' training, that is where my interests and enthusiasms lie.

I may say that I attended every session at the college and have never been unable to milk because of illness or any other reason, so I am genuinely keen.

Yours faithfully,
Alison Bryden

* * *

What I did not say was that my small-holding was two acres and my part-time job was one afternoon a week.

# 1979

# OCTOBER

I delivered my letter that afternoon. My parents, who were staying with us for a few days, came with me. We drove the back way, four miles through the quiet lanes to the Marford road. At the lodge by the great gates I asked the way to the office. We were directed past Home Farm to the house and beyond to the former laundry yard, now converted into offices.

'If it comes to nothing, it will have been worth the drive,' said my father, appreciating the landscaped gardens, the placid lake, and the neatly-clipped trees in the formal garden. A tranquil autumn sun shone on the picturesque cottages and the pale, mellow stone of the house.

Going into the office was a tall, lean man with a purposeful air. His red setter hung its handsome head out of the window of a white car in the yard.

The secretary paused at her typing, took my letter, and smiled.

Nothing happened for a week. Then I received a phone call from the farm manager who said he would like to come and see me.

I was picking nasturtiums for the kitchen table in the vegetable garden when the dogs barked and, when I came round the corner of the house, I saw the white car, the red dog, and its owner – the farm manager. Over a cup of coffee in the kitchen he told me what the job involved. I was inwardly dismayed. Not only would I have to do the relief milking for each dairy, but I would have to do the feeding of the cows and the scraping of the yards, which is done by a tractor with a hydraulic attachment, like a huge squeegee, on the back. I should have to return to the farm at night to observe cows bulling,[1] and this would mean going out four times a day. I would have to start milking at 5.00 am.

There were a hundred and fifty cows in each herd. My hours and pay would be exactly the same as the herdsman in charge of each dairy. I would be working two weekends out of three and have one day off a week, plus every third weekend. My holidays would be three working weeks (not twenty-one days) and no bank holidays. The imagined-idyllic farmhouse was actually on the main Riverton–Marford road, under the perpetual all-night glare of the yellow sodium street lamps.

I agreed to meet John Peregrine at the farmhouse at 10.00 am the next day.

I forgot to ask the salary.

I consulted my friends in a state of utter confusion, panic, and excitement. One thought the problems could be solved, another thought the work was too hard. I slept badly and woke at 5.00 am – milking time. I lay with thoughts of black despair, convinced that I could not do the job, and should not because of the younger children. I decided I would ring up in the morning and cancel the meeting. I would say, 'I'm sorry, but I don't think I can do it and I don't want to waste your time.' A pity, because I liked him, and the idea of working in a team of people strongly appealed to me.

With the grey dawn my convictions faded. And what were the alternatives? My future was a total blank, an emptiness so vast and meaningless to me that almost nothing mattered but a day-to-day survival. Desperately, I rang Margaret for advice: she did not reply. I rang Catherine for support: she was out. I rang my sister, Juliet. Her calm, soothing warmth filtered over the phone line:

'What harm can it do? You're not wasting his time. It's part of his

---

[1] Bulling is when cows mount other cows, it is one of the standard signs which farmers look out for as it shows that a cow is coming into estrus.

job. Don't worry about the children. My children hated the idea of moving here and now they wouldn't leave for anything. They're very adaptable.'

At 10.00 am I followed the white car into the yard of Hazelwood Farm, parked my car on the grass verge and went forward to meet Mr Peregrine and the man who was leaving, Owen.

Hazelwood Farm, our new home.

In the yellow-painted kitchen a mammoth log was burning in a fire-place set halfway up the wall. The house, unused except for two rooms, was large, light and well decorated. A strip of garden surrounded it on three sides, and yards, outbuildings and barns extended into the fields at the back.

Owen told me that he had found the job very worrying for the first months and that sometimes he had just wanted to sit down and cry. This appeared to be news to Mr Peregrine. Owen had been there three years and had not known how to milk when he started.

Mr Peregrine then took me on a tour of the four dairy farms with their milking parlours, yards, cows and herdsmen, who, with the exception of Bob, the oldest, gave me a quick, firm handshake, shot me a quick look in the eye, and avoided looking at me again. Bob had a longer look, tamped his pipe down and asked me how long my milking experience was and why I wanted the job.

I said feebly, 'I like cows.'

But Bob appeared to be satisfied and said, 'That's right, treat them kindly but firmly.'

The drive through the undulating countryside and the views to the Barrow Downs; the trees changing colour; the estate with its avenues of beeches and the parkland in which pheasants ran, or strutted, or flew in great profusion; these, in the sunshine, went to my head like wine. The milking parlours were immaculate, the yards were scraped bare and clean, and the cows were contented. I wanted the job.

We returned to Hazelwood Farm and sat in the car and discussed my salary – £4,500 – and my limitations (I would be unable to lift the one hundredweight sugar beet bags used on one of the farms) and the fact that I would need a great deal of help at first as I had never even scraped out a yard. Silence fell. At last I said, 'I'm not sure if you are offering me the job.'

'No, I'm not,' Mr Peregrine replied. 'I need to think it over because it *is* a risk.'

'I need to think it over too as there are problems I have to solve.'

He told me he was seeing another candidate and was then going away for a few days. And so we parted.

In the next days I visited the local schools, both primary and secondary, talked to my children, rang up friends for their opinions, and went to see an acquaintance whose husband works on the estate. I waited a week, in increasing agitation. At last, unable to concentrate on anything else, I rang the office and asked the secretary when I would be hearing about the job I had applied for, 'I'm going mad with suspense,' I said.

The farm manager rang soon after. He asked me questions about how I would cope with the children when they were ill, and what would happen if I could not do the job and was in a tied house.

Later, in the evening and after he had rung my referees, he rang again and told me I had the job: I had stepped off the precipice into the unknown. Would I fly, or would I crash to oblivion?

The children, aware of the decisions being made, had gone to the youth club for the evening. At 9.00 pm they burst in through the back door crying, 'Have you got it?'

On my grinning, 'Yes,' their faces beamed into smiles. Never have I been so grateful to them and their generosity to me.

# NOVEMBER

I was to start work on 3 December, but I was invited to attend the November dairy meeting, held monthly in the estate office. I set off from home far too early and had to sit for nearly half an hour on the top of Ivy Hill. The lights of Riverton twinkled on the plain below. There was no moon and the drive through the estate was black and quiet. I was the first to arrive.

We sat around the table: the farm manager; Philip (the dairy foreman); Bob, Graham, Greg and David (the dairymen); and myself. After introducing me, Mr Peregrine distributed Dairymaid ICI costing forms to each person. This mass of computerised figures began to gradually make sense to me. The men discussed these figures: why one of the dairies seemed to be using far more concentrates for the cows than the others, why the milk yield was dropping much more than forecast in one dairy, whether a newly-adopted system on two of the farms was working, and why the calves from one dairy were not thriving as they should be.

Leave at Christmas was worked out, and the day I should start work. I said I should like to work on Christmas day but did not explain that it was because the children would be with their father.

I was to spend a complete day with each herdsman, following their methods and learning as much as possible about each dairy, before I began milking by myself. Days off were on a strict rota, which seemed complicated, but could be worked out for the whole year ahead. My day off for the next three months would be a Monday. This meant that when I had a Saturday and Sunday off (every third week) I got a long weekend.

Mr Peregrine showed some slides of farms he had visited recently and of the new dairy unit at Quincey's on the estate when it was opened.

At the end of the meeting I handed in my letter of acceptance to the contract, and that was that. Hazelwood Farmhouse, as I sped past in a hopeful mood, looked lonely and deserted. I could hardly wait to move in and light it up.

# DECEMBER

*The first week*

Yesterday, I moved into Hazelwood Farm after one of the worst weeks of gloom, despair, lethargy and pessimism of my life: the inevitable aftermath of splitting up from a marriage and the making of a new life.

My friends Margaret and Anne helped to move the few pieces of furniture I needed. The children were staying at Causeway House with Edward until after Christmas and the beginning of the term at their new school. My parents were buying Roger a moped so that he could continue at his present school seven miles from Hazelwood.

Three of the four students who were living with us were finding other accommodation in the new year. I had asked the fourth student, Susan, if she would like to come with us to Hazelwood. She could catch the bus to Riverton every morning to go to the technical college. We had agreed that she would pay for the cost of her food and help me as much as the other children would have to. She and Roger are sixteen, Elizabeth and Daniel are nine and ten, Andrea is eighteen and is in her first year at university.

Owen had left the log fire burning in the kitchen and by tea time I was established, with my geraniums in pots in the corners and one of the cats and one of the dogs for company. I lay in bed that night in great peace and contentment, glad to be alone, and happy in this house.

*Monday, 3 December*

Philip called for me at 7.00 am with the dawn. Every morning he visits each dairy: a journey of eleven miles. The first visit was to Home Farm where Graham milks, and a mile from Hazelwood. Without preamble Graham asked me if, at 9.00 am I would follow him in my van to a garage in the next village where he was leaving his car to be serviced, and bring him back.

Philip and I drove on through the park, still mysterious with pockets of the night, to Owlnest Farm which is Bob's domain, and where Mr Peregrine lives. Here, Mr Peregrine came in to talk to Bob and Philip and he asked me to call him John, as most of the men do.

At Quincey's Farm the radio was on so loud above the noise of the milking machine that talking was almost impossible. David milks there and I was told that he had hoped to be a clergyman, but had not got enough A-levels to obtain a place at college.

By the time we arrived at Honeybed Farm Greg had finished milking and was washing down the parlour. It was morning. We looked at a cow that had just calved and appeared to be slightly lame.

Philip drove me back to my house as the sun rose behind Ivy Hill, casting an apricot glow over the trees and fields. I had already had an egg for breakfast two hours earlier, so I cut myself a thick, cheese sandwich before meeting Graham, and using my van for the first time.

Returning from the garage, Graham talked about the people on the estate, especially one who was known to be big-headed and difficult. He assured me that he was a good chap really and it was unfair to prejudice me: I should no doubt find out.

I had been told to go to Owlnest Farm to give Bob a hand. It was a glorious morning, gentle and bright. Bob showed me round the buildings. He had planned to get the dry cows (those not giving any milk) in from the fields for the winter, but the electric fencer he needed to keep them away from the silage face was broken. I suggested he use mine, although it would mean my going back to Causeway House four miles away to get it. He agreed to this and I went, experiencing happiness for the first time for months. While we were fixing the fence, Bob confided that Philip was a good bloke, but cunning: he wouldn't like to say how, but cunning. He also said that John was so mean that he would switch his windscreen wipers off if he drove under a railway bridge. 'Of course,' he said, 'I get on with him very well.'

From Owlnest one can see over to the Downs. Marford lies in the intermediate valley and the views are extensive. I drove the dry cows in from their field. The Hereford bull had broken away from the herd and had to be diverted into a small paddock where another bull stood, roaring. Instructed by Bob to stand in front of the escaped bull and head him off into the paddock, I assumed a confidence I did not feel and did as I was told. I had some practice on the dairy tractor, and the ancient David Brown: I was slow and inefficient. Bob likes everything done well, and done properly. He told me to knock him up if I needed help at any time: he lives in a bungalow adjacent to the unit. He offered to give me some of his dry logs for my fire.

When I had eaten my lunch and written my diary, I went to bed for a few minutes. Two hours later the dog woke me, barking insistently. John was knocking on the door. He wanted to know where the MOT certificate for my van was, as Owen was supposed to have given it to the office and had not. He gave me permission to buy a torch and he provided me with a milking top, apron and wellington boots. I had to buy my own penknife, overalls and horse-hide gloves (for outdoor work) and these I bought in the afternoon at the agricultural suppliers in Marford. I took the broken electric fencer there to be mended for Bob.

I explored the estate and discovered the rhododendron gardens, and a disused quarry – now a lake where ornamental ducks swam within an enclosure. Squirrels ran across the road, rabbits scurried, pheasants strode the paths. It was like being on a nature preserve.

As dusk fell and the tall street lamps shed their yellow light over the surrounding fields, I walked to the foot of Ivy Woods with Brock, the dog, away from the noise of the unceasing traffic passing Hazelwood. A huge moon rose and hung heavy in the sky.

*Tuesday, 4 December*

I woke at 4.00 am, washed, had a quick cup of coffee, donned my overalls and duffle coat, and set off to Honeybed Farm, three miles away. Greg was already there and, with a notebook and pen in hand, I tried to follow his every move, and to absorb his methods. Cows do not like changes in routine and the smallest difference in the way things are done can affect their milk yield.

Greg used the kickbar on many of the cows, not waiting to see if they kicked but as a matter of routine. He was cheerful and pleasant but had not been told that I could not drive a tractor. 'Gawd,' he said.

Honeybed Farm is three miles outside the main estate. It is up a secluded valley and the farmhouse, which is let, and the buildings overlook a gently rolling patchwork panorama of typical English countryside with nothing intrusive in view. In the distance are the evocative Downs, smooth curves against the rising sun. It takes ten minutes brisk driving through the lanes to get home for 8.30 am and I was at the farm again by 10.00 am.

I watched Greg scraping the slurry and spreading sugar beet along the feed troughs in the cold, grey morning. He spread bedding out in the cubicles, fed straw and hay to the cows, and together we brought the dry cows in from the fields. We separated a young steer that had strayed in with them, collected a calf and put it in the calving box with its mother, and moved a heifer and a cow into the milking herd.

Philip arrived to collect three calves and take them to the calf-rearing unit in his van. So far five hundred calves have gone to the unit from the dairies this season (since September).

Two builders employed by the estate were putting a slatted end onto the Dutch barn to make it more weatherproof. The wood used comes from the estate.

During the day Greg talked to me about the work and the estate. He said he loved his work (as did Bob yesterday) but said he wouldn't do my job for anything (as did Philip). There is a £5 bonus at Christmas for those who are new, and £10 for everyone else. Each employee is also given a Christmas tree and four sacks of potatoes a year. The farm workers are taken on a visit to the Royal Show, or the Dairy Show and, as well as going to Farm Walks, there are skittles evenings, discos, a harvest supper and a carol service in the chapel in the house. The dairymen get free milk: up to, but not over, four pints of milk a day.

After an exhausting day of merely looking, I bathed and wrote to Andrea in front of the kitchen fire. I ate my supper of bolognaise without the spaghetti for the third night running – food does not have much significance at this moment – and listened to the wind blowing the leaves in a rustling whirlwind outside the back door.

I am apprehensive about my capabilities to do the job, but not worried about the job itself.

*Wednesday, 5 December*
Another mind-blowing day with Bob at Owlnest. He is in his fifties and has a reputation for having a mind of his own. We did not stop talking all day. He is extraordinarily efficient, dedicated and fanatical about his cows and his unit. The milking parlour is bright, light, warm and clean. He has an elaborate system of tail-tagging so that one can see at a glance (once you have learnt it) at what stage a cow is in her lactation and, very nearly, her life. He has invented his own recording system and the charts and graphs for the life histories of the cows cover the walls of his cosy office. The office is warmed by hot air from the engine room, channelled there by Bob.

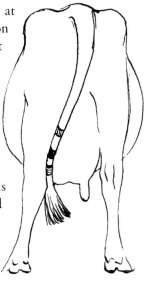
Cow with tail tags.

He told me about himself, his marriage, his children and his career which has been a varied one. He had strong opinions on all the people on the estate. Some were good. He learned to milk when he was four, doesn't believe in music in the parlour because he likes to concentrate on the cows all of the time. He is absolutely convinced of many things, but open to suggestions, of course. He takes pleasure in his battles with John, which he says he wins, loves his work and says he is a really happy man.

'I admit that, sometimes, when I come into the yard at night to check the cows and they take no notice of me – which means they accept me completely – then, well, I really love them.'

Bob has made a great many modifications to his parlour to improve it and, as well as obviously working hard, he enjoys a social life and is a member of the Lions Club, the Rotary Club and he organises flag days for charity.

It was not always easy to tell what he was saying as he smokes a pipe continually. Gripping it firmly in the centre of his mouth with his teeth, little drops of spittle flew off as he talked.

He feels that my job is a man's job, but he conceded that in some ways a woman would be better. He did not explain how. He was very kind to me, praising my slurry scraping, and tactfully leaving me alone while I was milking, or scraping, to get on with my bungling.

I was cautious about revealing some details of my own life as I see that this is a gossiping place, very similar to a village, and news spreads rapidly.

A cow went down with milk fever in the morning and had to be injected with a bottle of calcium. Another cow calved and had given birth to a large Charolais-cross-Friesian calf by tea-time. I met Harold, the arable foreman, and Malcolm, the calf rearer. I found out how to operate the pump to fill my van with petrol. I did not feel sleepy at lunchtime so I wandered round the yards behind Hazelwood, and I unblocked the gutter over the back door, and the drain in the corner which was clogged with old fat. By 6.45 pm I was home and opening a tin of ravioli for my supper.

*Thursday, 6 December, Home Farm*

Graham has been described to me as an easy-going chap, and the atmosphere is certainly more relaxed. Graham is in his early thirties, tall, dark and good-looking. He has been at Home Farm for seven years. He never uses a kickbar and his cows are quiet and easy-going also. He doesn't try to 'master' the cows as Bob feels it necessary to do. 'You never win anyway,' he said.

I helped him to pull a calf out in the morning when the cow began to need help. I ear-tagged it – badly.

One of the beautiful beech trees in front of the farm was felled and we watched from the dairy door. The workers on the estate have free wood for their fires. This is allotted to them and they have to saw it up and collect it. Many of them have their own chain saws and Graham seemed to expect me to be getting one (and to be able to handle it), a tractor and trailer, and a circular saw. The wood from the beech tree was contracted out, so despite their proximity to all that wood, nobody on the estate was allowed to touch it. There have been disputes over such incidents because, as well as the wood which is of value and therefore a realisable asset, there is a great quantity of good fire wood left.

Graham warned me to watch Rufus, the red setter. He said he was very quiet when out of John's car but would take your hand off if you go into the car.

Tina, Graham's attractive, smartly-dressed wife, came in to say 'hello' while we were clearing up after milking tonight. She works in the nearest market town and helps Graham run the social events on the estate. They have no children and want them.

The herdsmen are able to run their dairies as they wish, within certain boundaries. They know little about each other's systems, never visit each other's territories, and they are all exceptionally independent characters. I perceive that John has a most difficult job, and has to be a skilled diplomat.

*Friday, 7 December*

Quincey's Farm lies on the fringes of the main estate in an exposed position on the edge of a shallow, bowl-shaped plain, which rises to the foot of the Downs, two miles away. Until three years ago the old farm buildings were derelict. When they were demolished, a purpose-built dairy unit for one hundred and fifty cows was erected.

The building won an award for its design and the way it blended into the surrounding countryside. The passages, the cubicles, the yards and the pens are in straight lines, enabling greater efficiency and ease of work, yet David appears to work a longer, harder day than the other dairymen.

Harold, the arable foreman, went on a work-study course, and asked David if he would agree to a work-study project on Quincey's. David refused, affronted because he felt he had already simplified his system sufficiently. However, he alone scrapes out twice a day, which in itself means washing off the tractor twice, opening all the doors, swapping the scraper for the loader and the forage pusher, and cleaning the open yard twice. Perhaps there are reasons for this that I shall discover for myself?

The cows are fed in a central forage trough and not self fed from a silage clamp. As they eat, they push the silage away from them and it has to be pushed back to them twice a day.

David keeps his cows clean and comfortable. He does not approve of Bob's method of bedding them on sand, 'It's not natural to make a cow lie in a cubicle, and certainly not on a beach.' He has no outliers in the muck in the passageways, and he said, 'You must make sure there are enough cubicles by 2.00 am, when nearly every cow will be resting.' Only his dry cows are tail-tagged, although he trims the tails of newly calved cows to differentiate between the milkers and the near-to-calving cows.

He believes in an eye for an eye, and if he is kicked he will retaliate. 'I'm the boss and they know it.'

David is an extrovert, quick-witted and humorous, with high standards and strong opinions. He is ambitious and does not intend to remain a cow man all his life. He has three young children and he said he often fell asleep in the evenings: he was so tired.

Recently, John gave each herdsman a time-sheet to fill in. David considered this to be an insult. He told me that at Christmas all the workers on the estate, but no spouses, are invited to Lyndon House for a drink. If you forget to address Lord Elroy correctly during conversation he will remind you that he has a title. I said I could pull my forelock with the best of them. According to David, John makes all the decisions for the farms.

I was introduced to Geoff, the driver of the tractor and trailer which delivers the silage each morning to the forage trough. Geoff is a young man with a face from a Botticelli painting. David himself is short and fair, with a ginger moustache and badly bitten fingernails. In the afternoon I scraped, pushed the silage back and did some milking. The radio is an integral part of the milking and belts out Radio Two from the beginning to the end.

*13 December, work*

By chance I had joined Lyndon as my long weekend was due, so on the Friday evening I packed my suitcase and, very early on Saturday, I travelled north to see my sister and her new-born baby for the weekend.

As the weekend progressed I grew more and more nervous about the following week. The journey home was tedious, and I was lonely and afraid that evening. I was glad of the company of Brock.

The house is perishingly cold. I have a paraffin heater in my bedroom and one in the kitchen to supplement the heat from the log fire. I slept badly because I was afraid of oversleeping, and arrived early at Owlnest.

Bob had left everything ready to switch on and begin. With my notebook propped up in a dry corner I began. Philip came in at 6.00 am to see if I was all right, and John called in at 7.00 am. Checking and cleaning up after milking took the most time, as everything must be done in sequence. At lunchtime I shopped in Riverton and bought paint for the kitchen walls (though when I am going to have time to put it on I do not know). I drove into the yard at Hazelwood and calves scattered in all directions. They had somehow escaped from the large barn in which they are reared in groups of forty after they have been weaned at the calf unit. I was forced to use the radio which is installed in the vehicles of John; Harold, the arable foreman; Philip, the dairy foreman; Jim, the young stock foreman; and myself

I bleated feebly, 'Lyndon 6 to Lyndon 5.' Jim replied immediately and, within two minutes of my explanation, was driving into the yard, followed by Philip who had heard the message an his radio. It did not take long to round them up and I left Jim checking them over as I was already late for the afternoon milking.

Half way there I remembered that my indispensable notebook was still in the house. I returned, pocketed the notebook and, in my hurry not to be late, I jumped into the van, put it into what I thought was reverse gear – and it leapt forwards into the wall. I reversed hastily and, not being aware of what I had done wrong, did it again. This time the van backed away from the wall but refused to drive forward. Once more I had to use the radio to contact Philip, who later on used a crowbar to lever the bumper away from the wheel. I still had my own car until

Christmas and I used that for the rest of the day. I hoped earnestly that no one else, especially John, had heard what had happened.

In the evening I was invited out for supper by friends who lived fifteen miles away. I longed to go to bed instead, and was sure I looked haggard with exhaustion. None of the people there seemed happily married, not even a newly-married couple. Perhaps I am better on my own. Adjusting to another person is not easy.

I fell into bed at midnight and was up again at 4.30 am. Nervous energy keeps me going. The milk tanker comes early to Home Farm so I started milking early to finish in time. Henry the tanker driver is a small, cheerful, friendly man. He grasped my arm when he talked and called me 'love'.

The tractor drivers are based at Home Farm and receive their instructions for the day in the cathedral-sized barn which houses the cows in one half, and the machinery and a straw-covered mountain of potatoes under the other. John introduced me to Norman, one of the tractor drivers who had come into the dairy to look for a brush. Norman gazed at me as if I were an enormous curiosity, which I suppose I was.

Philip was to come every day to make sure I was getting on all right and to help me until I had speeded up and could do everything myself. He scraped out, moved the silage fence and bedded up the cows. John came into the parlour and turned off the overflowing water tap which I had forgotten to turn off. Graham told me that he was always switching off lights and turning off the water. I began to feel definitely submissive and in awe of John. He told me to fill the empty mineral container which he said Graham should have done. When Graham appeared to fetch his daily milk, John told him so. A look crossed Graham's face identical to that I have seen on the faces of my children when they think they have been unfairly accused of a minor misdeed: a sulky resentment, not very strong or deep. He replied that he had filled them but the cows were eating the minerals very quickly.

The parlour is scruffier and harder to work in than Owlnest and the hose is not pressurised. At the back of the parlour there is a large tank of water. Buckets of water from this sluice the floor and have to be carried the length of the parlour and also up and down the steps into the 'pit' where the milker stands during milking.

The collecting yard has been adapted from the old, original farm buildings and, although it is covered, it has many awkward corners, difficult to scrape and resultingly smelly. Many of the cows prefer to lie in the muck although the cubicles are well bedded up and cosy.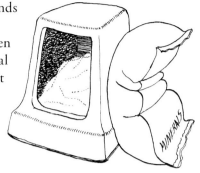

Graham does not bother to cut the cows tails and they are long and filthy, but he feeds them well. Graham thinks that Bob rations his cows 'something cruel'.

I asked John for his petrol-pump keys so that I could fill up my van. I am not allowed a key myself. He said they were in his car. I thought about my hand being taken off as I reached for them, but although the dog growled softly, he wagged his tail and did not move.

Bob rang to say how well I had done and that he had told John so. I am milking like a zombie and not taking anything in. My head is so crammed with information that I have no space left for worry, or sorrow, or anything but simple survival.

I slept for six hours last night: a record for some time. David scrapes out the cubicles before he milks, so I was driving the tractor at Quincey's soon after 5.00 am. Philip arrived at 6.00 am and I started the milking. Each cow has a number freeze-branded on her rump. When the corresponding number is entered on the control panel of the electronic feeder, the correct amount of cow cake falls automatically into the mangers as the cow enters the parlour. This is a different system and it took me some time to adjust to it. I failed to notice a valve which should have been turned off. The overflow jar filled up with milk and threatened to block up the milk pump. I turned the machine off and rushed for Philip's help.

There is a much greater sense of isolation at Quincey's. The unit and yards are completely unoverlooked – which I like. I pottered about during the morning: absorbing, loitering, practising on the tractor (swinging the scraper over and back), and oblivious of time. Home through the park, a separate pleasure, beautiful and calm in the mild and sunny morning. A letter from a friend awaited me, enclosing a cheque for a bottle of whisky as a token of admiration for my courage. Sometimes even I think I am brave, or is it foolish?

Rereading my notebook over lunch, I discovered I was already late. I should have been scraping out again before milking. The time-table at Quincey's is out of step with all the others.

In the calving boxes two cows had begun to calve. Two sets of feet protruded. One looked normal, the other looked strange. I thought the calf was coming out either backwards or upside down. I began to milk and checked the cow frequently. Half an hour passed and no progress was made so I used the van radio to call for help. Philip did not answer, but John did. He was in the vicinity and came over.

We were pulling the calf out when Philip arrived. He said I could get on with the milking. Happily, John realised I wanted to see the calves born and said I could stay. He told me to examine the second cow and I slid my arm up inside her to make sure the calf was in the correct position to be born. I added my weight to the ropes round its feet and out it came, to be slapped and pummelled alive.

A hailstorm drumming on the roof drowned out even the noise of the radio. Philip helped me to clean up and said I need not return to the dairy tonight. On my way home through the darkness of the park I was passed by John in his car. Using the radio he told me to stop as one of my headlights wasn't working. He asked me to open the bonnet and I had to confess that I could not remember where the knob which opened it was. I could see he didn't believe me. How humiliating: Roger and I had opened it once, so I knew it must be somewhere. Without saying anything, John leaned over the dashboard, opened the bonnet and put in a new light bulb.

*15 December*

A labour camp in Siberia could not be harder work than Honeybed Farm. The cows have a reputation for being nervous and difficult in the parlour, which itself is old-fashioned, hard to work in and not easy to keep clean.

A family of cats appears at the end of each milking for a dish of milk. They are kept there to keep the rats down, which once overran the place. There are two plaintive, scraggy kittens which I would catch and take home if I had any energy to spare.

It is Greg's weekend off and I am at Honeybed for Friday, Saturday and Sunday. Next weekend I am at Home Farm and then it is my weekend off. Philip milks at Owlnest and Quincey's when Bob and David have their weekends off.

The first milking at Honeybed was chaotic. I was getting along slowly but pleased that I was managing without the frequent use of the kickbar, when John called on his routine visit to the dairy. I said there was some overflow of milk into the jar and I did not know why so, on his way out, he pulled the plug out from the bottom of the overflow jar and drove off, unaware that the ball valve in the jar had flown up with the intake of air and cut off the vacuum. The jar is in the dairy, not the parlour, and I had not seen him do this. All I knew was that the milking clusters dropped off the cows and there was no suction. I spent an hour trying to find the cause and failing; I had to radio for help. John was too far away and Philip was off on Fridays, so John suggested I contacted Greg, who lives a mile from his farm, unlike the other dairymen, who live close to their work. Greg's house is owned by the estate and is in a village. He was still in bed when I knocked on the door, but he came back with me cheerfully enough and found the cause of the trouble immediately. To catch up on lost time I did not go home for breakfast, fortuitously having brought a flask of coffee with me.

The cows at Honeybed have a midday feed of cake and sugar beet pulp and because the sacks of pulp weigh one hundredweight, I cannot lift them by myself. Philip would be allotted this job, but it was his day off. John had arranged to fit it into his schedule. Because I was behind with the work and there was so much to do, he stayed on to help, which was a good thing as he drove the tractor and discovered that the brakes on it were non-existent.

The farm is built into the hillside and the yards are on differing levels and have tight corners and several slippery slopes. This is the only dairy tractor with a cab, as all the yards at Honeybed are open and exposed, with the exception of the collecting yard whose roof is so low that it is not possible to drive the tractor under it. This yard has to be scraped by hand with a squeegee.

John scraped the yards and then shut the cows up there while I scraped the cubicle house. We bedded up the dry cows in their separate barn, and we collected the sacks of cake and pulp from the barn on the lowest level, and carried them to the troughs on the loader. It was 1.30 pm before I had finished.

I went to see the children in the evening. Andrea had arrived home from university and they all came back with me to Honeybed for an hour. Andrea drove them home in the car as she will need it to ferry them around in the holidays.

Working three consecutive days in one place does give continuity, but the rest of the weekend was no easier. I took my breakfast with me on each day and worked right through again, eating my breakfast in the Dutch barn. I built up a barrier of bales against the wind, so that I could look at the view. I shed a few tears for the past, but was well satisfied with the present.

The auger, which fed the hoppers the cake, stopped working: I had to stop milking, find a ladder, climb up into the loft over the cows' heads, remove the blockage and shovel the cake down the chute which fed the augers. Considering these disturbances the cows milked quietly and well. While John and I were talking in the silage yard one of them came up and licked my hair.

Norman helped with the sugar beet on Saturday. I bashed the blade of the scraper against the wall and bent it. Norman stayed on to mend it, although I'm sure it was his lunch hour. With great precision and delicacy, he manoeuvred the tractor to position the blade against one of the barn supports and battered it (not too successfully) with a block of wood, not having a sledge hammer handy. In such ways has everyone been kind.

The tractor drivers do not like mending the dairymen's tractors because they think they do not look after them properly. The tractors are sprayed so often with water, which gets into the hydraulics, and the slurry is so corrosive, that this is why the brakes never seem to work.

My first job on Sunday morning was to get a cow which had calved the day before into the herd. In the dark she walked out of the box as far as a narrow, uphill-sloping passage and collapsed with milk fever, blocking the passage with her huge bulk. I searched for the flutter valve and bottle of calcium and needle, and injected her. After a bit she staggered up and went off to the silage face. I tried to head her back to her calf in the box but gave up as she kept trying to return to the food and I feared I was upsetting her more. One is not supposed to milk a cow with milk fever as milking would accelerate the drain of calcium from the body to the milk. When John came to help with the beet we put her back in the box without any trouble.

I let him shift the bales of hay and straw as I struggled with them yesterday and nearly cut my hands on the string. They have to be humped from one end of the barn to the other and are unusually heavy. I shall have to wear my horse-hide gloves for this job.

We stood watching the dry cows munching their hay.

'I had an idea it would be better to employ a woman for your job,' John said, 'because it's a terrible job following on behind everyone else and their systems. I thought there would be less aggro if a woman did it, and that a woman would be able to get away with murder.'

'I don't want to get away with murder,' I protested. 'You mean I'd be using the fact that I'm a woman.'

'Yes,' he said. 'For instance, Greg won't mind that you haven't scraped the silage yard.'

This was not quite fair because he had come early and we had had to shut the cows up in the silage yard before I had had time to scrape. I pressed my lips together.

'You haven't spread the bedding out properly for the dry cows either,' he said with a sidelong glance.

I wondered why he hadn't told me when I was actually doing it. I had done it as I had seen Greg do it but, of course, I couldn't say so. I wanted to do everything well and I explained that as I didn't know very much, then I had to be shown. John believes in always going to see prospective employees in their own homes and he will travel across country to do so.

'I had a good many applicants for your job,' he said, 'including several women. It isn't any good choosing someone with a lot of experience. They have definite ideas of their own and find it too difficult to fit in with the others and don't like being told what to do by the other dairymen.'

My inexperience was therefore an advantage, and if I had ideas of my own I was prepared to subdue them until my ignorance was less profound.

John said that he managed all the farming of the estate, nearly three thousand acres, and ran the four dairy farms as a whole.

'I miss the practical side of farming and I could easily spend the whole day in the office because there is so much paperwork, but I get out as much as I can because I do like to know what is going on in every part of the farm.' He does not appear to miss anything. 'I find the job totally absorbing, and I like the fact that I never know what is going to happen next. I have made some disastrous decisions, but some of the land is particularly hard to manage: Hazelwood land is wet and difficult, for example.'

He is there to make it pay, and in effect to make the whole estate viable, as the farms support the rest of the estate.

The milk tanker driver talked to me while the milk was sucked out of the bulk tank. It was not Henry who is on a different circuit.

'I came home one day and found my wife had gone off with someone else. She took half the furniture; just cleared off. I lost two stone in a fortnight, I just couldn't eat a thing. I've got the children. I'd been married seventeen years, you know. I never suspected anything. Later on, I went out with a woman, but she got to want me to live with her. I shied off from that. I didn't want that. I didn't want to take on her children, seeing all the problems and the long rearing of them.'

His eyes became very sad, and his mouth very bitter, as he talked of his wife. Driving the tanker was a relief job. He usually worked a shift system driving heavy lorries down to the coast, laden with yoghurt and dairy products. The milk tanker he was driving that day picked up milk from eight farms at a time and then returned to the base. He made about three journeys a day. Some drivers picked up from sixteen farms in one load: it depended on the size of the farm.

*19 December, integration*

It was my day off yesterday. I had a vision of myself in a dressing gown, trailing around the house in a deliciously aimless way, and I was determined to fulfil this image. Unexpectedly, I woke at 4.00 am, so I wrote my diary, slept again and it was still only 8.00 am when I breakfasted. I pottered in my dressing gown, writing Christmas cards, wrapping parcels and relaxing.

At noon I discarded the dressing gown and went shopping. I had to use the van, with permission from John. I slept in the afternoon and Andrea and Elizabeth came for tea and painted the kitchen for me in the evening. Going to bed at midnight – far too late – I looked forward to the morrow.

Artificial insemination has begun and any cow seen to be bulling, or on heat, is kept back after milking for the AI man. The numbers of the cows seen the previous day are chalked on a board, or written in the daily diary, or on a scrap of paper for me to see. It is only too easy for my concentration to slip when I am letting the cows out of the parlour and to pull the cord which opens the gate and forget that I am supposed to be diverting number '27' into the AI pens instead. Philip's wife is ill and he is away from work looking after her. John noticed I had one cow in the pen when I should have had three. I had looked at the wrong board. We searched for the missing cows in the yards, no easy task among one hundred and fifty others and, trying not to cause a panic, extricated them and drove them into the pens to await their insemination.

The milk pump ceased to work while I was rinsing through the pipes, but Bob had warned me that it might, so I did not assume it was my fault this time. It was put right during the morning by the manufacturers, who operate a round-the-clock service.

Two cows escaped through the barriers to the bulls while I was on the tractor. They careered over the lawns of John's house. I managed to get the cows back and hoped that the holes in the lawn were not irremediable.

Bob had asked me to help him sort out the dry cows and return the ones near to calving to the milking herd. He helped me to feed them and bed them up. They are in a separate yard at the side of the main buildings. I was requested to go to the office. I no longer go home for breakfast so I ate my honey sandwich and banana in the park on the way. A jay flashed its colours among the trees. Pheasants scratched around the newly planted saplings. The smooth grass verges sweep tidily up to the well-fenced fields. The felled trees are cleared away rapidly and there is an aura of tranquillity and good management.

The secretary took down the details of my marital status, children etc., for their records. I asked her for the make of the oil fires in my house, as I can not order fuel until I know.

Back at Owlnest I met the retired calf rearer who lives in one of the lodges, and Bert, a tractor driver who was cleaning out the bull pens with Norman. Milking at night went easily and John said he would look at the cows at night for me, to save me the four-mile journey. On the way home I passed through Home Farm where all the farm tractors are parked for the night; clumps of monolithic giants, huge, powerful and silent in the headlights of the van.

### 21 December

Home Farm, the centre of most activity. In the adjoining section of the barn the potato sorters and packers work in a huddled group beside the Sally-Ann, a cylindrical stove which adds its roar to the chatter of the women. One of the women is the owner of a small Jack Russell dog who has previously been the mate of my Jack Russell bitch. Sirius is on heat again and I went to ask her if I could use the dog again. Mrs Elder did not recognise me in my overalls, climbing over the dividing I barrier.

The hay and straw are stored above the silage at Home Farm and the bales have to be thrown down from a great height. Philip, back at work, helped me to drive a cow out of the calving box and into the herd. Some cows leave their calves reluctantly, but most are eager to return to the herd and familiar surroundings. Every day the silage overhang has to be forked down. It forms a cliff, sometimes ten feet high, of chopped grass, or lucerne, or maize pressed into a solid mass. The face at Home Farm is sixty feet long and to grapple the overhang down is hard labour. I heard that I had not done it properly at Honeybed and a huge wad had fallen on the electrified wire which controls the cows' feeding and broken it.

The entrance to the lagoon into which all the slurry is scraped was blocked by an impenetrable mass of dirty straw. With Philip holding on to the end of a rope tied round his waist, John ventured out onto the apparently solid surface to fork it away. A former student had nearly drowned there once, up to his neck in slurry before someone heard his cries. Philip wanted to go to Quincey's to help David, so he handed the end of the rope to me. I leaned over the wall, basking in the mild and sunny morning, while John, bending and straightening rhythmically as he worked, explained the forestry policy.

Forestry is a separate department. For a period of fifty years no trees were planted on the estate. There is a gap between the mature trees which are being felled today and the next ones. Some plantations are deer-fenced to protect them and all individually planted saplings in the park are fenced against deer and cattle. There is a small herd of muntjac deer in the park, as well as fallow deer.

I let water into the vacuum pipes during washing in the evening and everything ceased to work. I drained the whole system but nothing happened and I was still puzzling over it when Graham came to see if anything was wrong. He had seen that the lights were still blazing and the noise from the engine sounded odd. The sanitary trap had filled up and the engine had nearly overheated. He sorted me out and left me humbly grateful.

Today I received a Christmas card from Lord Elroy. It was a coloured photograph of his four children. The message inside said:

> Welcome to Lyndon, Alison, I look forward to meeting you.
> Elroy

John showed me where there was a pile of left-over wood for my fire, in the woods near the forestry department. I took Brock with me in the van to collect it. It was dark and the pheasants had gone to roost so I let him run in the park. For one and a half miles he ran at twenty-two miles per hour running for the joy of it, his sleek black body gleaming in the headlights and his great spotted paws pounding the road.

Going out in the morning has an air of unreality. The roads are deserted and unfold like a stage set. Cats eyes glitter from the hedgerows by farms where barns glow with the night lights for the cows. Thin ice sheeted the yards at Quincey's. The cows, though quiet for milking, tend to be nervous and panicky in the cubicles. They can so easily slip on the ice when being transferred to the collecting yard. Their teats are clean and soft, just as well because the udder washers are useless and only a thin trickle of water comes out of them.

I don't like scraping out twice in a day, but tractor driving after breakfast was a pleasure; a new skill. It was cold and I wore my new horse-hide gloves for the first time. The downs were distanced by a winter haze and their outlines bore a resemblance to the Yorkshire dales.

My visit to the dairy that night was worth the effort as a number of cows were bulling and I wrote their numbers on the board for David to see in the morning.

The system is very different at Honeybed and I take a long time establishing any sort of method. I let one cow out that should have been kept back. Another started calving. John pulled it out when he came on his rounds. It was a bull calf. Later, the cow had another, a heifer and therefore a free-martin and unlikely to be fertile.

I admired the view while I was hand scraping the collecting yard. My hands were numb with cold, but forking down the silage made me hot.

The tractor would not start. I hunted in vain for the Easistart spray and gave up and radioed for help. Nobody else being available, John came. The battery was flat and the charger was not working. John worked out why, mended the charger and started the engine of the tractor. He left me to scrape the yards and came back later to put out the sugar beet. Meanwhile, a cow began to calve in the cubicles, not a desirable place because the calf drops in the dung passage.

The calving box at Honeybed is nothing but the old cow byres with the partitions removed, and more than two cows in there makes a crowd. Already in there were three cows and the twin calves. There was nowhere else to put her so that is where she went. I left her to settle down and finished the work. The calf had retreated inside her and rather than leave her until I came back in the afternoon, John decided that we must examine her and, if necessary, get it out. Some cows are easy to halter and quiet to handle. This one was not. In her efforts to avoid us she broke the water pipe. John had to trek across a field to turn the water off and phone up the estate plumbers to ask them to mend it. With unending patience he caught the cow, tied her up, and with an effort we pulled it out. The cow refused to look at it. The calf looked wet, weak and lethargic. By this time I was in the same state.

I had left home at 4.45 am and had returned for lunch at 2.20 pm. I hurried my lunch and drove back to Honeybed under a gloomy, thick sky. A pall blotted out Marford in the valley. The calf was lying cold and wet in a draught into which it had stumbled. The cow would not let me get near enough to her to draw off her colostrum to give it to the calf. I moved it to a sheltered corner, and that night, on my last visit to the farm, I saw that all the cows and calves in the box were lying down and the calf was lying up against its mother. Rather than disturb them all and risk them careering about in the semi-darkness in the confined space, I left it and hoped that it had fed. A light, powdery snow was falling, covering my solitary tyre tracks in the thick, white frost. The next morning, at Home Farm, I heard that Greg had found the calf dead. He thought it had been trodden on.

*23 December*

A long, exhausting day on my own at Home Farm. The worst part is the silage face and throwing down the bales of hay and straw, and heaving them into the racks. John forked down the dry cows silage (in a separate clamp) and he mended the hand squeegee. There doesn't seem to be anything he can't or won't do. Perhaps checking up on me and helping at the same time is a good way of finding out how the men work. I hope it makes him more sympathetic to them. He told me that the men could have anything they want for the dairies, not the same story I have heard from the men. When Graham hurt his back John milked at Home Farm for a week and he said he found it very, very hard work.

An old cow was in labour in the cubicles before I went home for supper. I put her in a box without any trouble and went back at 8.00 pm. She had not progressed. The calf was in the normal position and I gathered the ropes, disinfectant and bucket of hot water and pulled the calf myself with a strenuous effort. It was dead. I tried for several minutes to start it breathing but it was no good. This was a disaster. Perhaps Philip and John would think I hadn't tried hard enough, or done the right things. Pondering, I looked at the cow and saw another pair of feet sticking out of her. Taking no chances I radioed Philip. He gave the cow a bottle of calcium, and jabbing the lolling tongue of the unborn calf, whose nose protruded from the swollen vulva, with the needle from the flutter valve, he said that was dead too. The two limp and pathetic bodies lay in the thick straw and the cow bled slowly, red oil dripping and sliding down the afterbirth hanging from her vagina.

John was predictably dismayed when he saw the dead calves in the morning. He inspects every part of the dairies before coming into the parlour to say good morning, so he is well informed before he sees the herdsman.

The tractor at Home Farm, a battered blue Ford, would not start. The motor turned over lethargically and I was afraid of running the batteries down. Absolute silence in the barn. On Sundays in winter the tractors are put away in the potato barn and no one is around. Philip was out of contact, milking at Owlnest, and it was, I believed, John's day off. Graham was out. Nothing but the barking of a dog and, far away, the church bells ringing.

I was thinking, 'What the hell do I do now?' when I glimpsed a figure lurking in the potato barn. It was Norman, who lives close by. I asked him if he could help. Solemnly he tested the tractor and said he would need some jump leads. At last I understood the cryptic message left by my predecessor, 'Don't let anyone borrow the jump leads in the van.' Steadily, without hurry, Norman unlocked the potato barn and drove one of the big tractors out of the barn, through the dry cows yard and into the silage yard. A water pipe hung low from an overhead beam but instead of knocking it aside he stopped the tractor underneath, climbed on the bonnet and tied the pipe carefully to the beam. He connected the tractors together with the jump leads as if for a strange kind of coupling, and started my tractor.

I had almost completed the work when John appeared. He had been working on the beef unit. I said belligerently, 'You had better not look too closely at the silage face, because I'm not going to do it any better *whatever*!' He immediately went to look at it and said it wasn't too bad. Graham walked in and said that he never had any trouble with the tractor.

The calves at Hazelwood were out in the yard again and we think someone must be letting them out.

The Christmas staff reception is tomorrow and I shall start milking at 2.00 pm to finish in time.

*Christmas Eve*

There was just time to wash the cow smells out of my hair and have a bath before the reception. The first person I saw as I walked across the lit-up courtyard, self-conscious and uncertain, was John. He accompanied me along the gallery and introduced me to Lord Elroy who stood at the entrance to the library, welcoming his workers. The flames from a fire in the hearth were reflected in the shining baubles hanging on a tall, beautiful Christmas tree. The room was filled with a mass of best-tweed-coated backs, muted checked shirts, and knitted woollen waistcoats in browns and greys and sombre greens. A few striped suits betrayed the presence of the office and managerial staff. Lady Elroy, her hair flowing freely from her high forehead down her back, wore an expensive knitted suit of a rust colour, but her large eyes were reserved and showed no warmth to any but her children, who handed round the peanuts and crisps and mingled confidently with the guests.

Leather-backed books lined the shelves, photographs of the family were propped on the desk in gilded frames, and the Greek philosophers painted on the ceiling looked down, unsmiling, on the scene. John thanked our hosts, and Lord Elroy made a speech, commenting on the past year in all the sections of the estate. He welcomed me to the staff, and spoke well and simply, standing very upright, but not totally at ease. He has a pleasant, intelligent face and must be about thirty-seven years of age. The atmosphere under the veneer of civility and bonhomie was one of extreme cynicism from the independent-minded farm workers.

One of them said to me, 'Last year I sent a note saying I could not go because of pressure of work. So they said I wouldn't get my bonus. So I said, "What, not get my bonus when I'm doing my job?" and they gave me my bonus.'

Attendance, if not actually compulsory, is requested. The worlds of those present are so far apart I do not see how they can ever imagine each other's lives. After a decent interval of socialising and drinking, we filed out into the gallery to form a queue in front of a white-cloth-covered table on which was a pile of envelopes, a number of wrapped bottles of wine and spirits, and labelled parcels. Rows of pheasants lay tidily on the floor. Lady Elroy placed her hand briefly in the roughened, hardened ones of her employees and Lord Elroy handed each of us an envelope. I did not discover who received the bottles and parcels. The children leapt about gaily and in an orderly procession we passed through the double doors gaping onto the cobbles of the empty, frosty yard.

*Christmas Day*

The first Christmas morning in my life that I have been alone. I woke at 4.00 am, even earlier than usual. An exceptionally hard frost coated everything with silver and starched the ruts of mud with cold. Each yellow arc lamp on the road was wreathed in a ball of mist, like illuminated candy floss.

The milking went smoothly, and Bob came to help with the scraping and feeding afterwards as he wants me to help him tomorrow. Only the essentials are done on Christmas Day, and as no cows calved, I expected to finish by 9.30 am.

I slipped out of the parlour to see the dawn. The stars were still shining in the clear, deep blue of the sky and all the valleys were shrouded in mist, with the trees rising from it in simple silhouettes. A divine morning and worth all the shit-shovelling to see it. I drove home through the cool, shadowed silver of the park, and found fog on the plain and thick hoarfrost on every surface.

I took the dogs for a walk on the Downs. Never can there have been so lovely a Christmas morning. The ramparts of the prehistoric earth-works, sleeked down from winter rains and the death of the summer's growth of tawny, fur-like grass, rose sharply from the plain, enclosing in their curves and folds the view of the countryside below. The frost had melted on the fields, which shone vivid green or brown in the brilliance of the sun. Fold upon fold, into the distance the mist lay piled and billowed against the far downs in mountain peaks, and the houses, churches and trees of this enchanted land floated on clouds. The rays of the sun fell in blue beams between the winter-stark trees, picking out the grey, fluffy seed pods of the old man's beard in the woods that clothed the hillsides.

I lay on a slope and the sun was warm and the wind gentle. I was sad for a while and cried. In the evening, leaving the quiet, warm barns and the clean, scrubbed dairy I discovered that although the ground was glassy with ice, the condensation on the van windows was not frozen.

*Boxing Day*

My parents are staying at Causeway House for Christmas, with Edward and the children. My father is putting shelves up in the kitchen at Hazelwood for me. The immersion heater is not working and John came to mend it, and stayed for a coffee and he met my father. When he had gone, and we were eating our lunch of bread and cheese, fruit and cake, I told my father that I thought John was attracted to me.

He was appalled at the implications. 'You must not get involved. You must say no whatever happens.'

I did not need to be told that my job could be in jeopardy, nor that my emotions were in a particularly fragile state after the disasters of the past year. What I did not tell him was that I was equally attracted to John. I knew I was vulnerable. I was fanatically determined not to have a casual affair with anyone. I had been severely hurt once, and so recently, that I didn't believe that I could survive another such experience so soon. Neither did I want to fall into the trap, reputedly common to divorced and separated women, of going to bed with anyone. I had to preserve some shred of integrity.

Why did I tell my father? I knew what his reaction would be and what he would say. I am afraid of myself, and perhaps I saw him as an anchor that would hold me to sanity and security. My fears were nebulous, but there was an excitement concealed within them that I could disguise from others, but never from myself.

# 1980

# JANUARY

*1 January*

The heavy metal-sheeted doors at Quincey's, propped open for scraping, act like sails in the wind and one blew against the tractor and cracked the headlamp. This was the first incident.

Sixty cows had been milked when everything was plunged into darkness and the only sound as the radio died was of the clusters falling off around the cows' feet and the inevitable splattering as the cows lifted their tails in unison at the interruption to their routine. I groped my way into the dairy and examined the switches by torchlight, but found nothing obviously wrong. I knew that the tractor could be connected up to the generator, but not how to do it, so I tried the van radio. There was no answer from Philip, whom I had already seen that morning, or from John, probably still eating his breakfast. It is taboo to disturb anyone on his day off so I was reluctant to knock on David's door. I tried the radio again and was still hopefully waiting for a reply when the headlights of Philip's van blazed down the blackness of the drive. All the radios were out of order, but he had heard the clicking of the switch and came straight from Honeybed.

In a few minutes, the tractor was turning the generator, the yellow pilot light steadied in its initial flickering, the lights went on, and the milking machine began its rhythmical swishing; then the same thing happened again and darkness descended. Philip told me never to touch the cows in the darkness. They might kick then from fear. He went off to get a more powerful tractor from Home Farm.

I waited, watching the sky grow lighter, while the cows in the collecting yard stood patiently chewing the cud, their udders growing larger and tighter and more uncomfortable as the time passed. A tree had blown down across the road in the park, and the tractor had to travel round the rim of the estate. It failed to start the motor and Philip was baffled. He left to get an electrician. The rain was sheeting down, and the wind was gusting forcefully when John arrived and worked out the reason for the failure of the tractor. The compressors for the ice bank in the milk tank had not been switched off before the tractor had been attached to the generator. When they had come on automatically the load had been too great and this had tripped a switch inside a box marked 'High Voltage: Danger.' While I watched, nervously, John untripped the switch and, before the electrician arrived, I was working again, hosing down the filthy parlour. New instructions are to be pinned inside each dairy so that this cannot happen again.

Because I was so late the AI man could not inseminate his cows, my hose had a slit in it which shot a powerful jet of water up my legs and soaked my trousers, and the wheelbarrow – heavily loaded with the midday ration of cow cake – tipped over under the silo hopper in the wind, and rain, and had to be shovelled back, arduously.

I enjoyed, and was stimulated by, the morning. It is interesting finding out how people cope when things go wrong, and how problems which, to me, appear insuperable, are solved.

Over to Causeway House to see the children for the evening, and later a deep, hot bath, an essential part of the day, before bed.

## 7 January

The children moved here during my last long weekend and life became a matter of simple survival again. Andrea used the car to take them shopping for new school uniforms, and to buy a pair of best trousers for Daniel to wear at the Lyndon children's party. Harold organised it and they enjoyed it.

We loaded the beds and essential items into the car in a number of journeys. Roger, Daniel and Elizabeth will sleep in the large downstairs room for warmth (there is an oil-fired heater in there which I hope will eventually be lit). Susan, not yet back at college, will sleep in the cosy room next to the kitchen. This, too, has a heater in it. I am the only one sleeping upstairs, in the smallest bedroom. It faces away from the road and the traffic and night-long lights, and is easy to heat economically. The curtains and some of the carpets I bought from Owen. My pictures and books remain at Causeway House until it is sold and we can divide them, so the rooms here echo and the walls are bare.

My van at the back of Hazelwood Farm.

Greg has given in his notice at Honeybed this week, and is going to look after the cows at a farm just across the valley. He says they are going to build a new parlour, although the old one is better than he has now: I believe him. The jars which collect the milk from each cow are overhead at Honeybed and the milk from a cow with mastitis cannot go into the bulk tank and has to be released from the jar. It pours out at head height in a splashing shower and, by the end of the three days there, I was stinking of sour milk. I wash my overalls, milking top, and rubber apron on my day off. I now wear rubber gloves for milking to protect my hands from the constant wet, dirt and chemicals. The slurry has to be scraped down a series of terraces which is unnecessarily time-consuming. But, when one has time to lift one's eyes from the mud, the stars are magnificent. The view is ethereal in the early morning. The sun rises from behind the monument on the Downs in a pearly shimmer, icily cold in the glittering landscape. In the evening the road sparkled with the diamonds of severe frost.

On the last day, I had to abandon the scraping because the hydraulics seized up. The agricultural engineer who was called out did not possess the necessary pump. I fed the cows by using the van to transport the hay and cake. Frustration and rebellion welled in me. I could do the job, given the proper tools.

The last few days have been bitterly cold and I faced, reluctantly, a thick, freezing fog one evening. I almost turned back to the womb-like warmth of the kitchen. In the box twin calves were newly born. The membrane was partially wrapped round the body of the last, and it was shaking its head and sniffling to free its nose of liquid. The mother lowed in the peculiar and tender note given only to their calves.

### 13 January

At 8.15 am the two younger children leave the house each day and catch a bus to the school from a stop fifty yards away. Roger leaves on his moped soon after, travelling in the opposite direction, and Susan leaves last of all to catch a bus to Riverton. I am never there to see them off, or to welcome them home.

Daniel and Elizabeth have to walk home in the afternoons, mostly on a pavement, but there is one narrow part of the hill which runs between high stone walls swagged with ivy and without a verge of any kind. I have said they must never walk home alone. If it rains they will be soaked by the time they reach the shelter of the house. I leave a note for them and a chocolate biscuit, and Roger and Susan join them after half an hour. I prepare the meal at lunchtime and Susan puts it on and serves it. The children lay the table and Roger gets wood in, or irons, or hoovers.

I enter, wearily, about 6.30 pm and hope for a few minutes respite before the bombardment of the day's problems. We eat together, sitting round the kitchen table in the warmth, and flickering light, of the huge, crackling fire.

*15 January*

The most severe frost yet, and my day off. I invited Tom and Jenny for lunch and proudly took them to see the dairies in the afternoon.

The trees were lacy with the frost and, because there was no sun, or blue sky, the landscape was grey, and white, and fawn, and lovely. The rich plumage of pheasants perching on fences glowed in goblets of colour against the monochrome of winter.

In the night it snowed and in the morning I was afraid I might not get through to Owlnest. Faint in the snow on the long drive were the tracks of John's car returning late from a meeting the evening before. All was calm and smooth in the parlour and, with the snow, the air was warm.

Philip told me that the tractor at Honeybed had been taken away to have its brakes and hydraulics mended. The milk tanker could not get up the slope to Honeybed in the snow and, to enable the tyres to grip (the tractor, being absent, could not pull it up), Greg spread a dustbinful of ashes over the yard. He discovered, too late, that the family living in the house had been burning old wood with nails in it.

The cows at Home Farm are giving so little milk that a mini-profile is to be carried out on them, and their food is to be analysed to find out if there is a protein or energy deficiency.

Three of the big tractors are muck spreading in the fields, the lines of dung clearly defined on the snowy ground.

The workshop on the estate used to be an aeroplane hanger and I was taken there to be shown where to pump up the tyres of the van. The former runway, a large, flat field above the valley and the lake, is used now as part of the farm, for potatoes, or corn, or cattle. I picked up another load of wood and drove home on a track through the woods running parallel to the village. On a small scale the scenery has perfection and there is a completeness about the landscape that is immensely satisfying.

Kilvert, one of the kittens I captured at Honeybed and brought home to treat his malnutrition, worms and gastric disorders, is tamed and improved. He has begun to play, and springs up the curtains I have hung over the back door to reduce the draughts. He sleeps in the cool ashes at the rim of the fire and has a yellow streak on the white of his fur where he mistook the heat and was singed. His appearance is unremarkable, even ugly, but his affection is unbounded. He lies in our arms on his back like a baby, touching our faces gently with his blackberry paws, and his eyes half closed with the intensity of his adoration.

I had a remarkable conversation with Susan. She talked for three hours, until midnight. Up to the age of eleven she said she was an 'ordinary' child; born more than ten years after her sisters and almost an only child. She and her parents lived in a conventional suburban setting. Her life was suddenly disrupted by her parents separation and divorce, Susan had to choose which parent she would live with, she now thinks that this decision is too momentous for a child to make. She chose her mother and they moved to a cottage in the country, a new environment, and a new school. She came home from school one day to find that her mother had tried to commit suicide, and from then on she was always afraid of going home. Her mother became ill and no one told her why, until shortly before she died of cancer, a year ago. Susan, with the help of her sister, had nursed her.

Her father had married again and Susan did not care for his new wife and felt she had no home, anywhere. When she was accepted as a student at the Riverton Technology College, I answered her advert for accommodation. She lived one hundred and thirty miles away with her mother. Most weekends she goes to stay with her married sister, who is not so far away. Susan is sensible and mature. She has had to be in the past, and the future is no different.

*19 January*

After working for sixteen days, with only two days off lost amongst them, my long weekend off is sheer bliss.

John had to attend a farm meeting all day on Friday and was unable to help me with the sugar beet. On his early morning check-up at Honeybed, he emptied three sacks of beet into the big wheelbarrow, and showed me how to start the John Deere tractor which temporarily replaces the dairy tractor. The wheels of the John Deere are taller than I am and I manoeuvred it slowly, and carefully, round the yards, uncertain of it and me as partners. I used the van to transport the six bags of cow cake up to the forage trough and to bring the bales of straw and hay down to the dry cows, after bedding up the cubicles and lifting two monstrously heavy bales of hay up into the racks. I tackled the barrow, but could see, after half a yard, that I would never get it up the dung-slippery slope with three hundredweight of beet in it. I rooted around for some sacks and shovelled some of the beet into them, and used the van again, and finally wheeled the barrow up the slope which taxed every muscle I possess.

Malcolm and Kevin, the calf rearers, collected a calf. It is their job when Philip is off. When the calf had been lifted into the truck and the tarpaulin fastened down, we stood in the yard chatting. Malcolm starts work at 7.00 am and works through until 4.30 pm. He has every other weekend off: that is one day off a week. He said we were better off than the workers on a nearby estate, who get only one weekend in five off (and presumably one day off a week as well).

Only two per cent of the calves in Malcolm's care had died this year. The dairymen are paid a bonus for all the calves still alive at the end of their first week, thus, hopefully, making sure that the calves are properly looked after in the first, vital hours of life before facing the further perils of a changed environment and food.

Of the particular calves that had died, Malcolm said, 'Poor little sod,' or 'Poor little bugger,' and sounded as if he really meant it. As more than five hundred calves pass through their hands in the autumn and winter months it is surprising that they are not too hardened to feel pity. It would be easy to get hardened. It is happening to me. Do I really care if some poor old cow with arthritis in her swollen joints can hardly rise from the cubicle, and can only tentatively let her foot down into the passageway with obvious pain? If she were mine, and giving several gallons of milk, what would I do?

With extreme reluctance I dragged myself out of the house in the cold, dark evening at 9.00 pm and drove four miles to look at the cows, shining the torch on the rows of recumbent bodies, standing quietly waiting for a cow to show the tell-tale signs of bulling, swinging the torch beam over the silage face and the cows still eating there, and, finally, sliding the door of the calving box back six inches and seeing a small, black and white calf suckling its dam, whose eyes shone like her silky, black hide in the dim light.

My second dairy meeting. With what ease I drove across the park and into the estate office yard, instead of hesitating outside as I did last time. Because the annual pay awards were to be discussed, the atmosphere was faintly aggressive. I knew that the men were out to make sure that they were paid what they deserved. I, being so new, not only to the farm, but to earning money, kept quiet and observed. The wages were discussed and settled at a twenty-five per cent increase and Bob, who had been prepared to fight for his expected twenty-four per cent, was disarmed. So everyone gets £5,700 a year, including myself. The herdsman at Honeybed receives less 'because of the differential' (there are fewer cows at Honeybed).

The question of cutting back in order to pay this increase arose, and John suggested an alternative to the calf bonus. Graham, rhythmically tapping his pen across his fingers, with his black brows frowning as he spoke, indignantly rejected this idea. After general discussion the calf bonus remained as it was, I had the impression that John had not expected anything else. To cut down the cost of the relief milker (emergencies and holidays), it was decided to train the calf rearer, Kevin, as he was eager to learn.

The next subject was holidays. David and Philip knew the dates they wanted and were given these. There didn't seem to be any priority. It is understood that we take our holidays at the quiet time of year when there are no calvings, and when fewer cows are going through the parlour, that is the summer. I had not thought of holidays and can fit in with anyone. The Dairymaid Costing figures were analysed rapidly, confusing me. The mini-profile at Home Farm had discovered that the cows were short of protein, so the cow cake order has been changed. The feeding policy for the next year followed. If the midday feed at Honeybed was abolished (praise be!), would the lorry delivering the then necessary brewers' grains[1] be able to crawl up the slopes

---

[1] After the first stage of brewing, when the malted barley has been steeped

and negotiate the bends, or would it have to dump its load at the crossroads?

With the relaxing of the atmosphere there was some bawdy repartee over a welding course John had been on. The meeting finished at 10.00 pm, by which time I could hardly keep my eyes open, though not because I was bored. One of the best qualities of the management is that John is always open to suggestions, criticisms, and plain grumbles and, as far as I can tell, he does try to improve, mediate or placate. However, first hand knowledge sometimes packs more punch. He said that milking at Home Farm for Graham had made him beside himself with rage at the inadequate washing down facilities. I reminded him that I had told him that they were practically mediaeval, and that sloshing water around in buckets, slogging up and down the steps to the tank of water, and controlling the flow of water from the hosepipe with a finger, does not fit the image of a progressive farm. The one and only bucket is used for all purposes, including disinfecting our hands and arms for calving, and for providing drinking water for cows in boxes when the drinking bowls freeze up. Needless to say, Bob has three buckets, each with a specific purpose.

The lagoon was emptied at Quincey's and, while I chugged about on the red Massey Fergusson, dwarfed by the giant blue Fords, a JCB on stilts scooped out the muck and tipped it into the waiting muck-spreaders of Norman, Bert, and Will. A huge pile of steaming dung and straw, cleaned out of the dry cow area by David, had disappeared, as well, by the end of the day. Philip came by on his way home and pushed back the silage against the forage trough walls. I noticed I was able to do the midday feed without as much effort and I can now fill a whole bucket with cake and spread it along the silage, where before I could lift two thirds, or less. The muscles in my arms bulge and a cow could stand on my stomach.

Although the puddles have been iced over, and the windscreen is blind with frost all week, I have not felt the cold and have exuded

in hot water to extract soluble sugars, a residue of cereal grains is left. This nutritious feed for dairy cows is highly palatable and nutritious, much sought after because of it contains concentrated sources of protein and oil.

warmth like a heated brick in a muff. If I keep the exit doors shut, except when letting the batch of cows out, the parlour is soon steaming with the body heat of the cows, and the warm water from the udder spray keeps my hands warm. Forking the silage down can only be done without a coat, or I am wet with sweat. I rarely wear my woolly hat, but my horse-hide gloves are invaluable.

One of the young gamekeepers stopped to help me saw up a log I was dragging to the van from the woods. He advised me to be wary of John and another of the men as he thought I might not be safe with them. I laughed and replied that I didn't think they were worse than anybody else, which he conceded. It is obvious that sex is on everybody's mind here. I have been told that one of the men has a pile of magazines in the corn drier barn that would make one's hair (or something) stand on end.

I paid my oil bill at the office today, £114 for two hundred gallons. The plumbers have fixed the heaters at last and the house is warm: marvellous. On the walls of the office were the maps of the estate, all five thousand acres of it, of which nearly three thousand are the farms. Further along the corridor the finances of the estate were being discussed behind closed doors; the losses, and gains, and the future policies which directly, or indirectly, affect all those who work here.

Elizabeth went to a friend's house for lunch and I took the boys out to a cafe. I was physically and emotionally exhausted by the Friday evening and did not wish to spend the weekend cooking. Catherine came and I shopped in Riverton and, on the way home, we fetched the milk from Home Farm where John was milking for Graham again. At night I went to a party, but I left at midnight, and slipped away into the lonely darkness, confused and unhappy. I am not used to being without a partner and I feel bereft.

*20 January*

Elizabeth is not happy at her new school and I slept uneasily, only too aware of the burden of responsibility I carry for us all, adrift on seas of uncertainty like Noah's Ark.

Awaking at 2.30 am I made a coffee and was trying once more to drift off to sleep when rustling noises outside, unidentifiable at first, but increasing into mooing and pattering, made it plain that the calves were out again. I telephoned the young stock foreman in vain, and, in trying to ring John, I muddled the numbers and woke poor Philip.

I woke Roger and, while he dressed, I flung on my dressing gown, coat and boots and leapt out of the house, and through the front gate to prevent the tide of calves sweeping out onto the road. Two groups were already running out of sight round the corner, but the rest were headed back. Roger guarded the entrance, and I set off up the deserted road to get them back. I had succeeded with one group of half a dozen when John arrived and, soon after, Jim. We squelched around in the mud and slanting rain, driving the majority back into the barn, where Jim stood on one of the racks and tried to count them. Twenty were missing and, after a further fruitless search, it was time for me to go milking. I was late starting, but the dawn, when it came, was rosy and fair. The children reported that on their way to school they had seen six of the men herding the missing calves along the road, none the worse for their wetting. I came home for breakfast across the saturated park. A towering beech had fallen; the remaining stump – a jagged splinter of ugliness – and another had been felled because its rocking had split open a stone wall in front of a bank of earth.

I scraped the yards at Owlnest very clean, pleased that I could do the job – when everything works properly. In the afternoon, a trailer-load of silage from Honeybed was delivered and put into troughs. Towards the end of milking, I let the milked cows out to eat it as I was instructed. Unfortunately, some of those still unmilked in the collecting yard saw them and followed them, braking through the electrified dog[1] which keeps them in, thus cutting short the milking.

*26 January*

Potatoes are being fed to the Home Farm cows. They are spread out in a long line in the troughs, straight from the clamp and uncleaned.

---

[1] A dog is an electrified bar which is pulled up behind the cows in the collecting yard, thus encouraging them into the milking parlour. A dog therefore eliminates the need for a person to do this job.

The cows wait eagerly at the gate and, when it is opened, they barge through, pushing and shoving, and eat with intense concentration, crunching the juicy white flesh, and the moist, red soil between their strong molars and their rubbery palates. They are provided with protein blocks which resemble enormous Horlicks tablets and their rough tongues rasp over these.

Harold does much of the welding on the farms and he has made a new gate for Home Farm and put Graham's initials in the design, a pleasing gesture. Graham has been away and not seen it yet.

The tractor was difficult to steer, and kept swinging from side to side when I was reversing up the passageways. The front wheels pointed outwards, probably the result of bashing it into a wall. Philip offered to complete the rest of the work so that I could go to Quincey's to see the new herd arrangements. The herd there have been split into two, high and low yielding cows, and I pray I won't make a mess of the system and muddle them up.

John belongs to a club whose members are dairy farmers and managers, and each of the members is free to take along any member of their staff who is interested in the talks and lectures. Each month he asks if anyone would like to accompany him. I said I should like to go. Nobody else was interested. He picked me up at 1.00 pm and drove about twenty-five miles to a country hotel, where the meeting was held in an upstairs conference room. The manager of our neighbouring estate took the chair. John was one of three people invited to speak that evening on the future of dairy farming as he saw it. He had everyone (twenty men) roaring with laughter at his account of the silage making at Home Farm last year. I was the only woman present and was greeted with affable friendliness by all those to whom I was introduced.

On the way home John told me that his marriage was not happy. I did not believe him. I said that I would not have an affair, and told him why. I said that I had been in love with somebody who had rejected me and that I literally could not bear that experience again. I also said that I was not going to be responsible for breaking up his marriage. What I did not say was that I had fallen in love with him. He has been too kind to me.

One does not expect beauty in a cow house, but early in the morning, just before the dawn at Quincey's, I stood at the parlour exit door, the long, bare, freshly scraped passage stretching out in front of me. The shapes, patterns and colours of the simple wooden building, and the gates superimposed upon each other, made an abstract design emptied of life, but softened by the billowing of mist from the outside cold which flowed over the solid outer gates and streamed down the long passages.

Last thing after the afternoon milking, Philip pushed the silage back for me and, as he drove the tractor up and down the narrow lane, the twin headlights searching the empty spaces and blurring the light and dark together, the long rows of cows' heads were silhouetted against the light. Each cows' breath rose in dragons' smoke as their muzzles poked and pushed amongst the feed; one hundred and fifty tiny bonfires puffing into infinity.

It is tough at Honeybed. Five calves have been born there in two days and, to ease the overcrowding in the calving box, I took one of them down to the calf-rearing unit myself on Friday because they don't get collected over the weekends. Two were born in the cubicles and were plastered in dung. I had to drag one down to the calving box before I could start milking, followed by its anxious mother and two concerned 'aunties'; there are always one or two of these in a herd.

The AI cows, carefully sorted out and correctly caught by me, escaped from the AI pen by breaking down the gate and had to be recaptured with John's help in the morning. He also explained the best combination of gears to use on the John Deere tractor. This improved my technique considerably.

*28 January*

A disco organised by the farm workers was held at the Hazel Arms, a pub half a mile up the road from my house. I thought I ought to go, though going on my own was not much fun. People from all the departments of the estate, their wives and girlfriends, sons and daughters, crowded and jostled in the smoky, dimly lit skittles alley. I danced with Norman, and Henry the tanker driver, and I talked to various people.

Tim, the gamekeeper, explained his job to me. Four full-time men are employed to rear and look after sufficient pheasants for sixteen days shooting a year. This year, the first day's shooting was let to wealthy German and Dutch business men. In the past it has been the Americans who have been prepared to spend a £1,000 a day. At the beginning of the season up to four hundred birds are shot each day. The 'guns' are allowed a couple of brace each, and the rest are sold to shops, stores and hotels. Lord Elroy invites his friends down on some of the days. Towards the end of the season, there is a tenants' shoot, to which the tenant farmers, neighbours, local eminences and a few members of staff are invited. Lord Elroy stands them lunch at the village inn (which is owned by him).

Towards the end of the season the hen pheasants are not shot , but are preserved for breeding. Their eggs are collected and hatched at a game farm, and returned as chicks to be reared at Lyndon in pens. Any surplus eggs and chicks are sold. The young birds are released into different parts of the estate and become the responsibility of the keeper of that particular area. They consume forty tons of wheat a year, bought from the estate's own farm department. The keepers have to ensure the birds stay within the boundaries of the estate, and are ruthless in trapping, or shooting, anything that would hunt, or hurt, the pheasants, including cats and birds of prey.

Each bird is wing tagged and Tim reckoned that fifty per cent are never accounted for, having either escaped, been killed by predators, or died from wounding. I, myself, have been given a pheasant whose leg was gangrenous from a shattered bone and whose crop was so empty that it was obvious that it had eaten nothing for days, miserably hopping about in agony.

The 'guns' stand in a line, beside posts planted across a field, or drive, and the beaters drive the birds towards them, the art of their job being to get the birds to fly high over the guns when they break cover.

I sneaked away from the disco early, not as yet being very good at going out on my own, excusing myself with the thought that, as I was working on the next day, I had to get *some* sleep.

Earlier in the week Simon Bard joined us for supper. He began working at Lyndon on the same day as I did. Knowing he is new to the area, and suspecting he may be lonely, I invited him for the evening.

Bob, when hearing of this (for nothing goes unnoticed here) said sourly, 'You seem to be mixing with the top people.'

It appears I do not know my place – which is a lowly one – for Simon has a position of great responsibility as the assistant agent, the go-between for Lord Elroy and all the separate departments of the estate.

Simon is a young, good-looking, bearded man of twenty-seven, both sensitive and sympathetic to the problems of staff and employers. He is employed by a firm of estate agents and surveyors and lives in a house provided by Lyndon, adjoining the main house. Part of his responsibility is to keep the keys of the burglar alarm system, and to be on hand should the alarm go off and the police arrive. He would prefer a cottage outside the main estate to maintain some sense of privacy. As the agent he has to know something about every aspect of the running of the estate, from negotiating the price of timber and the arranging of its disposal, to the designing of a new calving box at Honeybed.

Simon's job is varied, he will send out invitations for particular shoots, and make sure the guests have a worthwhile day. He will order the blocking up of my chimney to reduce the fumes (which are no better). He does a great amount of paper work and not much practical work, although he is a keen horse rider and has had farming experience, and he would like to do more. It is vital that he should get on with a variety of people, be diplomatic and possess a retentive memory, and – most of all – be discreet. He loves travelling and has worked his way across America. We found our past had much in common and, in the present, we had a natural sympathy.

John was shooting on Saturday: the tenants' shoot. It was my weekend at Honeybed. He came up early and put the sugar beet in the barrow, but this time we both pushed it up the slope and parked it in a safe place until it was needed. Having bedded up the day before I did not need to do that again, and the dry cows' hay and straw was stacked by their yard, so all that I had to do was throw it down, jump down myself and cut the strings. Even so, I worked there from 5.00 am until 12.00 pm with only a few minutes off at breakfast time – 9.00 am – to have my bread and honey sandwich, banana and coffee. Now I always take a flask of coffee wherever I go and leave the house in the morning laden with flask, torch, tractor gloves, parlour gloves, apron, milking top, overalls, handbag, and, sometimes, the radio. I dared to use it at Honeybed. The milk didn't drop off too much, so I shall use it again. Owen said the cows would 'take off' if one put the radio on there. I like to find out for myself if things are true and, sometimes, suffer for my curiosity.

I inspected the calving box first, then put the lights on in the parlour, dairy and collecting yard. I spray the parlour, wash the filters, which have been soaking overnight in a disinfecting solution, and screw them into the pipe-line, switch on the machine, open the doors to the parlour and go and get the cows in. I round them up from the outside yards, calling to them, talking to them, encouraging them to keep moving, but avoiding doing anything to alarm them, which might cause them to hurry and slip on the concrete.

About 6.45 am the sky begins to change colour and, by 7.00 am, it is deep indigo and the stars are still shining within its depths. On this particular Sunday morning there were seven degrees of frost, and the most lovely sunrise. I went out into the collecting yard amongst the last few cows and watched the sky flood with the palest, softest pink. Thin layers of cloud radiated from the horizon and the whitened landscape reflected the colour of the sky. All the wood surfaces were a deep ochre colour. It was so breathtaking I felt a great surge of gladness that I was there to enjoy it, and sorry for all those people still in their beds and missing it. However, no matter how beautiful the sunrise on *my* day off, I am never sorry to miss that. The frost had frozen the slurry in the outside yards and coated every surface with crystalline opacity. The steps to the dairy were sheets of milky ice. The tractor skidded on the slippery slopes and I nearly gave up – but that would have been feeble – and it did not happen again.

A dry cow came into the parlour in the afternoon with a very full, tight udder and she kept shifting about as if uncomfortable. I checked to see when she was due to calve, which wasn't for a week, but I moved her into the box and, by the time I had completed the milking, she had calved, so I was pleased with myself. This was the sixth calf born over the weekend. One of them was not well and had not suckled, so Kevin took it away with another. He put the weak one under a lamp, gave it an injection, fed it glucose and water, and I took off the colostrum from its mother and delivered it, in a bucket, to the unit on my way home. The beams from the setting sun shone gold on the packed backs of the patient cows in the collecting yard, contrasting radiantly with the jigsaw black and white of their coats.

Greg is now off work with either tonsillitis or mumps. Rumour has it that he has to wear two pairs of underpants to hold his swollen scrotum. The men are full of glee and sympathy. Greg says he thinks he's got a hernia from lifting the sacks of sugar beet. His is now the only dairy still using beet and it is to be discontinued next year. Philip is milking for him at Honeybed until he recovers: I do not envy him.

I am writing this with a cat on each arm, my feet in the fire like Polly Flinders, Radio Two battering the air with its swooning love songs, piles of breakfast washing-up to be done, and the exceedingly pleasurable knowledge that out in the cold everybody else is beavering away at washing down parlours, shovelling up muck and sorting out problems. I am still in my dressing gown, the children have gone to school and I have played my mothering role by rising early and giving them breakfast. Today they had grapefruit, cereal and toast. I sewed up Roger's trousers, opened my ears to the talking of the younger ones, and now can enjoy an hour of real relaxation and peace.

This is an attractive kitchen, wherever my eye comes to rest there is something pleasing or interesting. I experience a great sense of well-being, and this is emphasised by the fact that it is well-deserved; I have worked hard for my time off.

Working solely in the dairies it would be possible to be unaware of all the other activities that are of equal importance to the finances of the farm. When John offered to show me the rest of the farming on the estate I eagerly accepted. He called for me at 2.15 pm and we went first to the beef fattening unit at the top of a cold, windswept hill. All the calves are kept until the calf-rearing unit is full. The remainder are then

sent to market. The new Friesian heifer calves, who will replace the old cows who have gone to market or died, are reared in the same group as the castrated Friesian bull calves, and with them are the Friesian-cross beef calves. When they are six months old they are grouped and fed according to their purpose in life and death.

We crawled under the electric wire to inspect the beef cattle more closely. The yards were scraped so clean it would have been possible to it eat a meal off them. The animals from this group are picked out for slaughter as they become fat enough, and none remain by the end of the winter. They were housed loose on straw and not in cubicles.

The cleanliness of the buildings continued at the other, purpose-built unit down on the plain. The wood it was built from had mellowed to a soft, silvery green. Young trees were planted on the unused grassy places and would, one day, hide the uncompromising outline. Inside the young beasts were separated into small groups, fifteen to a pen, and of roughly the same weight and size to avoid undue competition for food. The building housed one hundred and eighty animals.

The eighteen-month-old dairy and beef heifers winter out in the fields in two groups of a hundred because there are no buildings to house them. The yearling beef steers also winter out.

The calf-rearing unit has been adapted from all the buildings of what was once a complete farm, and sheds, barns and cow byre have been utilised and filled with calves of varying ages. I saw the weak calf from Honeybed here, doing well. I was immensely impressed by the high standards of cleanliness and care at all the units, and the health and well-being of the animals. The large, airy barn at Hazelwood houses the weaned calves and these run in large groups in thick straw, arriving in batches from the calf unit throughout the winter, until there is no more room.

Sometimes leaving the car, John pointed out to me the far-flung fields and farms belonging to the estate. He is experimenting with one corn-growing acreage and, instead of ploughing the earth, he is direct-drilling into the stubble to preserve the structure of the soil. He burns off the straw to kill the weeds and, by this means, hopes to grow corn without rotation. To facilitate the movement of the machinery, and in the interest of profitability, he confessed he had pulled up all the dividing hedges on one farm, and ploughed up meadows full of herbs and flowers. He had, however, drained land which was soured by ten acre lakes in winter, replanted hedges and preserved trees standing in the middle of fields.

There are many types of soil within the estate and, as well as the fertile fields, there is rough grazing land: one of the reasons for keeping the beef cattle. John said he would like to try organic farming, but to change over on such a large scale would be difficult. A complex spraying programme is carried out throughout the year on all the crops.

We drove home through the park in the dusk, turning off to look at a ninety-acre field near the lake. I picked up a dead hen pheasant recently run over and left. It was still faintly warm and its feathers were a soft, and speckled, grey brown. I've hung it in my woodshed.

Now I I'm going to write to Andrea, who is writing remarkable letters about her philosophy of life to me, and my father.

Daniel's letter to Andrea. He is ten.

> Dear Andrea,
>
> In reply to your previous letter to the motly [*sic*] crew, as I am one of them I thought I would reply, so hear it is. The lack of football pitches is not [a] problem, and we have a match soon and practice every Friday and I have met a lot of new friends. On Saturday Daddy and I went to [the] rugby to see Bath play Marlow in the John Player cup. And after ten minutes a Marlow man broke his ankle, it was ever so dramatic and he was in terrible agony. Anyway, Bath won 30–6 in the end. After the match I went to the Lyndon party and I won three prizes: yes, three, and I got some food. As for washing up, we all do some every night, or live on cakes and fish and chips. Overall we are managing fine.
>
> Lots of love,
> Daniel

*30 January*

Owlnest, and usually a smoothly running day – when I can get home for breakfast and be away at a reasonable hour for lunch. I suspect Bob does not think I work hard enough, 'especially as you get paid the same as everyone else.' As he is so efficient and nothing is done that does not have a point to it, and all the tools are in logical places and kept in them, it is the easiest dairy in which to work. John, living at the farmhouse at Owlnest, always inspects the cows for me at night, which I do not wish him to do, but am grateful for. So, this week, in addition to the usual jobs, I rolled back the sheet on top of the silage as requested. I threw the row of tyres which weighted it down into the field and heaved back the heavy roll of black plastic. I was still doing this when Bob appeared and hovered in the background.

'Have you done the cubicles?' he said. I thought it must be obvious I had done the cubicles as they were completely clean and scraped.

Bob has a green rake with which you scrape the dung out, and push the sand to the front of the cubicle and then scratch a bit back to cover the place where the cow's udder would lie. I realised he was trying to tactfully tell me that I hadn't done them properly. I climbed down from the silage. He showed me, once more, how he liked them done, and got it off his chest that on the day after my day there, he had to work twice as hard at them. I took the rake and did them all again, row upon row. I reached home at 1.20 pm and went straight into Riverton to do some necessary shopping and, that day, I did not sit down from 5.00 am to 6.30 pm. But my private life has nothing to do with work, and nothing to do with Bob.

John's day had been no better. On the previous evening a steer had caused an accident on the main road. Two cars were damaged, but no one was hurt. John had been called out because they were Lyndon cattle. After driving the animal back, he and Jim had tried to find out how they had escaped from the field, and were unsuccessful – until this morning – when a hole was discovered at the end of a garden backing onto the field. The steer had crawled through this gap and gone out of the front garden gate. An insurance company had to be rung up and a report written.

Vic, the new herdsman appointed to Honeybed to replace Greg, rang John and said he wasn't coming after all because the main room of the house allotted to them was too big, and the garden of the house next door too scruffy. Greg leaves in less than a month and there is not much time to start looking for someone else. John promised him that the room would be divided and a high fence would be erected between his house and his neighbour's garden.

The builders came to my house to put a new chimney pot on the kitchen chimney and I invited them in for a coffee. Walter, the older man, with a straight and honest gaze, had been through hard times: a marriage break-up and unemployment. He was grateful for his job but had no illusions about it, and held firm opinions on the 'bodging' of jobs he was ordered to do.

'Why don't we take the roof off and make a decent job of it, instead of all this patching, which isn't going to last anyway?' he complained.

He had been to the Middle East and abhorred the attitude to women there. He thinks everything is a compromise: marriage included.

The builders begin work at 7.30 am and finish at 4.30 pm in winter, and have every weekend off. In his opinion the agent's job was the most difficult and he thought Simon was doing quite well, and not making promises which he had no hope of keeping – a great failing.

The only thing that went wrong at Home Farm this week was the runner on the scraper catching on rough concrete and wrenching half off. I had to ask Graham for a spanner and he helped me to take it off completely. Later on Philip put another one.

I was able to strip off a layer of jumpers because it was so warm and mild. A calf born in the afternoon was stained bright yellow by the fluid in the water bag. A proper top has been fitted to the end of the hose – a great improvement – and Harold has welded the cluster hooks so that the constant bending to cut off the air intake has been eliminated. I took the radio and the milk dropped thirty litres.

Owen said the job was never boring and, so far, he is right. I was about to fall asleep at lunchtime when Catherine rang.

# FEBRUARY

*4 February*

My day off again. I woke as the children were getting up. I lay and listened to the noises they made. I have wondered what it is like when I am not here, and if they squabble or are upset, but they sounded cheerful and amicable, with some laughing and friendly scuffling in the bathroom between the boys.

Roger took Elizabeth to Tenterton on Saturday to buy a spare part for his moped. They walked four miles to the station in Riverton and four miles back. I took Daniel with me to Honeybed for company – and to help. The cab of the John Deere is big enough for him to sit in with me, and he watched the scraping, pushed the hand squeegee and distributed the bedding. I have since found out that it was illegal to have him in the tractor with me but I did not know that at the time.

I should have been at Home Farm for the weekend. I was at Honeybed on Friday, and I hated the parlour and decided that I was in real danger of being kicked by the unpredictable and nervous cows. The whole set-up is full of hazards. The feeding hoppers are diabolical. Apart from continually blocking up or falling apart, the manually operated handles are so far above my head that I have to stretch to reach them and then pull hard to release the cake into the manger, sometimes eight times for one cow. I was leaving for home, thankful that I would not see the place again for a week, when the phone rang in the office. John was supposed to be milking over the weekend as Greg was not yet back at work. He has never milked at Honeybed and I thought the experience might be revealing.

John said, 'Would you stay on at Honeybed? Because Kevin is going to milk at Home Farm and, as he has been there all week, it seems sensible to stay where you are.'

I was feeling very tired. That is the first time I felt like crying since I came to Lyndon.

John knows I don't like Honeybed. 'I've spoken to Philip, who is milking at Quincey's this weekend, and he will swap with you if you ask him.'

Pride stiffened my quivering lips.

'Not likely, that would be admitting defeat in a big way.'

Unexpectedly, the milking on Saturday morning was calm and smooth, and taking Daniel to help lifted my spirits. No calves were born, thus reducing the workload. John went to see Philip, and came to see me in the afternoon to find out why I don't like milking at Honeybed. He explained that the only way to justify the spending of £10,000 on a new parlour would be to increase the herd to one hundred and fifty cows, and then there would be further problems with accommodation and the collecting yard, etc.

The milk dropped on Sunday and it rained all morning. The yards were awash with liquid slurry running away from the scraper. It was like emptying a lake with a teaspoon.

Every week I take our washing back to Causeway House as that is where the washing machine stays until the house is sold. I go in my lunch hour when the house is empty. One of the old apple trees is down, and the elms are stark, bare and skeletal. The whole place has an air of neglect and scruffiness, with marrows rotting, buckets lying about, and leaves blown up against the door. Inside it is worse.

Harold, the arable foreman, has been showing too much enterprise. In conjunction with an agricultural firm he has been developing a new type of corn drill. Should the idea be taken up, he would market it and sell it. He has also developed a pigeon-packing enterprise, exporting pigeons to France. The estate does not approve, and Harold, living in a tied house, must desist or give up his job and move. Relations are not improved by this autocracy and quelling of inventiveness.

Pat, the young wife of one of the tractor drivers, paid a neighbourly visit. She said about one of the men that, 'He goes all round the world to get to Warminster.' She also made some pithy comments on the estate's owners and workers.

When Jim has a weekend off, John does the cattle for him. The hundred heifers at Loxwell had broken down the electric fence between the turnips and kale on which they were strip-grazing this winter. John asked me if I would help him to get them back after he had helped me at Honeybed. I am always glad to be involved in different jobs on the estate and said I would.

The field at Loxwell is on top of a hill, well drained in winter and consisting of ironstone. It is full of great grey lumps of stone, which look like cowpats until you drive over them. Winter barley grew there last year and turnips and kale were drilled as a catch crop.[1] In April maize will be sown. The cattle have a shed for shelter and live on turnips, kale and straw. I drove John's car slowly along the ridge while he cut the string off eight bales of straw, and scattered them in a long line on the bare earth. He called the cattle, who came reluctantly out of the kale, along with the two bulls who were getting them in calf for the next season. We drove the remainder out, moved the wire and John mended it. I picked up, and ate, a rain-washed turnip, it was crunchy and delicious.

The heifers' different-coloured ear-tags denote each dairy, and they are returned to the dairies where they were born. This is much more interesting for the herdsmen, who follow the breeding of their own animals with dedication.

[1] Drilling is the process whereby a shallow trench or furrow is made in which seeds are planted in rows in the soil, before being covered up. A catch crop is a quick-growing crop planted between two regular crops grown in consecutive seasons, or between two rows of regular crops in the same season.

While preparing supper for the children, there was a knock on the door. Lord Elroy stood on the step, a long stick in his hand. I invited him inside and offered him a coffee which he declined. I introduced him to the children, who were gathering round for the meal. By one of those lucky chances which rarely happen, the kitchen was tidy and clean, the table simply, but properly, laid and bowls of soup steamed delectably. The fire burned cheerfully, and Mozart's *Horn Concerto* breathed its heavenly music from the record player. Lord Elroy recognised the music, said I had made the kitchen look very nice, and departed. He is undoubtedly good-looking, but a trifle stiff in his bearing, as if very much aware of his superiority to us lesser mortals.

I took Elizabeth to Brownies that evening. She has wanted to be a Brownie for a long time, so it might cheer her up. School is no easier for her, and, as the headmaster is part of the trouble, I cannot go to see him for help. Sometimes when she cries in bed at night, I go and talk to her for an hour, trying to comfort her. They were happy at their former school, and that makes it worse.

### 13 February

Graham is back at work after a hernia operation. He has been away for six weeks and is not supposed to do any heavy work. The only thing he is *actually* not doing is lifting the ten bales of hay into the rack every day.

The milk tanker arrived early at Home Farm, before I had finished milking. The filters had blocked up, the pump had failed, the hot water had ceased to run, and the end of milking was a filthy shambles. I walked into the dairy and found the tanker driver peeing into the drains. He apologised and I laughed and told him the problem was worse for a woman. Isolated as I am for most of the day, I can never be certain that some one is not going to come round a corner at an inappropriate moment.

Norman came in to offer me a sweet. I had to ask him to start the tractor again. I do not seem to have the knack. Every box was occupied by cows and calves. One calf would not suckle and I kept back some of the colostrum and persuaded it to drink from a bucket: no bottle being visible. I love the smell of cows, which is fortunate as, by the end of the day, I am saturated in it. I appreciatively sniff my smeared arms before sliding into the daily bath. When I arrive home at night, the children cry, 'Oh, you do stink!' I wash my hair almost every day.

From this week on, the calves born are to go to market, so, instead of being sent to the calf-rearing unit, they are kept at the dairies until market day. Their mothers go back with the herd for milking in the morning, and are returned to their offspring after milking at night. If there are several calves to go to market, we put two on a foster cow and do not milk her at night. The calves do well on this system and fetch more money, although it is extra work for the cow man. Some cows will not adopt a strange calf, and will butt it away and refuse to let it feed. The occasional cow will be violent and throw it around. We have to make sure this will not happen before they are left together.

John and Jim drove down to Devon to buy a North Devon bull to replace one of the Hereford bulls which went lame: it fetched £500 as beef. The new bull cost £1,000. The bulls go into the dairies next week and artificial insemination will finish, so I will no longer be required to go back to the dairies at night – unless a cow is due to calve.

I must have cleaned the cubicles satisfactorily this week. Bob came out to have a chat and heaped the van with large clumps of primulas, which he was splitting up. His garden is a showpiece – immaculate – and is sheltered from the wind on the hilltop, and the dairy's ugly barns, by a high beech hedge.

John's sister, Sarah, is staying with him and his family. She is nursing a broken arm and cannot drive, so she asked me if I could take her into Fishwickham. I invited her for lunch and we crossed the line of communication naturally and easily. In many ways, her life has run strangely parallel to mine.

Andrea came home unexpectedly at the weekend, planning to surprise us all: no one was there. I had travelled north to see my sister, and the children went back to Causeway House.

Lord Elroy has been persuaded that it would not be wise to make Harold sign an agreement saying that he would not work for anyone but Lyndon. John wrote Harold a letter selling him that they did not wish him to undertake anything which might interfere with his work, but, of course, he might do anything he liked in his spare time. Harold looked more cheerful today. John goes about whistling and singing. The attraction between us is electrical, but I see no way out of the thorns and the briars.

The snowdrops are clustering on the banks and in the woody copses near Pondtail Lodge. The pussy willow is out beside the lake, and lamb's tail catkins are dangling on the hazels. The flock of Canadian geese introduced by Lord Elroy were swimming on the lake and, as I stood and watched them, a tiny vole scurried and bobbed only a few feet from me.

### 15 February

A cow at Home Farm had severe mastitis. Her udder was full of gas, and today she went to the knacker's, on the advice of the vet. A live animal fetches more than a dead carcass, and she could have died within hours. The knacker's gave us £150 for her, collected her in a lorry and killed her on arrival at their premises.

I left Quincey's with a black eye: I tripped over the squeegee and the handle rose up and hit me, with great force, on my eyebrow, raising a pale green lump, and a violent purple stain has spread across to my nose. I look like a panda. I worked from 5.00 am to 12.00 noon, and from 2.00 pm to after 6.00 pm: a long day.

The Quincey's tractor is having a new engine and the Honeybed tractor, complete with new brakes and hydraulics, is taking its place. Being a bigger tractor it does not fit the passages and it is impossible to scrape clean. David left me a warning note about avoiding the hay racks.

A cow was trying to calve during the morning milking. The calf's head showed, a pale purply-blue with lack of oxygen. Just then John turned up on his daily inspection, and we pulled it out and swung it by its fluid-slippery hind legs, and hung it upside down until the mucus in its lungs and throat had drained away, and it sneezed and shook its curly, blunt head and blinked its long-lashed eyes.

The new Devon bull has been taken to Quincey's. He was in the same pen as the dry, but near-to-calving cows. One of them, excited by his presence, kept attempting to mount him, but from the front, so that she was in danger of tearing, or impaling, her udder on his horns. John helped me to separate them. The bull is a fine beast, lighter in build than the Herefords, and with a dark red hide and nimble-looking legs. I am apprehensive about the bull, his small, intent eyes followed my movements with concentration.

There are several odd things about Honeybed. The whole of today was good, from the pearly-grey dawn softly unfolding from the night to the final closing of the dairy doors. The drive there was lovely, whichever way one goes. The view is perfect. The milking, if it goes well, is quicker than the other dairies, and I usually have company and help at sugar beet time. Milking is a lonely occupation.

The North Devon bull.

The Honeybed bull has long horns, inconvenient in the parlour. He seems to be aware that they jab his neighbours and holds them aloft except when he is eating his cake, when the parlour is filled with rattling and clanging as he slots them in between the bars.

The sun was warm today, I wore a thin jumper and John his shirt. He asked me to go to Owlnest and help Bob to put the Owlnest bull in with the cows. All the way from the entrance lodge of the estate to Owlnest the smooth grass verges were pockmarked by the pounding feet of Bob's cows, which had got out and run almost as far as Maxford. Bob had tried to head them off by cutting across the fields – but failed. The unexpected freedom during the confinement of the winter regime went to their heads. In the dreaming sunshine we manoeuvred the bull out of his pen and into his harem.

*19 February*

Half term, and I took the children over to Causeway House to stay with Edward and to discuss the sale of the house with him.

Though I work such anti-social hours I have a need to keep in touch with people. I try to arrange evenings out; or meals in, so that I can sleep longer the following morning, although I still wake automatically at 4.30 am. On Sunday a few friends came for a simple meal and the last departed at 2.30 am. I never catch up on sleep and only begin to relax when I have two days off together. Sometimes I go to bed at 8.30 pm and, being a light sleeper, demand that everyone else is quiet, if not asleep, which is hard on the older children.

Singling out a calving cow from the multitude at Owlnest, I steered her into the box before milking. The steering is done by remote control, with the human acting as a rudder: step to the right and the cow move to the left, step to the left and the cow moves to the right, the slightest movement being sufficient with nervous cows, whistles and voices being an added necessity with the more confident.

I checked the cow as her labour progressed, and when I heard her mooing loudly with pain and effort (not a usual occurrence), I fetched the ropes and a bucket of disinfectant. Approaching the box, I was horrified to see the newborn calf lying motionless on the straw. In a fever of activity, I stuffed my fingers down its throat, pushed straw up its nostrils, pummelled its ribs, and swung it to and fro by its hind legs, as high as I could lift it while its head dragged limply on the ground. It weighed about ninety pounds. At last, its staring eye blinked and its breathing began. My legs trembled with the effort and I was filled with jubilation.

Bob gave me two loganberry plants and some strawberry runners. At lunchtime, on my way home through the park I waved to Tom, a tractor driver; Simon, the head forester; and Graham, Philip and

Jim. They all waved back and I had a happy sense of belonging and of contact with the outside world. A long-standing friend came for lunch. She said she was really worried about me. When I returned to work, I told her to follow me back to the dairy to give her some idea of the place I worked in. The limpid sunshine alighted on the leaf-covered ground, between the green-grey saplings, and on the blades of winter wheat springing vigorously from the fertile, red earth, and I wondered how anyone could be worried about me in such a beautiful place.

John was at a conference on grassland management today. Philip told him that he had never seen me looking so tired as on the day I gave myself the black eye – now changing colour each day.

I planted the loganberries and the strawberries. The garden at Hazelwood surrounds the house on the front and sides, and at the back the barns and yards adjoin it. On one side the six hens I inherited from Owen are fenced off, and on the other there is a screening fence so that I have some privacy from the road. Someone cared for it once, as various shrubs and trees testify, but now it looks sad and devoid of affection, and this I hope to rectify.

*23 February*

An aeroplane has been hired to distribute fertiliser over one hundred and twenty acres that were too wet to drive a tractor on.

Another weekend at Honeybed and I took my breakfast to Cuff's corner, and walking up the sandy track, ate it among the snowdrops. Clustering in the hollows and spilling down the banks, they symbolised hope and new beginnings. The unfrequented path, winding up through the edge of the woods to a village, had been swept by heavy rain and channels of pure golden sand were exposed beneath the stones and soil. A warning to be careful of the cow in the box made me wary as I fetched her out for milking. I found out that on the evening before she had not let anyone enter her box, but she left her calf meekly enough today and was quiet to milk.

The bull roared in the parlour, growling like a lion. He shook his head, prodding the cow next to him with his horns, which made her jump and cringe. Number '85' lashed out twice and caught me in the back: I was just too far away for it to hurt. Greg's arm had been broken by a cow. The day before, at Quincey's, whilst I was bending down sneezing, I was kicked so severely on top of my head, that I thought my neck must have been shortened by a couple of inches. My greatest fear is of being kicked in the mouth. I also think I should devise a dairymaid's breastplate, because my chest – another vulnerable area – is on a precise level with a cow's foot. A cow will kick for several reasons, mostly predictable: tenderness of teats because of mastitis, chapping or injury; a few cows are permanently ticklish and will always kick, or merely trample about, jiggling their udders and making it difficult to put the clusters on; there are cows that stand rock-like, though they have fearful wounds, and these appear oblivious to all necessary ministrations; there are also those who kick for no apparent reason whatever.

Bob has an old cow which he is using as a suckler cow for some of the calves which are going to market. I took one of the Honeybed calves down to Owlnest. The cow looked bony and poor. Why do they bother keeping these cows? Why don't they cut their losses? In fact, *this* cow was serving a useful function, but I have been told that John won't get rid of anything on four legs – and some hardly have that. John says it is the dairyman's decision whether to keep them.

Living in such large groups, in such unnatural conditions in winter, is hard on the animals, and they suffer from stress, no matter how one tries to alleviate it. A few develop liver failure, or other organic diseases, and some, at the bottom of the pecking order, lose weight. A few go downhill for no particular reason, but recover dramatically in the spring when they are turned out.

There is one such beast at Home Farm. Last week, as it crawled miserably into the parlour, I asked Philip what was wrong with it.

'I've just treated it for double soles on its feet,' he said, explaining that the feet had grown over and under and made it lame. I was aghast at the thought of treating it for anything. This week, John was there when it crept in to be milked. He could not understand how he had not noticed it (probably because it spent most of the day lying down). It made him very angry just looking at it. The poor creature was sent to the knacker's and was put out of its agony. The report from the knacker's showed that its liver had almost disintegrated, its kidneys were as big as footballs and its lungs had begun to collapse.

A tiny muntjac deer ran nimbly across the road by the Owlnest turning, and this morning, when wreaths of fog were hanging low in the beech coppices near Home Farm, I saw five Roe deer, heads erect, standing fifty yards away. I stopped the van and we stared at each other for three minutes before one moved off, without anxiety, and, as one, they bounded lightly away through the slender tree trunks and over the leaf-covered drives, their boldly striped rumps snow-bright in the haze.

In the box at Home Farm on Sunday morning, a cow lay flat on her side, thrashing the churned-up straw in her effort to rise, and in danger of her life from the weight of her stomachs pressing on her diaphragm. My first instinct was to pass the decision on to someone else, but I suppressed this and gave her a bottle of calcium for milk fever. The cow was wedged across the narrow box, putting me in a perilous position as I inserted the needle and watched the contents of the bottle drip slowly down the rubber tube. There was no answer from Philip when I used the radio and no one was near.

The cow, when I returned to her, was completely prostrated and I thought she was dying. No day off is sacred when a cow is dying, so I tried to ring John from the call box at Home Farm, but it was out of order. I ran back to the cow, my apron flapping round my legs, and forced her head up on a bale of straw and wedged another under her shoulder, trusting that she would not roll back in her struggles and crush me against the wall. Suddenly, she made a convulsive effort and was on her feet. I hurried back to finish the milking, at the fortuitous moment that both Henry, the tanker driver, and John appeared. Henry helped me start cleaning and John went to see the cow.

After breakfast I made her move about the box. I saw that she was lame, and found that she had bad mastitis in two of her quarters.[1] I rang, once more, for advice. The more powerful drugs are kept at Quincey's so John brought a supply over. I milked out the liquid from the bad quarters into a container to stop the bacteria contaminating

---

[1] A cow's udder is divided into four separate quarters, each with one teat.

the straw, and put tubes of antibiotics up the teats. John injected her with Penbritin, and she stood drooling, dull-eyed and miserable.

I never look at my watch until the work is done, as when I have completed every task I am free to go. This means that there is never any period of the day when I have nothing to do; it also means that I cannot leave until all the tasks are done. The herdsmen have slightly more flexibility because they can put aside certain jobs one day and make them up on another. They have more ultimate responsibility than I do, but, whereas I can leave a problem behind me when I pass onto the next dairy, they have to face it until it is solved. I never feel the urgent need to hurry because it is 12.30 pm or 6.30 pm.

I can tell the time at which the dawn breaks or dusk falls. The day I am home before it is quite dark heralds the spring. Not having to go out in the evenings is wonderful.

There are two indispensable items of farm life: one is a torch and the other a penknife. I attach my penknife to a long string tied to my belt and keep it slotted into my boots or socks. Even the cows straggling tails are cut with the knife. I would not normally cut the cows tails myself, presuming that if they are long and dirty that is how the herdsman likes them. But as Greg is leaving next week, I have cut all the cow's tails at Honeybed, thus setting the pattern for the new man – I hope. I enjoy cutting their tails and was sawing away at one bedraggled, stringy tail when I found I had cut into the actual flesh, making the cow angry and myself sick.

Every year the young stock are moved from one part of the farm to another, a distance of three miles along roads and lanes, but bypassing a couple of the villages. I was curious to know how this was managed and, though not asked, or expected, to help, for the dairymen are exempted from most operations if not directly connected with the dairies, I was welcomed because I had a vehicle. I drove to Home Farm to pick up four of the men: all hands available had been summoned.

Harold, talking to Jim on the radio, said, 'There's been a bit of a fight to get into the van behind.' This amused us as the van in question was mine.

In good spirits we drove in convoy to the field where the cattle had been wintering. They were rounded up and persuaded to enter the lane. Two vehicles went ahead, dropping men off at vulnerable places such as open gateways, gaps in hedges and road junctions. Jim's truck brought up the rear and, as the hundred cattle passed them, the men then ran across the fields – a short cut – so as to either fill another gap, or get a lift further up ahead.

The narrow lane dipped down into a valley, wound over the river beside a water mill, up the other side and along a ridge to the farm. All went well until they reached the bridge, where the cattle formed a dense, immobile pack and refused to cross. By shouts, yells and persuasion the leaders moved hesitantly over, but in the general panic, two of the animals broke the fence and fell down the banks into the river where one was washed over the weir. I was ahead of the procession in a place where the grass verge widened, and here we held the oncoming cattle while Harold, Jim and three of the tractor drivers ran to and fro beside the banks of the river, trying to drive the animals out. The river is not deep, but it is muddy. Yelling and throwing sticks had no effect, but after half an hour, Jim and Harold appeared on the hill, each hauling a bedraggled yearling by a lasso. We moved on and I parted from them to go to the afternoon's milking at Honeybed.

During the cattle drive, Harold shouted out the orders, and was referred to as Bionic Man and Bigmouth (behind his back), but Jim was actually in charge, as it is his department. Harold is very cheerful these days, and John says the atmosphere on the farm is good at the moment.

The last two weeks have been exceptionally mild and dry. At Hazelwood Farm the men are putting up a fence to contain the waste ground, and here we will be allowed to put Cinnamon, our pony, who is still at Causeway House. The fence posts are of pine and the crossbars are of elm, all are from the estate and treated with preservative.

Cinnamon, our pony.

# MARCH

*5 March*

I stripped out the clear, yellow liquid from the sick, old cow at Home Farm (the one who had given birth to two dead calves) and, after milking, I took the injection and tubes for her teats out to the box, only to find her laid out again, moaning pitifully. I knocked on Graham's door.

'Christ!' he exclaimed when he saw her, and injected a bottle of calcium straight into the milk vein for a more instant reaction. She did react instantly: she heaved herself up and he nearly lost the needle. He stripped, tubed and injected her, and told me he didn't understand why she was so ill. 'It doesn't tie up.'

That night I reached home at 7.00 pm – exhausted. On my next day at Home Farm the cow was still boxed, but a message said she was recovering. Once more I found her on her side. Nothing came out of either quarter with mastitis, indicating that she had lost the use of both these quarters and was therefore useless as a milking cow. John rang the knacker's. I asked what would happen if she couldn't get up. He said that, if possible, they would take her alive; but, if not, they would shoot her, cut her throat to bleed her, and so save the meat for animal consumption. As she was full of antibiotics, the meat could not be passed as fit for human consumption unless forty-eight hours had elapsed between the last dose and her death. As there is a great difference in the price one gets for meat for human consumption, as opposed to dog meat, I wondered if some people were tempted to keep quiet about the antibiotics.

I was apprehensive before the lorry came. We managed to get her on her feet and up the ramp of the lorry, where she was jammed in with a live cow and a dead calf. The knacker man said they would try to keep her alive for the three days until the antibiotics were out of her system, and then kill her. Of all occupations I would least like to be a knacker. It is wrong that money should come before mercy.

There is another bad case at Home Farm. A cow had had twin calves, both dead, and the afterbirth was retained. This happens fairly frequently and the afterbirth usually drops out eventually. This did not happen and, when I was passing the farm, I saw the cow in the crush,[1] waiting for the vet to remove the afterbirth. To my surprise the afterbirth was still limply swinging from her vagina the next time I milked there. By this time it had begun to stink. She is an outlier, encrusted with muck, and with this revolting rope of bad meat dangling round her legs – thoroughly unpleasant to milk. It is not sensible to cut it off as the other end is attached to her womb, and the weight of it is supposed to aid its expulsion. The average life span of a cow in a herd is four calvings.

No-one else wanted to go to the dairy club meeting this week so I accompanied John. The lecture was on the facts and figures of milk production in the EEC and compared us with other common market countries. It was intellectually stimulating. Because John has taken me into his confidence, I am learning about the overall management of the estate. Snatching four hours sleep, I was at Quincey's and scraping out by 5.00 am. I dropped my vacuum flask as I stepped out of the van and, bereft, wondered how I would survive for the next four hours without a hot drink.

The new bull is lame and has to be kept on straw because the concrete is hurting his feet. Any cows seen bulling are put in with him. He spends a long time courting the cow, licking her, nuzzling the vulva, resting his head on her quarters, and nudging her while she pivots round, but the serving is like a goat's – almost instantaneous – one quick thrust and it is all over.

---

[1] A crush is a construction designed to limit the movement of an animal so that it may be safely examined, or a procedure performed.

Philip, less forthcoming than the other dairymen, has a stolid reserve and a dry sense of humour. He passes on information, but never gossip. He is patient, kind and never loses his temper. I respect his knowledge and experience, and I learn from watching the way he does things. He wastes no time and is quietly efficient. He gives no praise, but he would notice if I did not do a job properly. He forgot himself one morning, and gave me a nod and a wink as he came on his daily inspection. At Owlnest he cheerily bade me, 'Clean out those cubicles – properly, mind,' and we exchanged a conspiratorial smirk; he, too, has had problems with those horrible cubicles.

Tom and Jenny invited me to the cinema. It was good to be in the normal world again, for I feel inadvertently submerged by Lyndon, it has completely taken me over, mind and body. Now, on my days off, I go to Causeway House to clean up in preparation for the sale, which is an extra emotional and physical strain. Nor am I making my life easier by my own actions: rather the reverse.

In the unromantic backyard of a garage in Riverton, collecting a van from a service, John told me that he wanted to marry me. I knew, of course I knew, that John loved me. Gossip had told me long since:

'He's crazy about her.'

'The farm manager is knocking off the new milker.'

I hurtled into danger with my eyes wide open and I was years ahead of John in experience and pain. I knew that in his present state of uplifted happiness he was impulsively rushing into areas of undreamed of anguish. I thought that when he assured me that he would stand by me, whatever happened, he was being naive, and had no idea of the pressures he might have to bear. Apart from no longer believing in marriage as a ceremony, I am determined to live on my own for a year, and to retain some space in my life. I am most afraid of precipitating a situation with which I cannot cope, and of being once more plunged into the morass of despair from which I am only just recovering. To wait seems the only sensible action, but I fear that John is too straight and direct to deceive, or wish to deceive, and will act accordingly. No one can be unaware of his feelings, but only I, and now my children, know of his intentions. There is nothing I hide from the children, not only because uncertainty is worse than knowledge, but because we are all in this together, struggling for survival and some sort of peace. I trust them to not say anything to anyone.

And so we have become lovers – such happiness.

*6 March*

I am writing by the kitchen fire with the sunshine streaming through the panes of the window and the cats curled together on one of the chairs. Apart from the pressure of all the things I must do today, I am peaceful and happy, the pleasant, slow swing of the upward pendulum.

The dog mated at Christmas and gave birth to four healthy puppies a week ago. One was a breech, and would have died – as happened in the past – by getting stuck half way, but Roger, with gentle fingers, pulled out the tiny, mouse-like Bonzo and saved its life.

Greg left Honeybed Farm for his new job across the valley. David suggested a farewell drink, so it was arranged that all the dairymen, including myself and Philip; the calf rearers; Mick, the beef rearer; and a few of the wives should meet at the local pub. We contributed to a kitty, and John presented an engraved tankard to Greg – who became somewhat merry. It was a jolly and relaxed evening, and I talked to Malcolm's wife, who is not happy and wants to be independent, but does not know how she can be.

The herdsmen always leave me a note to inform me of my duties, and the general state of affairs at the dairy. Greg's last note to me before he left was:

> One hundred and three in milk.
> Two steamers.
> No. '308' in box with three calves.
> Milk AM and PM. Calves to go on Friday morning (market).
> Keep the good work up, hope to see you *soon* (enytime) [*sic*].

This epistle carried me through another hard day's slogging at Honeybed Farm.

Although the barn at Owlnest is a gloomy place to work in, with its dreary, damp-looking, sanded cubicles, instead of the yellow-strawed ones of Home Farm, Quincey's and Honeybed, it too has moments of charm. One morning, well before dawn, a bird began to sing. Only the dim lights, which are on all night, illuminated the vast spaces, but from somewhere high in the rafters came the beautiful trilling and singing of a blackbird. Birds come frequently into the parlour between milkings; to pick up the crumbs of cake which have fallen from the hoppers, and, occasionally, I have seen mice searching for food. A flock of chaffinches flew into the forage passage at Quincey's to peck the corn from the maize silage, and collared doves strutted and cooed and began to nest on the ledges in all the barns.

It was at Owlnest that a fiery sun rose behind the east end of the barn, so that all the slats and cross bars were outlined against the brilliant reds and oranges of the sunrise; an irregular pattern which resembled the east window of a cathedral. The red light shed warmth on the cobwebbed, corrugated iron walls, and the whole barn glowed. The wooden struts of the cow stalls stood thin, black and vertical, a maze of crosses before this glory. Even the iron posts in the parlour have beauty and subtlety. All the parlours have large windows so that, although shut away from the outside world most of the time, we do not lack daylight and sunlight. When wet, the standings shine like pebbles under water, an infinite variety of colours in a microcosmic world. I wish that I could paint the lighting effects, which entrance me, or capture the fleeting subtleties of colour in what must be the most mundane of subjects.

I stand in the pit on a lower level from the cows, my head at the height of their bellies. As dawn comes, the daylight between their legs, and the space between the cows in the collecting yard, increases as fewer and fewer are left to be milked; it makes an abstract pattern and tells me that this long milking is drawing to an end.

Along the concrete track leading to the edge of the field opposite the milking parlour, I sat in the van and ate my breakfast of the usual honey sandwich, banana and coffee. Here the fields drop away to Laggus Farm and, through the bare branches of the ancient oaks, the mass of Lyndon House is perceptible, a soft, dove-colour in the silver sunshine. Rhythmically circling the ground was one of the big Ford tractors, distributing fertiliser granules on the ninety-acre field in the valley. All the colours were gentle and soft. I did not envy anyone in the world.

When I came to start the tractor for the scraping, the engine refused to turn over. By great good fortune, Norman, on the Ford Tractor I had been watching, was turning into the yard to get a fresh trailer-load of fertiliser. He looped a chain onto the scraper and pulled the dairy tractor out of the shed. Then he gave me a tow, saying, 'Do you think you can manage? If not I'll get Bert. And – for Gawd's sake – don't run it into the back of the fertiliser spreader.'

I did not.

The tractor at Quincey's is back from its overhaul. The clutch is so stiff that even the men are aghast at the effort needed to control it. Having told me about it, I fancied they were waiting for my reaction to it, or to see if I could manage it at all. Having tried it, I thought that I would be justified in refusing to use it. I was so incensed by it that I composed an essay on it while attempting to control it. Every few minutes it was necessary to put it out of gear to rest my shaking leg, and the fear of involuntarily driving backwards into the lagoon if my foot slipped was a sweat-making possibility. Apparently, nothing can be done to improve the clutch; it will have to wear in. I thought grimly that I might wear out before it did. During the course of the day at Quincey's, one has to change the attachments on the back of the tractor several times: the forage pusher to the scraper, then to the loader, then back to the scraper, and so on. The tractor needs precise handling for these operations, and I normally enjoy exercising my skill, but now it is frustrating and a strain. Philip, with kindness, came to complete the last part of the driving for me: I nearly went down on my knees in gratitude.

On my way home on Sunday morning, I went to welcome the new herdsman at Honeybed, Vic, and his family. They had moved in the previous day. A pile of logs had been brought up for them, but the promised fence to cut them off from their squalid neighbours has not yet been put up. Vic said they had not had a day off for nineteen weeks, and he and his wife looked tired and worn. His former milking parlour was an 'abreast' at floor level, so most of his day was spent bending down. Honeybed is a distinct improvement on that. Their old car stood in the unfenced front garden, the children played as his wife sorted the disorder in the kitchen, and Vic dug a few holes in the earth and carefully replanted clumps of winter-deadened plants that he had brought with him.

This week Lord Elroy returned from Switzerland: healthily tanned. His chauffeur fills his Mercedes with petrol from a pump at Owlnest, and we occasionally see it smoothly cresting the curving drive, glinting immaculately.

My day off is on Wednesday for the next three months as the rota has changed. My long weekends cease until the next quarter, but when I have a weekend the time is pleasantly split into shorter sections: Wednesday off; work Thursday and Friday; Saturday and Sunday off; work Monday and Tuesday; Wednesday off. It is a long time in between weekends off.

A cow in a box at Home Farm turned savage in defence of her calf. I waited prudently until John arrived before I ear-tagged the calf. He took a hay-fork into the box with him and drove the cow out, while I stood behind the door, nipped in quickly and shut the cow out. She charged around outside the box, roaring and pawing the ground. Once she was safely back in the box, she tossed the straw in the air over her back. I was careful to leave a warning note for Graham.

My chimney is still causing trouble and Simon the agent, and Stuart the builder, came to inspect it again. The stack leaks and creates a blockage of air when the wind blows. This is now on the list to be rectified. Later on, while I was pruning the roses in the garden, Simon appeared again. He had had a puncture almost outside the gate. He did not know where the tool kit was, nor how to change the tyre, so, for once, it was my turn to come to the rescue and I helped him put the spare tyre on. He asked if he could come round sometime, and, guessing that he might be lonely, I suggested lunch the following day. He is finding his job hard going, but knowing how gossipy the estate is, he did not want to tell anyone, but simply needed someone to talk to. I told him I had heard nothing but praise for him, which is true, and that everyone knows he has an exceedingly difficult job; I hope this encouraged him.

All the time I have been writing this, John has been spreading fertiliser on the fields opposite my house. He stepped in for one of the men who is ill. Yesterday, he explained to me how the grain is sold. It is important to catch the market at the right time as it fluctuates throughout the season. Representatives from the large grain-buying firms come to persuade him to sell to them. He used to make these decisions on his own, but he now involves Lord Elroy and his agent as the responsibility is too great and the gains and losses too large. Grain is sold throughout the winter to balance the budget.

When my van was only starting reluctantly Philip brought over the battery charger during milking, and showed me how to put the leads on: another thing learned. I put the tractor on charge afterwards.

*12 March*

Because I am unable to do any gardening at Causeway House, I paid a man to prune the roses. These he pruned vigorously, but well; but he cut back my lovely forsythia to almost nothing, which would have been so pretty this year.

Susan rode Cinnamon over here to the newly-fenced paddock.

Great, uncontrollable tidal waves of slurry sluiced down the slopes at Honeybed and the tractor came to a halt in the middle of one; I assumed it had run out of diesel. Maintenance of the tractors is done by the herdsmen, and I do not have to think about oil and diesel. I bedded up the cubicles until John came to do the sugar beet and he showed me how to fill up the tank after bleeding the system. We moved as if wading in the sea, the thick, brown slurry was ankle-deep and heavy.

The weekend at Honeybed was no more enjoyable than before. The scraper came off the tractor in the barn, and I fiddled about in the gloom and filth, and manoeuvred the tractor so as to position the scraper in line with the hydraulics and fitted it together with a piece of wire from the parlour. Improvisation and ingenuity kept them together until John appeared to make a more permanent job of it.

Two of the feeders ceased operating and, in between batches of cows, I unscrewed the front of each feeder, cleaned them out and made them work again. The milk yield has plummeted, partly due to a new herdsman with new methods, and perhaps because the sugar beet has gone mouldy in the bags. John is complaining to the suppliers. A good Friesian-cross-Aberdeen-Angus calf fetched only £7 at the market last week (not one of ours) because it was born red – a genetic freak – and buyers are suspicious of red calves, believing that they could be Ayrshires, or other dairy breeds that do not fatten well for beef.

The children go to the local sports centre each Friday evening to swim. They have had tea and departed by the time I arrive home, so I enjoy a period of complete silence and relaxation, which, when I am sapped of all energy, is utter bliss. Last Friday Elizabeth was sick at 2.30 am and I could not go to sleep again. Daniel went to a rugby match on Saturday with Edward, and in the evening I painted Elizabeth's bedroom ceiling as I have promised to decorate her bedroom for her birthday on 1 April. Roger had his belated sixteenth birthday party at Causeway House and I gladly handed the responsibility over to Edward. The party will go down in the annals of the school, but Roger said, 'Never again – too much of a worry.'

*16 March*

The sick cow at Home Farm fetched £150; she must have been kept alive until the antibiotics cleared. A yearling at the beef unit was sent to the knacker's after unsuccessful treatment by the vet for suspected vitamin deficiency. When cut up it was found that it had abscesses all over its body, including one on its spine. A cow at Quincey's was thought to have meningitis, and a huge growth was discovered between its liver and kidneys. David had diagnosed the dreaded E. coli bacteria, it is in the very early stages, and she is being treated in isolation. David has used lime on all the cubicles to prevent the spread of infection.

The knacker's say they are receiving twenty-five cows a day for slaughter. As they are not able to diagnose a cause, there are many vets going there to try and find out why so many cows are dying. Lead poisoning is occurring in some areas.

A calf at Home Farm would not feed, clamping its jaws shut, and turning away from its mother as I steadied it against her belly. Eventually, I had to milk her, fill a bottle and dribble the milk slowly down its throat, because it would not suck. The bull at Home Farm injured his back, falling onto his spine after mounting one of the cows, and he is resting in one of the boxes. The bull from Honeybed has been imported to take his place. In the morning I found him lying cosily in one of the double cubicles with the female of his choice.

Philip is to have another demonstration of correct cubicle cleaning by Bob at Owlnest, and Bob told me that if he had time on his day off he would give me one too. I was *sure* I was doing it properly this time. The day there dawned bright and frosty, but later turned grey and wet. Bob did not come out, but wondering when he was going to was nearly as bad.

Edward came over in the evening to discuss the house and its sale and we all ate fish and chips

*22 March*

My weekend off. I have had time to catch up on the diary; my last day off being too busy. I cleaned the house and then shopped for a carpet for my small bedroom because Elizabeth is having the one in my room. I bought paint for my bedroom ceiling and collected the broken lawn mower: £24 for its repair. I am not yet in the red, but I must spend carefully as I also need a washing machine and a vacuum cleaner. At the moment I take our washing to the machine at Causeway House: a drag.

I walked into a bad quarrel between the children one evening. It was impossible to detect the villain as everyone gave a different story, so I abandoned them to themselves, but I determined to sort out the bedrooms as the next priority. They are still sharing the big room downstairs for warmth and economy. The furniture is spartan and they amuse themselves playing with large cardboard boxes, as all their toys are at Causeway House. Roger went to Boulogne on a day trip with the school, reaching home long after we were in bed. On the kitchen table he left two delicious sticks of French bread.

The silage clamps are huge, empty spaces as the end of winter approaches. Silage is transferred each day from Honeybed, where there is a surplus, to Home Farm. The condition of the cows is dropping. Semi-organic fertiliser is being spread on all the grazing fields in preparation for turn out.

I was ear-tagging a calf at Honeybed and sprayed the navel with antibiotic purple spray it to prevent infection, when I became aware of its mother staring at me intently. I bent down to remove the afterbirth in the straw and she charged me, knocking me against the wall and sending me sprawling in the straw. I squeaked – with surprise more than hurt – and scrambled to my feet; not having anything else to hand, I walloped her head with the afterbirth.

The hoppers were more infuriating than ever, choking up with wet, solidified cake, which I removed by sticking my arm up the tubes and clearing a way through the slimy, sticky mass. I scraped the yard very clean and, by 11.30 am, I was sitting in the sunshine. John brought my former tutor from the agricultural college to see me. Two students from the college are spending a fortnight on the estate's farms studying farm management, and the tutor visits them regularly.

Jim, the young stock foreman, had a bad quarrel with his wife and came to work with a severely scratched face. He had a long talk with John, and asked to have a week off to try and sort out some of his difficulties.

The tractor at Quincey's is no better: it is well beyond the call of duty to have to use it. Even Philip says there is no pleasure scraping out there, and he now hand scrapes the cross passages to avoid damage to the partitions.

Once a month Lord Elroy goes on a farm walk, accompanied by John, Simon and the agent. The Range Rover drew up as I was collecting my flask and leaving Quincey's. Lord Elroy said, 'Good morning Alison.' I knew that I had left everything in perfect order and was quietly satisfied.

All the cows on all the farms are going through the parlour and the milkings are long. Although no calves had to be cared for, it was still a ten-and-a-half-hour day at Quincey's, and I was anxious to get home and make Andrea's bed and to tidy the house to make it more welcoming for her return from college. I had just completed the preparations when she arrived. She is sleeping in Elizabeth's room until Susan goes home for the holidays. Andrea helped me to move the carpets and I bought a single bed from an old people's home for £5. We collected it in the lunch hour and I tried not to think who might have died on it. I crept downstairs on Mothering Sunday and, blinking in the kitchen light, found a card, three feet square, on the table from the children, a cake made by Andrea, fudge made by Daniel, and sweets and chocolate from Elizabeth and Roger. I was deeply touched, especially as I have had to nag them severely in these tough times, and have been brutally forceful. To spoil the pleasure of these gifts, I almost fell over a dead calf spread-eagled in the filth and muck of the open yard at Home Farm. One of the outliers had unexpectedly calved in the night and the calf had probably died of cold and exposure.

One of the dry cows had blood and mastitis in all quarters. Thick red blood oozed out from one teat that I gently squeezed, and watery blood from another.

Graham said 'Stick her in a box and treat each quarter for mastitis.'

To my faint surprise she was still alive the next morning and Philip repeated the tubing of her teats on his morning call.

Pangs of uneasiness and guilt assailed me as one poor animal stood patiently waiting in the crush to be collected by the knacker's. She had a badly cut teat after calving and was difficult to handle and mastitis had developed in the cut teat. She also had 'whites', an infection of the vagina and was giving little milk. Nevertheless, as I drove the tractor up and down the passageways, and backwards and forwards over the yards, I did not like to think of her waiting for her death. The decision, in any case, was not mine.

The two students from the college, accompanied by Philip, came to do all the bedding up for me, which cut down my time. They are spending time with each department in turn, and are in the charge of the head of each department. During the afternoon milking the temperature dropped sharply and a hailstorm drove across the fields, prematurely darkening the waning light.

British Summertime began this weekend, and rising an hour earlier completely disturbed the cows' timetable. Philip said he had to boot them out of the cubicles at Quincey's, and none were waiting for me in the yard at Home Farm as they usually do. John says that a good cow man staggers the hour so that the change is not so abrupt.

The milk in all the dairies is falling steadily: a source of anxiety. The further it goes down the harder it will be to get it back up at 'turnout' when the cows go out to grass. There is enough grass at Honeybed to put the cows out, but the weather is not fit: it has been exceedingly cold.

The arm on the tractor which controls the scraper at Owlnest had broken, and I was warned by Bob to take extreme care in the cubicles because the scraper was swinging from side to side, endangering the upright posts. Before I had done one row Philip appeared with the necessary part and mended it. Bob said my cubicle cleaning was not too bad last week, so I avoided another demonstration.

In the evening I bought a Chinese take-away for Andrea, Roger, Susan, Simon, John and myself, and we sat nursing puppies by the fire in cosy informality. The late night was of no consequence because my day off followed. I slept late, collected Elizabeth and Daniel from school to save them the walk home, and went to feed the two beef heifers at Causeway House. Roger has been caring for them, travelling there each day after school on his moped to fill their hay nets and water them.

At 7.30 pm Philip, David, John and I attended a Grassland Society meeting at Riverton to hear a speaker talking of a co-operative he had helped to set up in the north of England. Once more I was the only woman present.

The wind blew from the east for the whole of my day at Honeybed. Since Honeybed faces east it was very, very cold; I was colder than at any time during the winter. I kept the parlour doors shut throughout milking and only opened them to let each batch of cows out. My foot rested like a block of ice on the clutch while scraping, and I pulled the woolly hat, that I rarely wear, right down over my eyes. I wore my overalls as well as a windproof jacket and I was still cold. Yet the wind was not violent, but barely perceptible, thin and searing in its intensity. The cows stayed in the cubicles all day and the silage yard was hardly worth scraping. A thin layer of ice on the troughs, broken by the lightest pressure, and icicles hanging from a gutter were the only visible signs of the cold. Heavy snow fell in the north. I ate my breakfast in the van. There is no hot storage heater in the office as at Quincey's. I shopped in Marford on my way home.

It was Vic's first dairy meeting that night. His opinion was that the cows were moved around too much at Honeybed and really someone should be scraping out while milking was progressing. Of course, we all agreed. The idea of actually having some one to do that brought smiles of disbelief to our faces. John is continually looking for ways to improve conditions at all the dairies, and particularly at Honeybed, but without spending much money, so little progress is made.

The students have costed the beef enterprise and found that it is losing money, which may mean complete reorganisation of that department.

The possible reasons for the drop in milk were discussed and it was decided which dairies would have the lucerne, grass or maize silage this year. The merits, or otherwise, of teat dipping, or spraying with disinfectant were thoroughly aired, and so was the possibility of doing our own artificial insemination. We agreed unanimously that the Milk Marketing Board did a good job with AI and that it was not financially worthwhile sending anyone away for training; although most of us would like to know how to PD or pregnancy diagnose.

I planned to sleep in the lunch time of my day at Quincey's – knowing that I was going out in the evening – but was disturbed by an acquaintance calling. At night I drove to see a friend who lives thirty miles away and returned at 1.30 am – very nearly falling asleep on the way home. Foolish and dangerous, but not surprising, as I had been awake since 4.30 am. My eyes were swollen with lack of sleep the next day, in spite of being able to sleep on until 8.30 am.

The sensual pleasure of two days off together is unvarying. If I do the chores in the house first, then I please myself. I cut the lawns, removed the broken panels of fencing which had been blown down and askew in the wind, then burnt the bonfire of weeds and brambles.

John helped Roger to service his moped in his lunch hour, and Margaret and Christopher, who had been shopping in Riverton, brought their lunch and ate it with us. I fed the calves in the barn at Hazelwood with John, and when the children had gone to spend the night with Edward, I began to paint a mural of Liquorice Allsorts on the bathroom wall. This has been mulling in my mind for some time.

On Sunday morning I slept on, drowsing, until 8.30 am and then prepared a meal for friends who were coming to lunch, and whom I wanted to show round the estate: an activity which gives me great pleasure.

### 31 March

The cow with E. coli at Quincey's is back in the herd and I was supposed to milk her on three quarters and throw the milk, with its residue of antibiotics, away. John, in the parlour at the time, unwittingly released the lever and the milk went into the tank in the morning.

In the afternoon I milked her out on all four quarters by mistake, but I remembered to reject the milk and the pus from her bad quarter. What effect that will have on the cow I don't know. I was annoyed with myself and thought I would be even more annoyed if I were David. The day after, the thick cable, which stretches down the length of the forage passage to prevent the cows getting in, broke and it took David two hours to mend it. Had I been there, fixing it would have been my job.

The injured bull at Home Farm is out in the paddock, convalescing. His replacement is a young bull who has little hope of reaching the larger cows due to his unfortunately short legs. He should seldom be needed as most of the cows should be in calf by now.

One of the cows stinks abominably. For yards around her there is a warm, foetid smell. She is an outlier and covered in slimy muck and is highly unpleasant to milk. She is losing condition and would be on her way to Barkers[1] if I did have any say in the matter. Heavy rain blocked all the drains and Home Farm was awash; lakes of slurry formed and made scraping tedious.

One of the tractor drivers, Ron, the spraying expert, stopped to talk to me. He came here from Cornwall and is not impressed with this county. John took Andrea and Simon on a tour of the farm because Simon said he would like to see the estate from the farming point of view. Andrea was suitably impressed. I collected Elizabeth and Susan from Brownies, went to a school manager meeting and fed the hungry heifers at Causeway House as Roger is ill in bed.

---

[1] 'Barkers' is the name of the knacker's yard or abattoir.

John and Bob are engaged in a battle of wills at Owlnest. There is a surfeit of grass but it is too wet to graze. John wants to strip graze the field, thus minimising the spoiling of large quantities of grass and the possibility of bloat, although this may poach or trample the ground along the fence line. Bob hates strip grazing and says he will put the fence up, but he will not move it forward every day.

John says, 'If I say the cows will be strip grazed *they will be.*'

It rained heavily today, putting off the moment of truth.

The cow parsley and garlic are emerging on the banks and in the woods, but apart from the lilac buds swelling and the willow trees changing colour, few trees look anything but bare.

I picked up some spare wood for my fire from the Hanger workshop. Harold was breaking up some metal containers with welding equipment, burning it apart. Four of the men were there, working on the machinery. Bert said I could have his share of the wood.

I was able to go on a walk on a local farm with John on my day off. Philip spent the morning with the vet and could not come. The farm was on heavy, clay, flat land. The milking parlour was almost underground, with no windows and only a limited glimpse of the outside world. In summer it would be a dark and dreary prison.

We fed the heifers at Causeway House on our return. Honeybed, when everything goes smoothly, is now the easiest place to work. Milking is quicker there because there are fewer cows, despite the antiquated system. I have speeded up with scraping and there are no more dry cows. The last dry cow calved yesterday. The grass up there ripples silkily in the wind, and the pussy willow is yellow with pollen.

Andrea has gone to Paris to visit a friend. To catch the train to London we rose at 3.45 am and I drove to the main line station; I drove straight back to Honeybed, starting half an hour late.

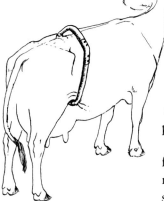

Cow with kick bar.

The feed of cake out of the parlour has been stopped – one less job – and with the help of John I had finished by 11.00 am and went home to sleep because we were all going to Catherine's party in the evening. Roger was in charge of the disco, and Elizabeth and Daniel helped with the preparations all day, and were allowed to stay up for a while in the evening. It was a thoroughly good party and I sank wearily into bed at 1.30 am and rose, equally wearily, at 4.30 am. I had asked for the day off, but Philip was not able to milk for me.

The sky began to lighten at 6.00 am: a beautiful sunrise and a calm, still morning. The water tank in the roof was overflowing: the washer had perished. I climbed into the roof with John and watched how he mended it. The mains water tap is in a field by a hedge and this had to be turned off. Treading on the earth and on the grass again was exciting as I have not had time to walk in the fields once this winter, and I am impatient for the spring.

The evening milking was bad. The cows were fidgety and dirty and I was unable to tube a mastitic cow. I had not been able to tube her the day before, and was determined to succeed. Even with the kickbar securely hooked in position, and a rope tightly tied round her belly, she jumped and heaved so much that the gate opened and she charged out, followed by the remaining batch, pulling the clusters off with loud bangings and clatterings. Fortunately, the rope came loose and dropped off in the silage yard, and the kick bar flew off in the panic. If it had not I would have had to catch her again, as she would not be able to lie down with it on.

I was hoping to have a solitary evening to catch up on the jobs at home, but several people called and I finally ate my supper, a pork chop, in bed.

On Friday it rained continually and I was wetted within, and without, as condensation forms in dripping blobs both in the parlour and in the cubicles in the buildings at Quincey's. In between the heavy, menacing downpours there was brilliant sunshine and violent gusts of wind. The covering on the vent on the roof came loose and banged ceaselessly in the afternoon, alarming the cows who were consequently mucky. Geoff came to borrow the scraper and he climbed onto the roof and held the covering down with a couple of old tyres as a temporary solution. Harold brought his brother to see round the dairies. I hoped he thought I was doing a reasonable job.

The Devon bull charged David when he was feeding him his cake in the box so he let him out with the cows. I had to transfer the bull from one group to another. The next day he was so lame again he was returned to his box. His feet are too soft for the punishing concrete.

'Did you have any trouble with number '41'?' asked Geoff.

I said I hadn't, and he told me that she had been so wild the night before that David had been unable to milk her. Geoff is learning to milk in the afternoons and will be used as a relief in the holiday period. With the bull confined to a box, I have to return to the dairy at night to check for bulling cows.

The blacksmith shod the pony on Monday. He used to shoe her for us at Causeway House, and while I held her we talked of the vast changes in my life, and the causes, since I last saw him. He said he had never married, although he had been in love with a girl and she with him, but she wouldn't marry him because he didn't have enough money.

He agreed that should not matter, and that too many people thought too much of the material things in life. He said he had never had a holiday, and did not want one. 'Life is a holiday,' he said, smiling.

He came in for a coffee, and as he was leaving, offered to help in any way he could. He charged £10 for a new set of shoes. I am lucky I can afford to keep the pony, but it is for Andrea I do it; a link with our former stability.

The silage outside Home Farm is completely finished and little is left in the inside clamp. Geoff and Colin bring a load over from Quincey's each day. The cows went out for the first time on Sunday. On Monday, when I was there, they clustered round the gate when they came out of the parlour and stood in a solid mass, waiting for the gate to be opened. If it had been frosty they would have to have waited until the frost was off the grass. They are only allowed out for a short time until their stomachs have adjusted to the change of diet. The yards are strange without them: empty and quiet.

The rain poured off the roof in waterfalls this morning. The smell of the wet earth, and the feel of the soil beneath my feet when I fetched them in for the afternoon milking, was invigorating. No wonder the cows leap and run. Most of them had soil-covered heads where they had found 'wallows' and rubbed their faces in the earth. I drove them back over the main drive from Deermead, a twenty-acre field, channelling them between two stretched pieces of fencing wire which they believed was electrified, and so avoided touching.

On the far side of Deermead the JCB was clearing drains which had been blocked when a pond was filled in. The water off the fields was diverted to a small lake among a copse beside the field.

The decision to put the cows out at Owlnest has been delayed because of the heavy rain. The grass there is long, lush and thick. Philip has strung the electric fence out across the field in a neat, straight line. Part of the remaining silage face fell down on to the wire in the afternoon and had to be shovelled back. I was warm enough without my long johns on.

Bob borrowed my van to go to the doctors and came into the parlour to see me on his return. He smelt very clean and soapy. He washes his hair every day. I wash mine every other day. Something snapped in the steering wheel of the tractor in the morning. First John and Philip examined it, then Harold was called in to mend it.

# APRIL

*4 April*

This has been a week of no sleep. On my day off I woke at 5.00 am, partly from habit and partly because there was a great deal to be done. Elizabeth and Daniel had their tenth and eleventh birthdays on the first and second of April, and I organised a secret treat. Without telling them, I arranged an outing to see Julian and Clare on the south coast. I had to borrow the car from Edward, taking him to the station at 7.30 am and delivering it back to him at 11.30 that night.

We had a hilarious day, taking the ferry to the Isle of Wight. We caught a bus to Freshwater Bay where we ate our picnic and I was almost swept away by the undertow sucking powerfully at the shingle; I had to sit in soggy pants and skirt until I could change at Clare's house. She made us a delicious supper and we drove the long road home, tired, but happy and satisfied.

I was cold at Honeybed. There was a sharp frost, and a huge hole in the parlour ceiling. A lorry load of cow cake had been blown up the pipe into the loft and, instead of pouring into the bins, a proportion of it had blown onto the ceiling which had fallen in. I did not ask who had had to shovel it up and carry it back up the ladder into the loft.

John debated whether to let the cows out. The ground is wet, but silage is scarce. I said I would like to see one herd going out. The herdsmen like to see their own cows going out for the first time, so that, normally, I would not have had this chance. Because Vic is new to the herd it did not matter so much to him. John agreed.

First we had to check and connect all the outside electric fencing, which runs off a mains socket in the dairy to all parts of the farm. When the cows had eaten their sugar beet, we opened the outer gates and, walking in front of them to prevent a stampede, we led them out to the field. When they had seen us in the fields with the fencing posts and wire, they began to be excited and moved rapidly up and down the yards, lowing. Once in the field they went into a frenzy of delight, leaping, bucking, galloping, tossing heads and tails in the air, and racing from one side of the field to the other for twenty minutes before settling down to voraciously tear at the juicy, fresh, clean grass.

Spreading sugar beet.

We watched them until they were quiet, and checked that none were injured and that no udders were damaged. I could not repress a shudder at the sight of the chunks of turf thrown into the air and the deep holes sunk in the grass by their pounding hooves. They were lying down when I fetched them in and their udders and legs were clean and dry for the milking. They will be in at night for some time yet.

The wheat at Hazelwood is being sprayed a fortnight late because the weather has been so wet. John took over the spraying in the lunch hour, and in the evening, to complete the job. The man who delivered the spray said it was the best drilled wheat he had seen and it was a month ahead of the other farms in the area, which pleased John. He is not worrying about the lack of silage, and this I find amazing. What happens if it does run out? The sun shone all day but I was too tired to feel warm. My friend Ruth and her daughter Emma from the north of England arrived for a visit, just before I reached home at night.

*9 April*

I had done nothing to prepare for visitors and the house was untidy and uncared for, and I had no chance to improve it while they were with us. I was completely stretched at work over the weekend, and when work eases on the farm, I also tend to relax at home and am far less inclined to keep going. Ruth and Emma followed me through the estate on the way to Quincey's in the afternoon, and after they had gone on to Riverton I spent a long time trying to detach the scraper from the tractor, but without success, and was resigned to pushing the long, heavy row of silage back to the cows by hand, when John arrived with a large hammer and not only separated the scraper, but pushed the forage back too. It was a beautiful, mild spring day; the land in the distance was washed over with a pale sunshine. I was so tired that I went to bed at 9.00 pm in spite of having visitors.

The Easter weekend was warm and sunny. A severe, sharp frost on the Saturday was followed by glittering sunshine all day. Milkings are now very long, particularly at Home Farm where the cows are so slow for me, but the milk rose steadily over all three days there. I forgot to put the milk arm in the tank for the first few batches of cows: I was appalled to see the milk gurgling thickly down the drain when I went to pour myself a coffee.

The cows went out after their feed of potatoes on the first day. On the second day I opened the gates straight after milking, and on the third morning I fixed open the gates and races[1] to the field called Cathill One so that they could amble out as soon as they had been milked.

---

[1] A race is a narrow passage, or enclosure, defined by a hedge, or an electric fence. The livestock must pass through it individually, such as to a sheep dip, or alternatively, it can be wide enough to guide the herd to different pastures, or back to the farm.

The injured bull in the calving paddock has to be fed cake and hay each day. The replacement bull sees him as a threat and roars menacingly when he passes along the race beside the paddock. They face each other across the flimsy fence, heads lowered, pawing the ground. I boot his fat backside to move him on.

One hundred and fifty cows spread evenly over an undulating field is a pleasing sight. In the afternoon, when I was getting them in, I seemed to share the Easter break. Far across the fields one can see the rows of parked cars belonging to the humans of another existence, those who have come to wander through the gardens of Lyndon, opened to the public for the season. I was faintly envious of their leisure but a sense of satisfaction came from the fact that I belong and they are only onlookers. Ruth and Emma joined them and strolled in the greens for the afternoon.

The cows take no notice of me as I advance through them, calling them in, then one by one they heave themselves up and move towards the gate until they are funnelled into an indistinguishable mass of bobbing black and white backs. There is a copse at the far end of Cathill One and it is necessary to walk round this to make sure the cows are gathered in. On the way back I picked up dead wood for my fire and shed my jumpers, rolling up my shirt sleeves to feel the warmth of the sun on my arms.

Daffodils are in flower, the tender green of the hawthorns is sprinkling the hedges, and Bob's primulas are a happy, springing red in my garden. On Saturday evening, impatient to begin the spring, I hauled the lawnmower on to the grass and cut the lawns round the house, the entrance verges and the strip of grass bordering the road. Ruth cooked us steak for supper and Emma and I went to buy the chips.

On Easter Sunday morning, in great need of calm, peace and space for myself, I went in search of the mausoleum, which stands in the rhododendron gardens near to Home Farm. After the morning milking I drove up the track towards the quarry and wandered among the trees, shrubs and leaf-covered, mossy ground, past one or two rhododendrons already in flower, until I came to the mausoleum. It's domed roof was shadowed by towering trees and I lay on the ground, gazing up at the canopy of branches. The pointed buds of the beeches were pale with protruding growth but the weird, harsh, spiky branches of the Spanish chestnuts were devoid of any evidence of spring, and only the coniferous trees bore any green in their loftiness. Primroses starred the banks and foxgloves and bluebells pushed their leaves through the spongy ground mosses.

I slept in bed in the lunch hour and was calm again.

The estate agents who are selling Causeway House for us have stipulated the necessity of shutting the hens up in the stables so that prospective buyers will not tread in the droppings. To comply with this absurdity I went over there in the evening and shut them up when they had gone to roost. We have to keep the food and water hoppers filled up, and I strawed the floor to give them something to scratch. I mowed the lawns while I was there because I possess the only lawn mower.

Andrea is home from Paris and she helped me with the bedding up at Home Farm on Easter Monday. Ruth and Emma have departed. I took Andrea to show her the mausoleum and we picked up a van load of wood for the fire – an endless task.

I had asked for a day's holiday this week in an attempt to catch up at home, and was allotted Tuesday, the day I am at Owlnest. I did not miss those cubicles. I slept for seven hours and woke at 6.30 am, feeling almost normal. In Riverton I ordered a washing machine and a second-hand vacuum cleaner. I have paid more than £200 worth of bills this month: electricity £112, oil £75, and the carpets and bed I bought from Owen.

One of the foresters is having our smallest puppy, and he came to see her. The puppies are becoming noisy and harder to keep clean.

I was tidying the garden when Malcolm, the calf rearer, leaned over the wall to chat. He was waiting for Jim to make some pens in which they would dose the young cattle before turnout. He is having trouble with some of his relations and sounded thoroughly fed up. His cat is missing and his children are upset. It has been seen around Hazelwood. I said I would look out for it. John and I, setting off to a Grassland Society meeting in the evening, espied the cat, caught it and returned it to the delighted children. The meeting was interesting, though not well attended, I was the only woman present. The speaker had come from Scotland and had built up a thriving farm from bog land. He had had three bouts of brucellosis which had decimated his herd each time. He estimated he used ten tons of silage per cow per winter and did not turn out until May.

The calves were bawling at Hazelwood when we arrived home. All the racks were empty and they were hungry. Clad in old coats and boots, asking Andrea to help, we fed them. She tossed the bales of hay down from the stack, I carried them to the calf barn and lifted them up to John, who humped them over the doors and into the racks. The doors are jammed shut with the build up of dung and straw which is so deep that the calves can look over the tops of the doors.

My day off was so pressurised and busy that it was not enjoyable. A veterinary student who lived with us last summer came over for the day. Within minutes of finishing her cup of coffee at 8.30 am she seized the new vacuum cleaner and, in an hour, the house looked more presentable. We spent the rest of the day at Causeway House, tidying up the yard to entice prospective purchasers. Roger cleared out the old tack room and the rest of us heaved dried dung into a tidy heap. The lawn mower refused to start. The hens are contented. The sadness of the task hardly penetrated my mind: it had to be done and the urgency of doing it in such a compressed portion of my time removed much of the emotion I would otherwise have felt. I discovered a row of good cauliflowers and we had cauliflower cheese for tea.

The carpet layers came to lay my white, impractical, but luxurious, carpet in my bedroom. The children, tired and cross all day, played in the barns all evening and said it was 'Ace'.

## 15 April

I forgot to put two pairs of socks on for Honeybed and my feet were numb with the cold, but the day gradually warmed up and I ate my sandwiches and coffee in the sun. There was no midday feed, the slurry had all dried up, and the scraping was relatively simple. The long, straight track to the farm was bleached and dusty, the muddy potholes of the winter now dried and whitened, like blown out craters.

A man from the Ministry of Agriculture appeared to ask permission to trap a badger and test it for TB. I told him I would ask the farm manager. There are a few badger setts in the banks bordering the upper fields of Honeybed.

The dairymen ease up after the winter, and the tractor drivers begin to work longer hours. One of the men was fertilising the lower fields when I drove away from the farm in the evening. The dairymen worked all over Easter, but the tractor drivers had time off.

I returned to Causeway House to cut the lawns with a borrowed mower and the evening smelt of summer, too evocative to be anything but painful. The prunus is out with its delicately petalled blossoms, and the daffodils that I had planted gleamed under the fir trees. The smell of cut grass bruised my memories.

Hazelwood Farmhouse looked homely, friendly and welcoming as we turned into the yard. Elizabeth's big, black teddy bear sat on the windowsill, silhouetted against the cheerful orange glow of the room behind. It is very different here, but no less likeable. The biggest change is at Quincey's: instead of scraping out for an hour before milking, I let the cows out of the cubicles and into the collecting yard, then I can start milking – marvellous. They have to be contained in the cubicles and feeding passage after milking in order to encourage them to eat more silage, and are then let out *en masse,* there is something of a scrabble because they are so eager to be out in the open air. For some time they remained unsettled, cantering from one side of the field to the other, heads up, tails up, udders bumping. It takes three hours to milk them, from the first cluster on to the last off, not counting the washing down of the plant, or getting them in. Perhaps it is the length of time the milking takes, which necessitates a high degree of concentration and is done without any break, which makes me so tired. Perhaps I am winding down after the arduous winter. The scraping was quick, there was no bedding up to do, and the remnants of the straw stack, with the left over, half sodden bales, had been dismantled and tidied away by David. There was no midday barrow pushing to be done, and only the silage to push back. It took me a long time to fetch the cows in. Three years ago, the whole herd was bought in when in calf, so the cows are all the same age. Thus they are all comparatively young, and there are no oldies to steady them and lead the way. A white cat playing in the hedge on the far side of the field intrigued them and most of them broke away to inspect it, they are skittishly silly and uncooperative. The Young Farmers Club from Marford arrived for their evening out, complete with sausage rolls, sandwiches, cakes and coke. John gave them a talk on the history of Quincey's and I faded away home when they began to tour the building.

Going to Owlnest was like starting all over again. The system has changed so much that I was uncertain whether I was doing the right things, and I was slow and without method. I saw Bob yesterday and he showed me the way to let the cows in and out of the fields and the parlour. I did not sleep well, and was there early. The cows are out at night and I had been told to drive to the first gate on the drive, collect a container from the water tank in the middle of the field, and then round them up using the van. The container holds magnesium crystals in it to prevent the cows getting staggers, or magnesium deficiency, and has to be filled up each day. Once I have 'drawn' them into the neck of the paddock, I must 'nip smartly' (Bob's words) out of the gate nearest to the bungalow, set the electrified gate across the drive and move the hurdles to form a race into the collecting yard. I must get the calved cow out of the box, and then I could let all the other cows in.

When I opened the first gate along the drive it was, at first, too dark to see any of the cows anywhere, but the headlights of the van picked out the dark shapes on the grass and, very slowly, they began to move in the direction of the buildings. Bob uses the tractor and they respond to that, rising immediately from the dewy ground when they hear the noise of the engine. My van meant nothing to them. Merchant's Close and Hanging Ground are two large, connecting fields, used mainly for night grazing. Slowly, the dawn lightened the sky and, by the time I had obeyed all the instructions, it was light and then I rounded up the stragglers in the lovely spring morning.

On the top of the hill the length of Merchant's Close stretched ahead, sheltered on half if its length by plantations of fir. Hanging Ground, its slopes dotted by magnificent, ancient oak trees, sloped to the corn fields and valley below, where the beautiful front of Lyndon still slumbered amongst its lawns, lake and daffodils.

Today, the milk topped the thirty-thousand-litre mark, brimming to the top of the tank. I turned the motor on at 5.45 am and turned it off at 9.15. The sun rose at 7.00 am, painting all the wooden surfaces a burnt orange. The huge barn is empty, silent and scraped bare. The cubicles lie clean and cold. The collecting yard was covered in a thin layer of liquid slurry.

I searched for a sheltered place to eat my breakfast, wandering through the old yard where the original dairy herd had been kept. The three sides of the square surround a central, weed-covered yard, and the iron standings stood awry. The red-tiled roof sagged over broken pavings. I sat down in the scoop of a horse chestnut's trunk in a fenced-off corner of the field, facing east, warmed by the sun. I thought I would be quite unobserved, but had swallowed only the first bite when one of the big tractors, with the burly figure of Bert at the wheel, entered the adjoining field and rapidly approached, spreading nitrogen pellets. I smiled and waved and, by his third circuit, I had eaten my breakfast and was back at work.

I was loading bales of straw on the tractor to take them to the racks in the field when an unfamiliar car drew up. Two advisers from a cow breeding centre had come to assess the cows and advise on the bulls to use next season. John and Philip invited me to join them.

In the warm sunshine we walked slowly round the herd, inspecting udders, feet, rear ends, backs and all the other qualities of a dairy cow. The main fault of the Owlnest cows was their udders, some were rather light in the forequarters because the ligament holding the udder had dropped at the back and let the udder sag. The men moved on to Honeybed, and I drove the tractor into the fields for the first time. The straw provides roughage and counters the laxative effect of the rich new grass. I dropped the magnesium containers into the water troughs. The grass shone silkily and it was like riding a boat on a smoothly rolling sea.

The day at Home Farm was slow and muddling. Graham had told me to stand and shout for the cows as they still had access to the yard and cubicles, but there was no need. They came slowly gliding up through the dim, early morning light. Keeping the parlours clean is much harder. Any splashes of muck dry quickly and set viciously hard. An atmospheric change has taken place, because up to now, no matter how warm or windy the day, the dung was always moist. Now, despite the cold, it is flaked and stiff and dry and is difficult to scrape and scrub. From milking, the cows went out over the main drive and into the race leading past Deermead, Cathill One and Two, and on to Golden Gate. When the tractor drivers arrive for work at 7.30 am they take down the wires across the drive and shut the cows in the yard. I let the remaining cows out in one big batch at the end.

I checked that the gates were shut all round Pond Ground, and reported some broken fencing to Philip. I fetched some fencing wire from the workshop for him to mend it with. There is now no silage in the clamps at Home Farm. The yards are chalky white and bare.

Graham was in his garden, digging. His house, just across the yard from the dairy, is picturesque with mullioned windows and diamond panes, and there is an old, cobbled yard at the back with a patch of grass and a vegetable garden. But he has no privacy at all.

Andrea is back at university. We had a perfect drive there and it made a lovely day out, the road swooped over the downs and we stopped for a picnic in a wood where primroses, blue and white violets, and windflowers trembled in the wind. We lingered in Burghclere chapel to look at Stanley Spencer's murals, and in the bright, dry sunshine I talked to her about John and myself and the problems all of us face, both now and in the future.

I cut all the lawns at both houses, gardened for three hours, caught up on housework, and sold the last puppy. I cleared a derelict shed in the yard at Hazelwood, and made it waterproof.

I brought my old – and honourably retired – goat over from Causeway House. She is not a good specimen, but her overshot jaw gives her a perpetual smile, and I am particularly fond of her.

*23 April*

The builders Walter and Paul took one of my chimneys off and rebuilt it in another attempt to stop it from smoking. I sat in the garden and sewed.

At 6.30 pm John picked me up to

go to the AGM of the Dairy Discussion Group which this year was held at the house of the farm manager of an adjoining estate. Very few people were present for the start of the farm tour, and we climbed onto a straw-bale-covered trailer on the back of a tractor, and were driven at speed round the bends, and up and down the hills of the estate. More and more people joined us during the evening, which was mild and still; the distances blurred into nothingness. We were shown the beef unit, the heifer-rearing unit and two of the dairy units. Neither of the parlours had windows, and were dark and dreary. At one point we jumped off the trailer to examine the grass in a field. It was discussed knowledgeably; I looked and listened in ignorance. The farmers, managers, and advisers were assured and confident in themselves, but not afraid to admit their mistakes and blunders, and to ask for advice from the other members. The heifers were considered to be too fat, but a field of silage grass received high praise.

John is the 'wag' of the society and made us laugh frequently. When it was dark we returned to the house and were given drinks and a meal. I had no idea what they thought of my being there, but all the men were pleasant, friendly and not at all condescending.

Four hours of sleep, and off to Honeybed. Getting the cows in from Tower Three was the only smooth part of the day – and the most enjoyable. The gate out of the parlour opened twice by itself, with the usual clashing , banging and stamping as the cows rushed out, pulling the clusters off as they went.

I gnashed my teeth in fury at the inefficiencies of the system. The hoppers had not been filled up and half way through I had to set the augers rumbling.[1]

I lay in the barn to eat my breakfast and fell asleep in the sun for a few minutes. I am trying to live a *normal* life, but I am working completely *abnormal* hours. The two are not compatible, nor ever can they be.

John was mending the water tank when I arrived in the afternoon.

---

[1] A hopper is a trough through which feed passes into a chute. An 'auger' is a type of chute with a rotating screw conveyor to supply the feed.

A chance remark of his upset me so much that I went off to get the cows in with tears streaming down my face. I cried until four o'clock, unable even to start milking, so I was late home. John came to see me then and we talked it out. He decided that he would have to see Lord Elroy because the rumours about us are spreading, and can do nothing but harm to us and to the farm.

The dairymen use their tractors to get the cows in, but not knowing the fields I am reluctant to use them, imagining myself getting bogged down in wet places, tipped over in holes and hollows, or running out of control on hills. Each farm is divided into several large fields, or paddocks, so the cows stay in one field until the grass is eaten, and then move to another. Rounding them up from a twenty-two-acre field takes at least half an hour. I would like a dog, and I am surprised that none of the dairymen have one. John would approve. The milking at Quincey's was easy and relaxed. The air in the morning was cold and starry, and warm and sunny in the afternoon. The downs beyond the village of Oliver were washed in a pale heat haze. The huge, flat fields, the gleaming grass, and the slow-moving cows coming from all the far corners in a chequered pattern, then merging into one, was impressive. Larks sang, and, in the hedgerows, the blossom of the blackthorn unfurled its snowy petals.

The Lyndon estate has been *recommended* (one cannot enter) for the Bleddisloe Gold Medal for the best-run estate in the country. The judges look for management, conservation and tree planting programmes, maintenance of buildings, progressive farming, and relationships between landlord and tenants, among other aspects. On the day I was at Quincey's two judges were coming to see the estate. Everyone had been asked to 'do their bit', and the builders had spent the previous day tidying up, although the estate is always tidy. Simon was to escort the judges round various departments in the morning, including a visit to my chimney as an example of a worthwhile maintenance job. John was showing them the farms in the afternoon. I waited in suspense, keeping the parlour sprayed very clean. I had put on a clean apron and blouse. When the car stopped outside I was milking smoothly and efficiently. Two paunchy, elderly men with beetling brows, exchanged a friendly greeting and passed on into the rest of the unit. In the very next batch, the last cow to come into the parlour had been bulling all day and she was in a complete lather. The bull pushed in violently after her, and throughout the milking tried desperately to mount her in spite of the metal barrier between them. This caused a tremendous disturbance and there was a chaotic outbreak of noise, and volumes of shitting from all the other cows, so that everything, including me, was spattered with muck.

David was gardening all day, accompanied by his two little boys, and his baby sat in her pram in the sun, watching. Back at my house I gardened until the arc lamps took over from the sun. I knew that John had gone to see Lord Elroy, and in an agony of apprehension, found comfort in physical activity.

John said, 'I have something very serious to say, Lord Elroy.'

'You aren't leaving, John?' was the instant response, which gave John a little reassurance. John explained that he had fallen in love with me, and that he wanted Lord Elroy to hear this from himself and not through rumour. To John's enormous relief, Lord Elroy was both kind and understanding. He did not try to influence him, and only suggested that if he had made up his mind it was better to act, and to act quickly.

A peaceful start at Honeybed degenerated into a repetition of my last day there and I was mad with anger, focussed partly on the cows – a rotten and untrustworthy lot – and partly on the parlour itself – which is dangerous and difficult. I always begin with cheerful optimism, convinced that this time it's going to be really good. I start off liking the cows (as I basically do). I feel I have an empathy with them, I feel a warmth towards them, and a sense of satisfaction in working with them that is not easily described.

All day a cold, drying east wind soughed through the farm, and the dry, hard sunshine hurt my eyes. Brock came with me when I put the magnesium in the troughs, and as soon as the cows saw him approaching, they converged on him in a swift and menacing mob. A field of grazing and reposing cows was in an instant transformed, and the dog fled before their aggression.

The tenant at the farmhouse came out, full of indignation, because some badger had been trapped. She said *they* had no business to give permission. I sit on the fence with regard to this controversy. I said it was to prevent TB in the cows, which, if it occurs, can devastate a herd. Reactors are slaughtered and no cattle can be moved off the farm until further tests prove that no other cows or animals have it.[1] This can take months. This argument had no weight with the tenant who said that milk was so sterilised these days that TB could not be passed on. I have a feeling that if any of her family were threatened with TB she would have little mercy on the badgers then. I have my milk straight from the tank. When TB was suspected at Owlnest some years ago, the cows that were reactors were not even allowed to give birth to their calves, even those due to be born immediately before the cows were slaughtered, healthy though all the cows appeared to be.

Every animal at Lyndon is being tuberculin tested for the annual compulsory test. Each animal is tested twice within a few days. It is a mammoth task.

Norman and Harold had a row this week. Harold told Norman that he wasn't driving his tractor properly and Norman was so angry that he threw his knife at Harold's feet. Harold refused to be bullied and told Norman where to get off. John heard both sides of the situation, without condemning either. Later he called all the men together, to thank them for the effort they had made in catching up on the work delayed by the weather. Norman thought they were in for a 'bollocking' and had turned his back on John, but when he found he was being thanked he turned round again. John went to see Harold to thank him especially as foreman, and heard that Norman had been to apologise to him.

Fred, a big, burly tractor driver, knocked on the door of my house and asked to use the telephone. His tractor was stuck in the mud nearby. The older tractor drivers wear caps in their cabs. The younger drivers go bare-headed.

I cleaned out the drain at the back of the parlour at Honeybed. In

---

[1] A reactor animal is one that has failed the tuberculin skin test. If reactors are found in a herd, this is known as a herd TB 'breakdown'.

it were two dead mice, a baby rat and a great deal of sludge: no wonder it smelt. The rest of the weekend there was cold, but uneventful. I was home by 10.30 am, but back for 2.30 pm, allowing for an extra half hour to fetch the cows in. Home by 6.30 pm and over to Causeway House with the mower. I am not sleeping well (not surprisingly).

The milk tanker comes early to Home Farm so I have to be there by 5.00 am. The cows were in Greenmoor, under the trees. This beautiful field is sheltered by the trees that crowd down to the fence which girds it, and it falls gently to a stream flowing through the centre of the saucer-shaped open area. A giant oak tree spreads its branches above the grass where the rack stands for the barley straw.

There are many wild cherry trees in Lyndon and I am entranced by the sight of these graceful, full-sized trees covered in a profusion of delicate blossom. The lilacs are budding and the horse chestnut tree near the Lyndon Arms is almost fully out, yet the beeches are only at the white, pointed bud stage.

Today I told John that milking one hundred and fifty cows unaided was stretching a person to the limits of human endurance, and was quite unreasonable in these days of supposed enlightenment. I was cross and tired, and do not accept that because I am a woman I am finding it harder. I still like and enjoy the job itself. With a visit to the dentist, family commitments and a number of incidents on the farm itself, I was on my feet from 4.30 am to 9.30 pm.

Unknown to me, and while I was collecting the children from Brownies and Scouts, John was having a long and serious talk with his eldest daughter, who had perceived that something was very wrong, and had bravely and directly tackled him and asked for the truth. Not wishing to lie to her, he had told her the truth and, from that moment, there was no further concealment. He talked to his wife and came to talk to me, and I talked to Susan and Roger. His daughter came to talk to me as I was milking at Owlnest, and, on leaving, kissed my cheek. I shall never forget that little gesture of understanding from an eighteen-year-old girl, and I was humbled. Tears come easily to my eyes and terror to my heart at the part I am playing in the destinies of so many people.

In the afternoon another visitor disturbed the rhythm of the milking. Bob entered the parlour and, leaning on the rail with a kindly smile, said confidentially, 'We all know what's going on, of course, but I think I ought to warn you that John will get the sack if Lordy gets to know.'

I thanked him for the information. There was nothing else to say. Before I left he offered me a couple of parsley plants and told me to be a bit harsh with the cows if they hang back and won't come into the parlour. Their cake has been reduced and the incentive to come in has gone. It is infuriating when they hang back, as if they have never seen the inside of the parlour, and have to be persuaded to enter.

By this morning's post I received a letter from a friend whose son, the same age and name as Roger, has been killed on his moped.

The time had come to tell the men. It chanced to be my day off. John asked everyone to be present in the Home Farm barn at the usual gathering hour of 7.30 am. He told the men, simply and straightforwardly, that he was getting divorced and was going to marry me, and that I was to continue working as before. He asked them to be especially kind to his wife, and then he turned and, in a dead silence, walked out of the barn.

One of the men told him later that he had never respected him more. It was necessary to tell the dairymen separately because they were milking at the time. John found it difficult to tell Bob. In the end he was prompted:

'I think you have something to tell me, John,' said Bob, puffing his pipe. 'Of course I shall support your wife; I am on her side,' was all he said.

# MAY

I escaped to Honeybed, grateful for the isolation. However, today the place teemed with men. Walter and Paul were building a concrete ramp to enable the brewers' grains to be tipped directly into the silage clamp so that midday feeding can be abolished. The silage yards have to be washed first, using a tanker and fire hose to remover the taint of urine, and dung. Philip was there, filling in the ankle-twisting holes in the collecting yards with quick drying cement. Will was keeping Norman supplied with the nitrogen he was using to fertilise the fields. The policy is to put a lot of nitrogen on in the spring, and less in the summer when it the ground is likely to be drier. If the ground is dry the pellets will be wasted as they need rain to dissolve them. Philip was the only person in whom I sensed a difference, an awkwardness. No mention was made to me on the subject uppermost in our minds. It would be stupid to deny that it affects the relationships between everyone on the estate, but, acutely sensitive though I am now, I detected no difference in their manner to me. In any case, if there was, I should have to bear it.

The mist was lying low in the valleys and slowly, slowly rising with the sun. I kept leaving the parlour to watch it change the world before me. In the woods the bluebells are pushing up on long, slender, sappy stalks. I intended to pick some, but hurried home instead. My mind in its present turmoil woke me at 2.30 am and I made a cup of coffee and wrote an explanatory letter to Andrea. It rained at Quincey's,

Cows in milking parlour.

the first time the cows' there have felt rain on their backs since the autumn as there are no open yards at Quincey's. They did not like it, and huddled near the gate, anxious to get back to shelter. Philip and the vet tuberculin tested each cow as it came out of the parlour in the afternoon. Hearing the noise in the passageway outside, the cows shoved into the parlour and milking was rapid and easy.

The swallows have arrived, while the blackthorns are in blossom. The cows are so clean that I don't have to wash them, but milking is still so slow that I took a book to read in snatches – something of which John would disapprove. He thinks I can't be doing the job properly if I can read as well; I deny this.

I have had to ask Edward to divorce me. We had planned to separate for two years, after which time a divorce is granted automatically if required by both partners. He is reluctant to divorce me for adultery, which are the only grounds on which one can be divorced with any rapidity – apart from unreasonable behaviour, and I would resist this.

John and his wife made an appointment to see Lord Elroy, who has the power to make decisions which could alter our lives. He has offered John the use of a flat in the complex at Lyndon House, because I do not want John to move in with me at this stage: it seems inappropriate for a number of reasons. His wife will be able to stay in the house at Owlnest until September, and after that she will probably move into the house they own which is presently let as a holiday cottage. John and I are to keep our jobs unless there is a deterioration in our work. I am not allowed to visit John in his flat.

'And,' said Lord Elroy, 'the farm manager must live in the farm manager's house.'

This means that, if I want to live with John when we are married, he must move back into his old house – which his ex-wife must leave – and I must leave my house and go to live with him in the house which his family have lived in for the last ten years. If *I* find this thoroughly distasteful, how much worse must this be for John's wife and children?

In many ways it would be more sensible to give up my job, but I want to keep my independence, particularly financially. To me it would be a disaster to give up the opportunity of doing this amazing job – which I am only just beginning to master – and has initiated me into another world, and is the experience of a lifetime.

A few days later the sensation we had caused was entirely eclipsed by the rumour that Lady Elroy had left her husband – and this appears to be the truth.

*8 May*

Elizabeth played in the gardens with the gamekeeper's daughter at the weekend. As children of staff, they are allowed to use the gardens any time they are open to the public: what a playground.

All the grass verges and lawns on the estate are being mown so the grass is smooth and short. The huge area of the park and gardens is perfection itself, rolling in sweeps of glowing green to the shores of the lake. The trees, shrubs and flowers provide an endless variety of colours and textures.

A pall of quiet lay over Home Farm on the Sunday: nothing moved. All the tractors were under cover in the potato barn, clean and silent. I can always tell when it is 7.30 am on a weekday at Home Farm because I hear the rumble of the tractors starting up and diverging to all parts of the farm. Brock, who is now very afraid of cows, refused to come with me to put the hay in the racks.

The gear lever on the dairy tractor packed up on the Monday, delaying me for an hour while Norman mended it for me, frustrating my desire to be home in good time for my parents' visit. John, thinking the gears might go again as soon as I used the tractor, continued with the scraping while I hand scraped all the awkward corners. That was my last day's work for six days.

My appreciation of time off has increased a hundredfold, and when the pressure of selling Causeway House has ceased, I will enjoy it even more. Counting even the times when I am exhausted, or stretched to the point of absolute endurance, I feel I am living with the utmost intensity and almost as if I have only a brief span of life ahead, as if every sense I possess is fully aware, open, alive and working. My happiness is tentative, my security unsure, but my appreciation of all the good things in life has increased beyond measure.

My parents are staying for a week, both to see us, and to look after the children while I go away for three nights and four days with John and the Dairy Discussion Group. We are going to Scotland to visit farms, the West of Scotland Agricultural College, and the farm owned by the *Farmer's Weekly* magazine at Conrick.

I took a customary cup of tea to my parents in the morning and, sitting on their bed in the privacy of their bedroom, I told them of the events so far recorded in this diary concerning John and myself. They were shocked, worried and supportive. John came for the evening and we talked: a probing, revealing and analysing talk.

Eight members of the club were on the tour. I went as a privileged observer. The others were on a business trip and the men who went, and the men we saw, were all intelligent and of a high standing in the farming world. I had no responsibility and an intense interest in the farms and in this man's world. My position to John was understood from the moment we were shown to our rooms in the hotel, John declared to everyone that, as he was going to marry me, he was going to share my room – which he did. We were the butt of some ribald remarks, which added to the good humour and amusement already apparent in the club.

The men wore tweed jackets, quietly checked shirts and patterned ties, and a few wore caps. On one occasion we ventured into a sheep market and the men instantly blended into the background. Nobody present could have doubted that the intruders were farmers: their clothes; their gait; their already sunburned faces; the wrinkles round their eyes from screwing them up to look into the far distance; their large, broad and roughened hands; their shrewd, all-noticing eyes; all these things gave them away. It was bliss not having to get up early, and to saunter down to an enormous breakfast and, afterwards, sitting replete in the back of the smooth, silent car, which carried us, without effort, to the next fascinating farm.

The way people run their houses is interesting; the way people run their farms is more so. There was the earnest man who was putting all his efforts into making money, without consideration of aesthetics or comforts. There was the couple whose house possessed every luxury, and whose generosity extended to a feast of cakes, buttered scotch scones and coffee on arrival – which was shortly after our breakfast at the hotel – and large glasses of whisky on our departure. With respect, we viewed the uniformity of their excellence: their superb cows, the tidiness of the well-run farm, the correct fences and complete walls, the acres and acre of beautiful grass and corn. In great contrast to this was the hill farm which an enthusiastic, well-built, bearded young man was bringing back to use after years of neglect by the previous owner. He took us, balanced on a trailer, on a rough track leading over the crest of a round-topped mountain swept by bleak winds and where no trees stood. He showed us a barren, humpy field, in which the rushes had been eaten down by hungry cattle, and only a few blades of green grass showed through the dried-up, spongy, dung-covered moss. He said he thought that it would be a good silage field because it was so *flat*. Unanimous convulsions of laughter burst from us as we considered the bumps, hollows and steeply falling valleys, but he was serious, and, over three years, he had done so much to reclaim the useless land that one could not doubt that one day it would be a silage field.

Four days of solid cow-talk made me reluctant to mention the word 'cow' for some time.

My parents and I went to visit the gardens of Lyndon. On our way home we were driving out of the estate and approaching the entrance gates when about twenty cows galloped out of the wood and headed onto the main road. I jumped out of the car to try to prevent them leaving the estate and my father drove back to the Home Farm dairy to tell Graham, who was peacefully milking. He turned off the machine and sped to the gates in his car. I had succeeded in rounding up the cows on the road, but they careered away through the woods. I raced through the trees to the field to examine the hedges and fences for the gap out of which they had escaped. One of the gates leading from the field into the wood was wide open. The cattle lorry, which had collected a dead cow that had died of bloat in the morning, had forgotten to shut the gate: gross carelessness.

Four cows have died on the farms since turnout. One of them died of magnesium deficiency or staggers. The knacker men say the cold wind is also responsible, as well as the change of diet to the rich grass. John went to a party given by Barkers to celebrate the opening of their new abattoir. A macabre experience, drinking wine where blood would be flowing on the morrow.

The electric fence at Owlnest had been broken down in the night by the cows, which meant gathering them in from the whole field of knee-high, sea-green grass. The herd climbed the sloping field in the dawn light, their sleek, supple hides rippling, their feet hidden in the grass. I had to move the electric fence to enclose more of the pasture, and had intended it to be in a beautiful, straight line, but it looped, broken-backed, across the field. Philip showed me how it should be done.

There is a surplus of grass at Owlnest, but a shortage elsewhere and eleven acres of silage grass has been strip grazed at Quincey's.

*14 May*

Suddenly it's warm. I'm lying on my stomach in the garden in what used to be the dog pen at Hazelwood. There was a large heap of white pebbles in the pen, and these I spread out neatly, and, as it is the most sheltered place in the garden, my geraniums are out here in their pots.

I am fond of Hazelwood, with its warm, red brick walls, white-painted porch, its doll's house front and its crooked chimneys. A hornbeam, a wild white cherry tree and a red may tree were once planted in the front garden by someone who cared. At the entrance to the yard, whose verges I have cut, there are two large, purple lilac bushes, some of the blossom of which now scents the kitchen and the bathroom.

One of the huge Dutch barns has been emptied of hay and straw. Ron has sprayed the docks and nettles in the pony's paddock, causing a quandary over where to put her for the next few weeks. She is already too fat, and putting her in with the calves in their paddock might give her laminitis.

Ron was spraying a field near Marford a few days ago, when a person in an adjoining cottage complained that the spray was drifting onto her garden. There have been so few days without wind that they had sprayed in desperation, when conditions were not ideal. John went round to see if there was any damage.

Yesterday, the first grass for silage was mown at Quincey's, today it is wilting, and tomorrow silage making begins. Driving past the workshop I could see the trailers and forage harvesters being prepared. All the men are involved in this operation and they will be working until 8.00 pm from now on as a matter of course.

A great part of the success of the farm depends on the silage, because the quality determines the how well the animals are maintained throughout the important winter months, and thus the ensuing production of milk and beef. The grass 'heads' at different times, depending on length of day, and not on the weather, so it is possible to predict with accuracy when it will be ready to cut. Once it starts to head, digestibility goes down and it will never make really good quality silage. Because of the shortage of rain this spring the grass has not bulked up, but it should be high in dry matter (i.e. not have so much water content) and this is good.

The vivid blue of the bluebells floods the woods and the unfolding leaves of the beech trees' springy branches sweep towards the ground. Horse chestnuts, thickly laden with white candles, stand proudly in the park and on the road to Owlnest, the branches of the trees knit their leaves together in an overhead arch beneath the sky. Pink campions and white mustard garland the banks and the smell of the white-rosetted garlic flowers drifts from the shaded copses. The yellow-green of the tiny oak leaves is misting over the gnarled and twisted shapes of the old oaks in the fields at Owlnest. So dry is the soil at Home Farm that in Deermead the wallows that the cows have scraped and pawed are now like children's sandpits. The top layer of sandy soil is nine inches deep, dry and pale brown. Underneath is yellow sand. We are thirty miles from the sea.

Dust rises in a powdery cloud from the track as the cows go in to milk and the dung that splashes on the walls dries rock hard. My arm muscles are strong from scrubbing every day. The potatoes are showing along the ridges of earth and the spring corn is covering the Laggus Field in sea-green shoots. All along the fence lines, and in the tree-planted patches, the weeds are sprayed, as well as the clumps of docks and nettles in the fields. I am afraid that the pair of lapwings nesting in Owlnest Park will never rear their chicks. When the cows have grazed it off, the field will be sprayed or fertilised and the birds will be disturbed or killed. The rhododendrons are beginning to splash their colours over the slopes by the mausoleum, and the honeyed scent of the azaleas mingles with the odour of the pines.

The cows at Owlnest were being TT tested in the afternoon and so great was the confusion that I took my newly acquired cassette radio with me and dared to use it. The extra noise made little difference, but cheered our efforts. I had to use a stick to prod the cows' into the parlour and prod them out, the doors were continually being opened and shut and the mess was universal – a hard afternoon's work. Walter and Paul were concreting the dry cows' yard, patching up the worst parts.

I have had a headache, off and on, for three days. John milked for me at Honeybed on Saturday afternoon while I slept. He enjoyed it, thereby convincing himself that I am making a fuss about nothing. The brewers' grains were delivered successfully. The lorry negotiated the new ramp and the grains slid off the huge, articulated container into a golden pyramid, faintly steaming with moisture which immediately began to run in little channels from this pile of aromatic remains of the beer-making process.

There is a pretty litter of kittens in the barn and the tenant wants Vic to drown them. I will try to find homes for them. Vic has given in his notice. His wife has not settled at the house, or in the village, and she has had 'flaming rows' with the squalid neighbour. Their children are not happy at the school – the same school where my children were so very happy, and to which they return at any possible opportunity to see their friends.

With two evenings spent out visiting friends, a lunch with Tom and Jenny, and with the children inviting friends over one day, we have had a social week. John and I also invited Owen, my predecessor, and Graham and his wife, with whom he is staying, for drinks one evening. I had my first whisky mac: very potent. Both Graham and myself were milking next day. Megan, the wife of one of the tractor drivers, came for a coffee. She is the mother of the children I saw when I was taking my application to the office. She is a tiny, delicate-looking person, attractive and alert. We avoided further revelations about John and me, but she said there had been a lot of gossip. She takes a keen interest in the lives of everyone on the estate, and makes an interesting coffee mate.

*16 May*

A sharp, perpetual breeze still ripples the drying-up grass, but in sheltered places the sun burns hot. I was so sleepy after milking at Quincey's that I ate my breakfast lying on the bank outside the dairy in one such sheltered place, and fell asleep for a few minutes, waking with the sun dazzling through my eyelids. When the long, slanting evening sun picked out the fading blue of the bluebells and the shocking pink of the campions among the trees, I came past Home Farm to see the silage-making.

Near the lodge I could see four tractors working over the pale, yellow-green of the wilted grass. Each was pulling a forage harvester spouting out a plume of darker green, chopped-up grass into the following trailers. These have hoods like babies' prams to prevent the grass from blowing over the back. Passing on along the drive I had to diverge onto the verge as three more tractors and trailers swayed towards me, returning from the unloading of their burden at Home Farm. The younger men were stripped to the waist, but the older men kept their shirts, waistcoats, overalls, jackets and caps on.

The big barn at Home Farm was drenched with the smell of mown, bruised grass; and the sweetish smell of the brewers' grains, the colour of wet sand and pushed into a deep, even layer on the bottom of the pit. The sides of the pit had been draped in thick, black plastic sheets. The trailers deliver the grass to the barn, slowly tipping up until the moulded mass of forage slides smoothly from the shining interior. Fred, in the Sambron [a small forklift truck], was picking up the piles of grass with the buck-rake, a monstrous implement of dragon-tail curves and prongs, and depositing them on the brewers' grains. The Sambron rolled back and forth on the spongy surface, its specially fitted wheel extensions gripping the grass to prevent slipping.

Each cow will eat at least eight tons of silage during the winter, and there are five hundred and fifty cows, plus the same number of young stock and beef animals. The men had offered to work on Sunday because the weather was holding, and because of the delays when the mower broke down. The ground was so unusually hard when it was due to be rolled that many stones remained on the surface of the soil, and these caused severe damage because they are invisible in the long grass. One breakdown is estimated to have cost £250 already.

Swooping down the steep hill to Hazelwood in my van, the beech hedges on either side were thick with the opacity of their pale-green, hairy leaves. The verges were creamed with the foaming cow parsley. When the tractors were put away and all the men had gone home, John came to me and we were happy and at peace.

John showed a couple from New Zealand round the estate. A message came over the radio that the cows were out at Owlnest. John cut across one of the dirt tracks, and from there we could see the cows in the wheat field. A closer look revealed that they were not cows [mature females] but in-calf heifers who had escaped from their field near Lyndon House by swimming across the lake, running through the woods, and crossing the potato field and so on into the wheat. The New Zealand couple were farmers themselves and were pleased to help. We rounded the cattle up and drove them back to their field.

We showed our new friends the dairy at Quincey's and inspected the sixty-acre field of silage there. Some of the grass has been taken off and the rest of it is wilting in long parallel swathes. A little field mouse jumped about at our feet. Two days later, all the grass will be safely under black plastic and old tyres, undergoing the chemical changes that will make it into a nutritious fodder for the winter, and Ron will be spraying nitrogen over the shaven ground to encourage the next cut to grow. John completed the tour of the estate by driving the car onto the rough grass in the park in front of Lyndon House so that we could admire the tranquillity of the lake with the little fishing stands jutting out into the water, the reflections of the trees, and the pretty cottage on the other side.

A ten-hour day again at Honeybed. The vet, with Philip and Kevin, came up to TT the cows. I had to bring them in again at 9.00 am, and run them in batches of ten through the parlour and into the AI pen, where they were then put into a crush which had been brought up for the purpose. Naturally, the cows did not like this, and sticks and tail twisting were sometimes necessary. I defy anybody to get a stubborn beast, weighing more than half a ton, into a narrow passage of which it is rightly suspicious without force. Great was the relief when all the cows were declared clear. A badger, riddled with TB, had been found on the adjoining farm.

The cat had moved her kittens to another hole in the hay. The tiny, black and white kitten – its eyes barely open – hissed, spat and spread its claws so convincingly that I was almost afraid to put my hand in and touch it.

The cows are still getting hay to eat every day. I moved the rack in to the next field by towing it behind the tractor. The track is rough, and the bales of hay fall off when the tractor lurches. The large calves in the backyard at Hazelwood have been taken away in lorry-loads to be put out for the summer on the farms, and the young ones at the calf-rearing unit have replaced them because they can sleep and shelter in the yard, and go out into the field next to it.

John drove the lorry in the evening and took Daniel and Elizabeth with him, much to their pleasure.

The three days at Home Farm were not, in any way, a pleasure, yet I had many moments of pure happiness. I used the tractor to fetch the cows in from Cathill Two and they came quickly and obediently. The milking was slow, bad and dirty. I am never sure if it is my method that is affecting them, I have tried to follow each dairyman's way of milking, but it seems to make no difference at Home Farm. They are nice, quiet, docile and very, very slow. If the milk tanker did not come early, it would not matter, but I don't like holding the drivers up as it adds to their day's length. Henry, the driver, is always cheerful and if he is kept waiting he helps to clean the parlour, runs the hot water in readiness for washing and likes to talk.

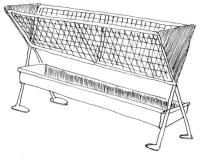

Hay and straw rack.

The tractor packed up again on Saturday morning, I left it in a sea of slurry and squeegeed the slop out of the path of the cows. Silage making was in full swing and everyone was working with a purposeful urgency and a sense of togetherness. The undercurrent of excitement was almost tangible.

Hurriedly making a picnic for Elizabeth, Daniel, John and myself, we set off for the Young Farmers rally at the agricultural college. John is the president of the local branch, and I enjoy going back to the place where I became a day-release student and sat in a class of leather-jacketed youths, at least fifteen years older than any of them. We ate the picnic on the edge of a lush silage field in hot sunshine and explored the stalls, exhibitions and competitions.

I was a little late for milking so John and Daniel went to get the cows and I went on to set up the machine and parlour. An ominous silence hung over the farm. Nothing moved: the roads, yards and barns were empty of people, tractors and action. Not long after we had gone that morning, one of the forage harvesters had picked up a piece of metal (which had flown off the damaged mower) and the metal had got caught up in the machinery and 'blown it up'. Ten minutes later, the remaining forage harvester had suffered the same fate. That was the end of silage-making for the day. Harold had taken charge and had organised the delivery of the forage harvesters to the town where they were being mended. To prevent it happening again, he took the hay turner out to separate the swathes of cut grass so that they could see, and remove, the bits of the mower. John took Daniel and went straight off to the town to see the agricultural engineers. Crises like this one are part of their business; before 8.30 am on Sunday, the forage harvesters were back on the farm.

I had hoped that, by the time I had finished milking that night, which was not until after 7.00 pm, the children would have been taken to spend the rest of the weekend at Causeway House, as arranged. They were still at Hazelwood. I drove them to Causeway House, too tired to speak to them. I bought fish and chips on the way home for my supper and went straight to bed. Because the tractor was not reliable, I walked to get the cows in. The race through which the cows move is made up of posts and a wire fence. It was broken by young stock barging through it and has not been properly mended, as it is one of those jobs that doesn't fit into anybody's duties. The wire is so loose and sagging that one cow automatically stepped over it into the lusher grass beyond. Four more cows followed, and, had I not been close, the whole herd would have gone. Getting them back took some time and I was in a temper before I began milking. The inefficiencies of the system, and the time-wasting efforts of trying to manage with inadequate equipment, begin to ferment inside me.

The cows were reluctant to enter the parlour because of the lack of cake, and this meant I had to go out into the collecting yard and encourage them. Sometimes a cow would go through the doorway and stop there, and I would have to push through the queue of cows waiting behind her, and by prodding, pushing, poking and shouting, get her to move on to her place in the parlour, then return to the smelly, dark, slippery collecting yard and round up the next ones. I was splattered with liquid cow dung. For the first time, I hit a cow, knowing it would not improve anything, but I was enraged at the system, and sure it could be improved somehow. When John came on his round of the dairy I was shaking with rage, so much so that he left abruptly, and I did not see him again until much later that morning. Minutes after he left I saw three of the men mending the race, and the day after Philip electrified the whole race. The agricultural engineers came to mend the tractor, and the split rubber tubes in the parlour were replaced, so they no longer came apart in my hands with irritating frequency: I was pacified. Because I am treading on other peoples' territory all the time, I feel unable to mend, move, change, or improve anything without permission. In asking for permission there is the problem of implied criticism. I presume that how I find a place is how they like it. Perhaps requests for improvements have been made, and not accepted, for reasons economical, or because they were considered to be unnecessary.

Another worry beset the silage-making: the forage harvesters were working, but the Sambron wasn't, one of the men got it working again, after a period of anxiety. Mick was the only tractor driver not working that Sunday. He said he would rather face John's wrath than his wife's, and we believed him. Throughout the day John was forking the silage on top of the clamp into the corners. The smell of the grass, the acrid fumes of the diesel, and the continual noise of the tractors rolling the grass high up in the airy roof spaces of the barn filled the parlour. It was so warm, particularly in the parlour where the body heat of ten cows is considerable, that I wore a bikini top. John said that Owen used to go barefoot in the summer.

By Monday, the cows had moved on into Golden Gate, the field furthest from the dairy. I fetched them by tractor, my confidence boosted by experience. Rolling and bumping over the uneven ground in the cool of the early morning, or the hot sunshine of the afternoon, I was happy and satisfied. To belong to an organisation such as this, to be doing an entirely worthwhile, vital job, and to remember, occasionally, that we are not just making money for ourselves and Lord Elroy, but feeding the nation, improving the land, and keeping the landscape as it is now for generations to come, is a euphoric sensation. Nuclear wars are a possibility, but not much of a worry to those so close to the earth that their noses are nearly pressed into it with the effort of their labours upon it.

To improve the milking, I rigged up a long length of orange baler twine, which the cows believed be electric fencing wire, and this kept them in a tight bunch in the collecting yard and stopped the senseless chasing around in the slurry. Quincey's and Owlnest have an electric 'dog' which can be drawn up by a winch in the parlour and this brings the cows up automatically, but the construction of the Home Farm collecting yard makes this impossible.

Ron, the sprayer, finished the spraying of the pony paddock, leaving a corner of the field to which the pony is confined. The huge tractor, its outspread spraying arms like dragonfly wings, trundled slowly over the thick carpets of docks and nettles, shedding its poison. By the end of the day, the buttercups were dying, and the dock leaves were wilting and crumpled. On the fields where the lucerne is growing, long strips are dying and it is believed that those portions received a double dose of weed killer last year, when the maize was planted in that field and the sprayer overlapped by mistake.

Just as the weeds are killed, so too is anything likely to prey on the pheasants. Hanging on the fence, in an unfrequented field, is a row of dead stoats, weasels, crows, squirrels and even hedgehogs. Pierced through their snouts by the sharp barbs of the wire, their tiny withered bodies swing in the wind.

The milking at Owlnest was smooth and swift. The cows amble meekly into the parlour without fuss. The builders were constructing another, much needed, calving box all day, working in the dark and silent barn, digging holes in the old, brick-lined floor and inserting huge, golden, splintery beams of fresh-smelling wood, and securing them with concrete. Bob wanted a partition for storing hay and straw, but John thought this was unnecessary and would add to the expense. When asked what I thought, I said it would simplify the system, cut out extra tractor journeys, mean less hassle, and, if Bob thought it was a good idea, one could be certain that he had given it much thought; the partition is being built.

Rain fell, the first for many weeks and turned the dried and crispy flakes of dung into a sludgy morass. It dripped all day from a grey sky, puddling the yards and thinly wetting the hard-baked earth and reviving the colours of grass and soil. Margaret came for lunch and I took her to see the rhododendrons. Despite the dull, damp day the banks of colour against the pine trees and the beeches are breathtaking. Some of the rhododendrons tower above one's head, their blossoms cascading to the ground. Everywhere there is the scent of the azaleas. Now that the trees are in full leaf and the may trees are laden with blossom, the park has changed its character. It is lush, smothering, heavy with growth, grand in design, shadowy and secure. The drives are tunnels of shady green, human warrens of vivid colours.

Jim, Malcolm and Kevin were dividing a group of young stock in the yard at Owlnest when I returned in the afternoon. They were separating the heifers from the steers and the yard was full of hurtling bodies, and the noises of cracking whips, gates and hurdles clashing and men shouting. Bob, pipe clenched in his teeth, stood at a strategic point, loudly proclaiming that he had come to help, as there was, 'So much noise you would have thought it was a bunch of bloody amateurs. It makes all the difference, an extra hand.'

The loaded lorry roared away and I rearranged the gates and hurdles. Rain began to fall heavily and I was saturated by the time I had got the cows in. I was glad of my flask of hot coffee.

## 25 May

Since the hot weather, it has been cold and dry, with no further rain. The ground is as dry as before. When the cows are walking down the dirt tracks the noise of their tails switching the flies makes a dry, rattling sound as the dried up clods and beads of dung swing about on the long hairs. The fields of barley 'that clothe the wold and meet the sky' are thick, soft and strokeable as the pelt of a golden-green teddy bear. All over the red earth of Loxwell the spears of maize are pricking through the ground like the stubble on a man's chin. In the gardens of the thatched cottages the last bright days of the wallflowers illuminate the borders and the lilac blossom fades and is replaced by the yellow showers of the laburnams.

Silage making has moved to Honeybed. I left the men working on the clamp and went to the dairy meeting, held this month in the morning. The breeding policy was discussed, as well as holidays, grass, mastitis, cell counts, and milk yields. Bob had got carried away by the breeding policy and had drawn up a chart so that he could see at a glance the conformation of each cow. To correct the faults in his cows he says he needs to use the semen of eight bulls. It is unlikely that he will be allowed to use more than two, because the farms are trying to establish a type of animal which will be seen throughout the Lyndon herds in the future.

All the herdsmen, except Bob, went to Honeybed with John and Philip to see the cows and assess them for breeding and culling. Vic was there, though he is leaving soon. He told me he would sometimes go and sit with the cows for half an hour and they do seem quieter. The cows were in Honeybed field, looking contented, sleek and glossy. Seen individually there are some good cows and a distinct variety of type. It is not often I have time to look at a cow from the side, I am nearly always at the rear end! One heifer was condemned straight away: she had conceived long after she should have, and had given very little milk since calving. She will go to market on Friday and will be dead on Saturday. Graham said, 'Poor little sod,' and I think we all felt a twinge of unease. David said there were one or two of his that he would not only be glad to sentence to death, but willing to do it himself, slowly and painfully!

A new man has been appointed for Honeybed. I was driving the cows in, whistling tunelessly and talking nonsense to them, when I became aware of four people watching from the yard: John, Philip and a young man and woman. They were being shown the dairy and the herdsman's house; the estate are going to put an extension on a small house nearer to the dairy and sell off the house in the village. Vic was given the chance to change his mind, but his wife did not want the new house either, although he was willing to move there. He has been to see about two jobs, but not liked either. When a tied house is involved with a job it adds another dimension to the whole business. It will be awkward if he fails to find another job within his two months notice. Owing to the general shortage of grass because of the prolonged dry weather, the cows at Home Farm are grazing the huge area of the park in the daytime, some of which is now sectioned off with an electric fence. The bull is not allowed out with the cows in the park, not to protect the safety of the public, but because on the other side of the fence is a group of irresistible heifers. He has to be confined in the cow stalls all day, and rejoins the herd in the paddocks at night. At Owlnest, Bob has removed the bull from his cows and any that have not now conceived will go as barreners to market when they go dry. This gives him a tighter calving index, is financially sound, but hard on the cows.

Lyndon fête is on Saturday. Anxiety and fuss over the cowpats in the park is causing minor irritation on the farm. It is feared that people attending the fête may not like evidence of country life on their shoes. Simon has asked John what he is going to do about it. Lord Elroy has decreed that the cows must not use the park, but the grass shortage is desperate and, in this case, the farms have priority. Today the mowers were out in the park, smoothing the turf and chewing up the offending muck.

I put the cows at Quincey's in the wrong field, but the lack of grass in all the fields meant that it made little difference. The milk is dropping at all the dairies and a dramatic plunge at Owlnest worried me, until Bob confided that it was his fault. The day before the cows had been shut in the top part of Stump Ground all day, an area nothing more than a small pack, or passageway, to the large field beyond. Bob had not noticed that the intermediate gate into Stump Ground was shut and that is why they had come so quickly, and quietly, into the parlour – they were hungry.

My sister Juliet and her baby came to stay for five days. Andrea came home for the spring bank holiday, which coincides with her birthday. The house is full, and luckily it was my weekend off. Saturday morning was passed buying clothes for the children in Marford. The afternoon was devoted to showing Juliet the whole estate. The men were making silage at Honeybed and waved cheerfully. John took us out for an expensive meal in the evening, much appreciated by me after our diet of fish and chips and packet foods. Occasionally, I long for a piece of home-made cake.

We celebrated Andrea's birthday with a picnic on the edge of the rhododendrons (we are not allowed to picnic in them) and, replete, we strolled among them, imagining what they would look like if the sun had shone. Later, on our own, John and I walked through the fields of Hazelwood to the edge of the wood. Alan, the driver of the JCB digger, had been digging in search of a leaking land drain, but had hit the oil pipe which runs underground. He had abandoned his search, and the digger, until a solution to the problem could be found. We peered into the deep hole, filled with muddy, clayey water and jumped from ridge to ridge on the churned-up soil. The fields so recently cut for silage were greening over with fresh growth, and the dogs ran on the perimeter of an invisible circle around us, mad with delight. A layer of cold air rested on the fields sloping away from the wood. It is cold for May.

Nobody worked on the bank holiday except the dairymen. I milked and John mowed twenty-five acres of grass ready for silage making at Quincey's on the morrow. Juliet and I made a picnic and went to find him in the lunch hour. I glimpsed the big, blue Ford tractor far across the fields and turned my van onto a rough track running

My Jack Russell terrier.

beside the field. We ate in a sheltered corner looking over flat fields to the rise of the sea-green downs. I climbed into the tractor with John. When he had cut several rows of swathes I drove the tractor, steering it astride the dying ribbons of heavy, silky, corpse-cold grass. Juliet had a turn, then we had to go: Juliet to Hazelwood; me to milking. We left John in the silent cab, sailing higher than the hedges and severed from the disturbances of urban life as effectively as if he were a satellite in space. I would gladly have lain down and slept on the wet parlour floor that afternoon. Missing my sleep in the lunch hour is not good.

Bob told me – with glee – that he has persuaded John to let him have his cubicles concreted this year. He had been to see Lord Elroy about them; £1,000 had been allotted to put new light panels into the barn roof, but Bob thinks the cubicles are the priority and I agree.

Edward took Juliet and the baby home, and Daniel to the north to visit his grandparents. Elizabeth is staying with a friend and Roger, a free agent, is inhabiting Causeway House. Susan is away for half-term, Andrea has returned to university, and I, after a period of hectic, but pleasurable, activity, have a brief space in which to mentally, if not physically, flop.

# JUNE

*5 June*

Causeway House is officially on the market, with its own glossy brochure. I went round to tidy the house and put flowers in all the rooms. Roger helped me. I cut the few clumps of thistles sprouting in the orchard. Going back is indescribably painful, but it must be done. On Friday I showed the first person round (Edward was at work) and they made a written offer, since then we have had an offer of cash, which we will probably accept.

Honeybed is the only farm where the tractor is never used to get the cows in. The fields are smaller and lie on a slope in a long string, with the exception of Park Field, which is a large, flat field from which the silage is cut. The field was bare, stalky and yellow-green. Round the edges, and beside the white, heavy-smelling blossom of the hawthorn hedges, the grass was long and glossy. Interrupting the line of the hedges are many lovely old trees, mainly oak. On other farms one sees the ugly skeletons of the dead elm trees, but few remain on Lyndon land, where they have been cut down and tidied away.

The sun glared down in the afternoon as I trudged across the wide expanse of baking ground. The feeling was akin to treading on virgin snow. In the nearby bushes a flock of starlings filled the air with their chatter, and the twigs and branches swayed and bounced under their combined weight. The cows, spread evenly over the field, moved sluggishly in the direction of the dairy. John, myself and the children had supper at Catherine's with a Japanese family who were staying with her. Roger cut her lawns.

My hands were numb with cold, and the grass grey with frost the next morning at Quincey's. Green patches dotted the field where the cows had been lying, and each recently-evacuated dung pat steamed against the sunrise, so the field appeared to be smoking with subdued fires. A pheasant with her chicks darted into the undergrowth near the silage clamp. I stopped the tractor and followed them. The chicks squatted silently in the grass and only when I was very close did they flutter up and scuttle after the hen. The men made silage there all day, bringing the grass from the fields under the downs a mile away along the road and down the drive. The Sambron broke down during the afternoon and the mechanic who came to mend it had not got the necessary spare part. John drove a hundred miles to Berkshire to get it, driving fast to reach the factory before it closed at 5.00 pm. The new part cost £1,000.

I was depressed all morning, affected by the sale of my beloved house, and full of doubt and fear for the future. My life is stratified like the soil, layered with sadness and happiness, anger and fulfilment.

Saturday was an amazing day. It stretched elastically into Sunday. I was at Honeybed for the weekend and, unobserved, was able to leave the outside scraping and skimped the washing down on Saturday so that I could go shopping, then have a brief sleep, and go to the wedding of Linda and Tony, in a pretty village on the far side of the downs. Tony is a herdsman and met Linda, as I did, at a Stockman's Club in my days as a mature student at the agricultural college. It was a second marriage for both of them, and the wedding in the church was simple, sincere and moving. The thatched cottages covered in clematis, the lilac trees, laburnams, peonies and irises made a cornucopia of loveliness as a backcloth to their happiness. I left the reception in the village hall at 4.00 pm and drove through the vale, past villages half hidden by the clumps of trees under the great sweep of the downs and the vast sky. John milked for me in the afternoon, and, even more generously, the next morning, when I slept until 9.00 am. By 6.00 pm John, Roger and I were on our way to the theatre to see *Oh! What a Lovely War* with our friends the Coventrys and from there to supper at their house.

The younger children went to the Lyndon fête while I was at the wedding. Before I left we had a crisis over a scout shirt for Daniel. It was his first official appearance as a scout and the shirt we had bought was too small (the shop's mistake). Catherine rescued us by taking the shirt to exchange at the shop before it shut for the afternoon. A friend of Andrea's – Jane – has come to stay for a week to retake her A-levels because her parents no longer live in the area. All the teenagers, Roger, Susan, and Jane will be taking exams this week. John came for a late breakfast on Sunday morning, he likes milking at Honeybed, which is sickening.

I was pottering in the garden when the phone rang. The store calves at Harvey's Ground had got out. Forgetting breakfast, we contacted Jim and set off to help him round them up. We heard cattle lowing in the rough woods that drop away from the edge of the lucerne field. We climbed through barbed wire into a marshy field where clumps of rushes grew and buttercups mingled. The electric fence was down and had been dragged about, a small group of young stock had gathered round Jim's unoccupied truck. Far over the other side of the field the cattle came pouring and jumping over the ditch from the wood, followed by Jim. He then started running rapidly in the opposite direction and it was clear that a gate must be open, so John leaped into the truck and I clambered onto the back and wedged myself in among the assortment of stakes, spades, buckets, crowbars and fencing wire, and the truck bumped and jolted over the ground until John made a wrong decision about the wetness of the ground and the truck sank to its axles in a bog. We abandoned the truck and went to meet Jim who had fastened the gate and was mending the fence.

We began to trudge back to the truck, which was out of sight. When Jim had started to head this way, John had said, 'I think we ought to be going this way, Jim.'

Jim didn't say anything when he saw the truck. He just looked. He is always laconic, and occasionally wears a wry smile. Both men tried to dig the truck out, but it was in too firmly. John took me home and fetched a tractor from Home Farm and pulled the truck out. He came home at lunchtime: hungry.

I heard Jim on the radio last week, very angry. He asked where *Mr* Alan was as *Mr* Alan had gone right through his fence with the JCB, thus causing him much extra work. He sounded choked with rage and actually swore, which is not allowed 'on the air'.

Catherine, the Japanese family, a friend of Elizabeth's, and John came for lunch, which we ate in the garden. The children sat on a rug on the grass, Roger and Susan perched on the rounded coping of the wall, and the adults in the former dog pen, where the vibrating red of the geraniums is beginning to show. Although the day had started so well, it built to a crisis involving Elizabeth and, eventually, John and me. I felt strongly that Elizabeth was getting distant and her behaviour was disturbed. In the quiet of the Sunday evening I had a long talk with her. How can she be expected to accept the dramatic changes in our lives, and how can a ten-year-old be expected to cope with them? Again, I felt under enormous emotional pressure, and the heavy weight of responsibility for all the people under this roof bore down on me. It was one of those bad moments that occur inevitably. Much worse, it badly affected John and myself. He, too, is in need of sympathy and understanding, and was unable to see that my plea for what I call my 'space' was not a rejection of him, but my inability to cope with anybody else leaning on me at that moment.

Monday at Honeybed, and part of Tuesday at Owlnest, are not days I care to remember. John did not come near me and nursed his hurt until I wrote him a desperate note and left it for him at the office. Despite the physical pain in my heart I completed the planting of all the tiny stocks, petunias, asters and antirrhinums; sowed seeds; trimmed the borders; wrote to Andrea; washed; ironed; cooked; and collected scouts and brownies from village halls as usual.

The last of the first cut of silage has been made. The men were filling the Owlnest clamp with lucerne on Tuesday. It smells differently from grass, but is still a warm, bruised smell. Before starting, the brewers' grains were spread evenly over the floor and I had to be careful to scrape the slurry past the mouth of the clamp so as not to foul it. All afternoon, during the hot milking, the trailers backed up the side yard and into the barn, deposited their loads, and drove out forwards. I was happy again by then. John came to me in the lunch hour and we talked our way through the problems besetting us. There is no doubt that our emotions are unstable, and liable to wild imbalances of joy and sorrow.

All the herdsmen at Lyndon were invited to see the new dairy unit at the agricultural college, and that evening we packed ourselves into two vehicles and enjoyed a critical viewing of someone else's set-up. The money allocated to the college had run out before completion of the job and the parlour had an unfinished air, nor was it as clean as any of our parlours, which surprised us as they are not short of labour and it is a teaching unit. The more I see of other people's farms and dairies the more impressed I am with ours.

The Principal provided sausage rolls, sandwiches and lager: much appreciated by everyone, especially as the evening became cold and the bats began to fly. John took me home, came in for a coffee and stayed the night. After the nights' exploding and exploring pleasures the next day at Quincey's passed in a haze.

It was warm enough to milk in a shirt at 5.00 am, and in the afternoon the heat was smothering in its intensity: a warm, woolly blanket of heat. I milked in my bikini top, without even an apron. Apart from milking and scraping out the collecting yard, all I had to do was to drag the hay rack from one field to another, and put magnesium in the water trough. I went straight to Home Farm where the herdsmen were meeting to discuss the breeding policy there. We stood in a group waiting for John, who had been to collect his new farm car. Norman drove past, towing a spraying machine on the back of his tractor. He did not give me his usual big smile and wave, and did not respond to a joke from Graham, leaving us puzzled. Harold drove by. He said Norman had backed his trailer, a new one costing £2,500, into a large tree on the lucerne field and buckled a large part of it. Graham said, with feeling, 'Christ, he'll be for it. No wonder he didn't seem very cheerful. Better not tell him [meaning John] before we've seen the cows. He'll do his nut.'

So, when John drove up, very cheerfully in the new car, no one said anything. I waited with interest to find out what would happen, but when I heard nothing after several days, I asked John what he had done. He wanted to know how I knew and he then told me that the damage would cost £250 to repair, and what a good job it had happened on the last day of silaging. He said Norman was accident prone and, on one occasion, had managed to knock over one of the huge, stone gate pillars at Home Farm. This time he had said nothing to Norman, believing that he had suffered enough and knowing well that Norman is a loyal, hard worker.

When the Sambron broke down at Quincey's, the men offered to carry on voluntarily and he said, again, what a marvellous team of men they are. I had met a man at the wedding who did contract work for Lyndon, and he had remarked on what a high calibre of men there were on the estate. He also had a high opinion of John.

Roger wanted to help me milk, which pleased me, partly because it helps them understand what I am doing. He fetched the cows from Shepherd's Ground while I prepared the tank and parlour, and then he stood in the collecting yard and sent every batch in so that milking was rapid and easy. The last cluster was on at 5.00 am and we were home by 5.45.

Because of the rota change over at the beginning of June I worked for fifteen days with one day off lost in the middle. On that day the children dragged me out of bed at 7.00 am by violent squabbling, but it did mean that I caught up with various tasks before setting off with John for a picnic and a beautiful drive to Salisbury Plain. We briefly stopped to sleep in a large wood in a glade of rhododendrons and bluebells in the hot sun. Refreshed and relaxed, we continued the journey to friends of mine who wanted advice on a four-acre field which had been badly trodden by horses and was a mass of buttercups.

Both Susan and Jane (Andrea's friend) have a step-parent and we had a long discussion one evening after supper, with all the children and John present, about the difficulties that arise in building new relationships, and the ways in which they could be avoided, or at least reduced. Another subject brought into the open was the sending of Elizabeth to boarding school, put into her head by friends. It is not possible financially anyway, but I wanted her to know the other reasons why I would not consider it. Knowing that we have to move house again next winter I thought she would then be able to leave the school where she has been so unhappy, and I have been enquiring at the schools in Marford. Now she says she wants to stay at the school. Her teacher says she is popular and she had no idea that Elizabeth had been so miserable, nor had she any inkling of the difficulties of her home life at the moment.

Two more little girls came for tea this week. I barely see them; Susan makes their tea. They ride the pony, play in the barns, play monopoly in the unfurnished rooms, and I take them home in the smelly, rattling interior of the van. They find our home exciting, as it is so different from the modern estates in which most of them live.

Cows in cubicles.

Daniel has burst into tears twice this week, which is unusual. I must try to find the underlying reasons. He is not good at expressing his innermost thoughts, and the only way to find out is to talk around what I think must be troubling him, asking carefully phrased questions, and hoping that when I hit on the right one he will nod his head instead of shaking it. This method means that I may be putting ideas into his head that he had not thought of, but I have not found any other way. Perhaps just by showing that I am aware there is a problem helps. I have no difficulty in imagining the things which might be causing his instability of mood and his almost hysterical highs. Roger has been releasing his own tensions on Daniel and provoking him in small ways. I take my tensions out on Elizabeth.

Susan told me this week she has decided not to marry someone she has known for four years, and has been seeing every weekend at her sister's house. She has never mentioned a boyfriend so this was a surprise!

Jane helped me to milk after Roger, and Susan the day after that. We watched a carriage rally in the park. It was not open to the public, and for a moment it was possible to visualise Lyndon as it had been in the past, when horses and ponies, groomed and polished to perfection, trotted briskly along the gracious avenues pulling broughams, gigs and pony carts beneath the summery boughs of the spreading trees beside the smooth, green lawns.

I took Susan to the rhododendron drive where the turf is now so thickly strewn with fallen blossoms that the patchwork of colour reflects upwards into the sombre greens of the hollow bushes. She and Elizabeth went with John to a concert in the evening. I was too tired. Earlier that day John took all the children to see the rally, and his flat.

Rain fell several times this week and the ground is moist, except for under the trees and bushes where it remains dry and powdery. In my small vegetable plot I have three loganberry and four strawberry plants from Bob, along with sweetcorn, tomatoes, cucumbers and courgettes. Lettuces are crisply curling, mint springs willingly beside thyme and sage, and my beans are ready to curl round the sticks I cut from the hazels at Causeway House. Against the fence are sweet peas. Poppy wings are poking through behind the row of primulas, and tiny radish seedlings unfold between the corn and the tomatoes.

A marvellous sunrise at Honeybed lifted my spirits until a cow in the front stall tried to leap straight out of the parlour over the restraining gate. The gate resisted until she jogged the latch and bolted out. I prevented the rest following her. My face tickled throughout milking and I discovered, by careful and intense scrutiny of the bars, that mites were crawling on them in multitudes: they had fallen from the cake loft overhead. John is certain that the electric vaporised fly killer, which is installed in all the parlours, will kill all the mites, but I am as suspicious of this as of the mites. It is supposed to penetrate the hides of the cows to give them protection, therefore I am certain it will penetrate *mine.* I do not intend to switch it on unless the flies are very bad.

Each parlour is painted in the summer. Vic and Kevin are to clean Honeybed parlour with a power hose and then paint it a dark blue. Bob is planning to paint his Atlantic green. Graham has already painted his a morning glory blue and silver. The painters are also at Hazelwood Farm and my house outwardly looks like a model home for the estate. I have no choice in colour schemes, but the windows are white and the guttering black, the doors are a stone colour, so it is all quite pleasing. The lawns have been neatly cut by Roger and the borders weeded to add to the effect. The beautiful red rose is out on the south wall.

The goat is eating her way through the rough patches of ground round the barns and the hens are content on their patch of garden. The cat I rescued from Honeybed is now a favourite, and we would not

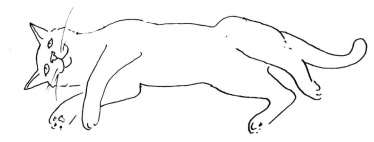

Kilvert, my cat.

part with him. He is the most relaxed cat I have ever known; he lies on his back and loves to have his stomach tickled – just like a dog – and his paws expand and contract in ecstasy, his eyes half-closed with the power of these sensual sensations.

Bob found one of his cows dead of a perforated ulcer. Did it die in agony, thrashing in pain? Or did it lie down quietly and give up the ghost? It must have suffered. Philip said it proved it was not worth keeping these thin, old cows and trying to nurse them better. Yet at Home Farm, when poor old number '14' came limping into the parlour with a new bandage on her foot, thrusting her protruding bones into position for milking and I told John she ought to go, that it was cruel to keep her, Philip protested and said she was all right for a bit yet. We examined her records and found that she had had ten calves and I was accused of being hard-hearted for wanting to send her to her death. I said that after using her for all those years, a merciful ending should be given to her. These old cows should not be milked to their last drop, no matter what they are suffering. So number '14' was kept back when the others went out to grass. Her eyes, which were luminous with old age and pain, will soon be clouded and dull with death. There is no nice way of dying for a cow. It is always a violent and frightening end: but some ways are quicker than others.

*13 June*

Harold is an expert at shooting and fishing, he used to shoot the pigeons on the estate which are classed as vermin, but this is no longer allowed. He is such a keen fisherman that he will get up at 3.00 am to go down to Somerset to fish. He presented a beautiful trout to John, which we had for our supper, and another time he brought us a large piece of smoked salmon.

Brock is leaner and fitter from his frequent early morning runs through the park. He runs ahead of the van like an arrow, diverting neither right nor left, ignoring the rabbits bobbing out of his path and the many pheasants in the fields. He once raced past a little owl perched on the fence at Owlnest. But he was in the van on the evening I crested the rise by the cattle grid and saw a deer standing motionless on the drive. I slowly stopped the van and watched the unconscious elegance and ease with which it walked off the road into the coppice. It stood with another deer looking at me, then, silently, and in apparent slow motion, they bounded into the deep shade of the wood. The glowing-green of a wet, dripping summer evening surrounded me, silent and without bird song, or the noise of working men.

Every year an expert on cereal diseases from Bristol is invited to Lyndon. Many farmers are invited to attend for the occasion, they can bring their own problem cereal, and can see someone else's. John and Harold showed him round the crops, and discussed what they ought to have done, or not done, and the other farmers presented their blighted leaves and withered shoots in the hope of enlightenment. The gaps in the potato field are not caused by bad seed, but by a bad potato planter, which was acquired this season.

The bull with the bad back fetched £400 as meat, so his summer of fattening was worth while. The two hornless bulls are together in a small paddock at Owlnest, and the horned bull at Honeybed is in with a few dry cows for company. The Devon bull is out in the park with the heifers. Cows are being dried off in all the dairies, a few at a time , either because they have come to the natural end of their lactation and ceased to give enough milk to be worth milking, or because they will be calving again in two months time.

The men start work at 7.30 am, take a lunch break of a quarter of an hour at 10.00 am, continue until 1.00 pm, when they go home for dinner, and are back for 2.00 pm. They have a short break at 4.30 pm, then they sometimes work on until 9.00 pm, although more usually until 7 or 8.00 pm. They are paid by the hour and the time after 4.30 pm is overtime, and therefore paid at £2.50 an hour. John believes they work these hours because they like them – and they want the money – but I believe they work because they have to. John has admitted that if they didn't work these hours they would not get, or keep, their jobs, so they cannot choose to work fewer hours and get less money. My wages are estimated on a working week of sixty hours, including overtime, with more hours in winter, and fewer in summer. I know that if the men did not work the overtime they could not live on their basic wages. I also know that their wives see very little of them in the summer, spring and autumn, and that this is one of the causes of the depression and loneliness suffered by many farm worker's wives. Perhaps they would be at a loss without the work, but that is the conditioning of the system. What time, or energy, is left for reading, hobbies or intellectual stimulation?

Only at Quincey's are the cows still eating hay. Shifting the rack added an hour to my work day. It rained all day and I was bedraggled and sodden. I rushed through milking in the afternoon because, as a treat, Susan had paid for John, myself and her to go to a concert in Marford this evening. It is the week of the Marford Music

Festival, most of which is passing me by. John is going to some of the lunchtime concerts and a musical evening at Lyndon House. I declined to go to this, preferring to lie low this year.

*17 June*

I am in the habit of writing a note to the dairyman when I leave at night so that they know what has happened during the day. The note I wrote to David this week was unintentionally disastrous. I said I had hustled through the afternoon's milking to go to the concert. Next morning John found David in a rage and told me. I felt very bad about upsetting David and physically sick inside. I decided I had to go and see him and find out why he had been so angry, for we all know that on special occasions it is permissible to hurry up the milking and John knew that I was doing so. Because of my relationship with John, I am extra sensitive to all reactions and aware that problems are aggravated by the situation.

I stayed an additional hour at Owlnest cleaning the dairy – one of the summer jobs allotted to me. It was sheeting down with rain and, across the yard, I could see two of the foresters cutting the nettles and weeds from the ground between the young trees in the enclosure beyond Bob's bungalow. They were wearing protective clothing and pushed and pulled doggedly at the machine, which sank into the soft earth as it chewed up the stalks of dock and nettle, droning mesmerically all day. As I scrubbed the walls, arms aching, it seemed to me that the peace and graciousness of Lyndon, and places like it, was built on nothing but the arduous manual labour of the masses. However, I was satisfied with my efforts, as were the foresters with theirs.

From Owlnest I went straight to see David, wondering on the way what I was going to say to him. I drew up in front of his house and he came out frowning and unfriendly. I apologised and he did not deny that he had been very angry, 'I've had a difficult time trying to keep the milk up on too little grass, and it's going to drop any time now, and it did go down, and I thought you helped it go down and I was mad.'

We talked of cows in general, hours of work, and jobs I could do apart from the routine ones. He said that if he had to ask me to clean the bulk tank, then he would feel he was not doing his job properly, unlike Bob, who hates cleaning the tank and will even ask Philip to do it. Here is another area where I tread carefully. If I clean something that one of them regards as his territory I am likely to be misunderstood and to be implying criticism.

David said that Lord Elroy had taken a party of people to Quincey's to show them the dairy, and one of the visitors had asked David how many hours he worked. David replied that he reckoned to work an average of seventy hours a week, and that he thought his reward might come in heaven, thus implying that it was not coming on earth. They laughed. He appreciated my going to see him and we parted reasonably amicably.

Harold has given John two more trout. It appears he does not like trout. Does he like smoked salmon? All today the men have been clearing the dung from the calf yard at Hazelwood. The JCB scoops it up and drops it into the waiting trailers which are hauled up Ivy Hill, past Home Farm, and into the park where it is dumped, a rich-smelling mini-mountain. Drizzle fell, interspersed with heavy downpours of rain or brief intervals of sunshine and clear, soft winds.

Driving through the park in the slanting rain was like swimming underwater in a vast aquarium. The canopy of trees blotted out most of the light, and where the light fell through the open spaces, the bracken glowed a translucent, aphid-green. The blue-green of the ash trees mingled with the now deep and glossy green of the beeches, and in the open fields the beautiful, soft grey-green of the barley contrasts with the harder, darker green of the potato field.

One of the fields of maize is heavily infested with couch grass. It was sprayed with a weed killer which kills everything except maize and its potency means that maize will have to be grown there for two years until the effects wear off. In spite of its potency it has failed to kill all the couch.

A great transformation has taken place since the rain. An inch of rain was forecast, and fulfilled in forty-eight hours. The paths that the cows tread, which were so dusty and dry, are now squelchy with mud and pockmarked with hoof-prints. At each step the mud squeezes up between the clefts of their hooves, and their legs are wet to the hock and splashes of mud smear their bellies and udders. They bear the wet with indifference, although the cows at Honeybed, sheltering against the hedge with their backs turned to the driving rain, were reluctant to turn into the wind to be milked. The milk went up at Owlnest, due to the fresh growth of grass which has increased their intake.

On the first of my days off on my long weekend, I took Margaret to see the rhododendrons. It is the first time since I came to Lyndon that I have been able to stroll on the 'largest area of mown grass in England' – according to Lord Elroy – and wander down to the shimmering lake. A gentle breeze, and warm sunshine, lent calmness and peace to our talk among the bridal drifts of blossom, and, after an hour, we drove over to the pleasure grounds and walked in the pinetum, an eerie place, where we were towered over by giant and solitary trees. Beside the lake the vast open lawns have been evenly dotted with excreta from the geese, and in the formal gardens at the front of the house, the sharp green outlines of the clipped yews emphasised the uniform red of the geraniums springing like jack-in-a-boxes from the urns on the balustraded walls.

John was singing in a Choral Society concert that night and Susan came with me to the concert, lending her sympathetic support to my qualms about meeting people whom John has known for years. On Sunday John and I took Elizabeth, Daniel and Susan to the seaside, meandering through the lush countryside on the way there, happy and relaxed. Although it rained at Lyndon we sunbathed and swam in the sea, and picnicked on the sand hills at Studland Bay.

*22 June*

I am so tired tonight that I have come to bed to write my diary and it is only 8.30 pm. Jane began her exams last week and Susan was ill. Andrea came home and I quarrelled with John. Our capacity to hurt and be hurt is total, but while still gasping with pain, we talk and keep talking until, somehow, sanity, reason and understanding return.

The morning milking at Quincey's was slow, and getting them in for the afternoon was slower. A neighbour driving his cows along the road distracted my cows, who charged round the field until I could persuade them to start on the long trek down the race to the dairy. The race, stretching out of sight, was a red ribbon of slippery mud. The tractor, whose brakes and clutch are still jerky and severe, scared me as it skidded in the mud. John and I were taking his eldest daughter, and her boyfriend, out for a meal in the evening, but I did not hustle. Not hustling during the evening meant a three-and-a-half-hour night, but Roger helped at Home Farm the following afternoon, and thought it was good fun. The milk is dropping more rapidly there and cake is being fed to some of the cows.

One of the cows had aborted last week and she is isolated until it is proved that she does not have brucellosis. The dead calf has to be sent away for analysis. The cow must be brought in last for milking and her milk thrown away. John thought the reason for the abortion might be the spraying of the fence lines by the forestry department. Their enthusiasm for neatness means that, for a while, every field is bordered by a harsh, artificial, yellow line of dead undergrowth. The farm and forestry departments are supposed to share the cost of the spraying. The verge to Owlnest was over enthusiastically sprayed, and in its entirety has turned yellow, making John extremely angry because he deliberately had the fence wired high enough for the cows to graze under it. The fence line is supposed to be sprayed *after* the cattle have grazed a field, thus allowing several days to elapse before they will be in that field again. The grass in Owlnest Park has to be re-seeded because it is not permanent pasture and is declining in quality. A total weed killer has been sprayed onto it and, when all the grass is dead, the field will be direct drilled and Bob should be able to put his freshly calved cows there in the autumn. Kevin, the calf rearer, is not happy in his job, mainly due to his workmate, who is known to be a 'worry guts' and is getting Kevin down. I am often thankful that I work alone most of the time, so I don't have the problem of an incompatible companion which must occur often on farms. Kevin, according to general opinion is a 'good stockman' and 'a good lad' – both the highest praise. If he isn't made happy he may leave, and everyone agrees that would be a pity. John has to find a solution to an apparent impasse.

Andrea rode the pony to Causeway House to spend her last night there, and to lend the pony to our neighbours for the summer. I went over to divide the furniture with Edward, mentally, if not physically, and brought back some of the still useful hens. Early in the morning of my day off, I picked up both Andrea and Edward and drove Edward to hospital for a minor eye operation and Andrea to Wales. She has a summer job as a riding instructor, cook and dogsbody at a small trekking centre. I was in the car from 8.45 am to 6.30 pm. To keep myself awake I stopped to pick strawberries for tea on the return journey. The hedges were glowing with wild roses, honeysuckle and elderflowers; the spires of foxgloves rose from barren banks where road works had destroyed all other vegetation. Dog daisies and poppies strewed the verges, and the stiff stalks and angular heads of hogweed topped the waving grass hedge.

I am at Honeybed for Vic's long weekend and I *cannot* like it, and occasionally I still hate it. The work there is easier and shorter than elsewhere, but the parlour depresses me, the ugliness of the utilitarian buildings made of concrete blocks depresses me; the weedy yard and the unscraped slurry depresses me. If someone really keen and enthusiastic were to go there it could be partially transformed. Vic is painting the parlour a dark and overpowering blue, in the assumption that it will not show the dirt. The mites are being decimated by the fly killer. I may be allergic to it as I have been sneezing frequently. There is a new milk pump, noisier but without the stench that the old one had.

Without premeditation, I decided that I was not going to milk a certain cow, number '409', again after this weekend. I will refuse utterly and completely, I feel so determined that I will accept the sack rather than doing so. With beating heart, I asked John if I could speak to him privately, and in the role of boss. I tried to explain why I wanted her to go. Firstly, she is awkward, difficult and dangerous to milk, and she is guaranteed to make each milking, which are bad enough to start with, decidedly unpleasant. She upsets all the other cows in the same batch, and I am afraid of having my face smashed in, or my arm broken. There is always a risk of that happening with *any* cow, but there is a far greater chance with her. I am not a coward, and I am not really afraid of her (though I was this weekend), but I have milked her for six months and she has not improved. She has a deep cut on her teat, which is one of the reasons she kicks. To cure it, she would have to be dried off, and as she is not in calf, and is giving a lot of milk, she could milk on for another year. John listened to me in silence, and then said he would speak to Philip.

Philip has now told me that she will go to market on Friday and I have milked her for almost the last time. She is a big fat boss cow and will fetch a good price for slaughter.

Hay is being cut on the surrounding farms, but it is dry for barely more than a few hours, and the farmers are getting desperate. We saw a field of hay being turned and turned to get it dry. It was baled at night, when it must have been far too damp.

The roses are out everywhere, flowering on cottage walls in an abundance of great sprays of reds, pinks and yellows; the flat elder blossoms in the hedges turn their creamy faces to the sun, and the delicate lace of the cow parsley yellows into seed heads, half hidden now by the swaying heads of the grasses, feathery and supple in the wind.

John inspected all the young stock last Saturday and I went with him. We started at Nuthills, which is down a sandy track by the cottage where Simon is to live. A more idyllic cottage could not be imagined, a tiny doll's house of a cottage, thatched and set in a pretty garden. It's lead paned windows peer out over the neat beech hedge to the wide view beyond. We strolled over the curving hillside to look at the heifers, one hundred and fifty of them, gathered in a group in the shelter of a belt of firs, sleek hides shining, long tails switching, jaws monotonously chewing, oblivious of the view across to the downs. The track where I sat among the snowdrops to eat my breakfast in February is now unrecognisable, it is thick with growth and alive with insects and sprinkled with the colours of campions and thistle heads. Alan, using the JCB, has dug out trenches across the path and filled them with stones to provide drainage for the water which washes the sand down the hill. John noticed that mildew was attacking the spears of corn in Cuffs Corner and noted down that it must be sprayed as soon as possible.

On the slopes above the lake, opposite to Lyndon House, the in-calf heifers were grazing. Their round sides and slightly bulging undeveloped udders proclaimed their fertility. Harold, Will and Bert were in the silage field, filling up the clamp at Owlnest. The calves were in a field of beautiful, thick grass mixed with clover. Many people keep their calves inside all summer, believing that growth rates are better, but the policy here is to put every animal out. The calves associate vehicles with food and came rocking over the grass to the car. From that huge field we could see Bob's cows grazing in the field above us, and the house, dairy and barns of Owlnest perched on the top of the hill. We skirted the estate and found the beef heifers in a rough field by the main road, one that would be costly and difficult to drain. In every field there were rabbits. There is a plague of baby rabbits. I am beginning to recognise the different grasses: cocksfoot and timothy, meadow grass and Italian rye.

*23 June*

Roger came to help on Sunday morning, zooming up the track of Honeybed on his moped at 8.20 am. He scraped the yards and sprayed the clumps of nettles and docks with the knapsack sprayer. We scrubbed out the dairy together. I am not alone in having help from the family: Philip sometimes takes his to work with him, and wives have been known to help with calvings, or with getting the cows in.

Vic is on the short list for a new job and the new man, Rodney, wants to start work. John will let him start work with Vic, and between them they are to clean out the calving shed – an arduous task, paint the dairy, and finish painting the parlour.

The panorama from the fields of Honeybed is the kind of image of England of which exiles abroad must dream: the rolling hills, the tall and beautiful trees, the orderly hedgerows, even the fields of corn and grass, and the pretty houses and cottages which jar not the eye, nor prick the conscience. I slept a long time at lunchtime and awoke dull, dopey and desperate for further sleep. I normally only sleep for ten minutes, sinking into a state of complete relaxation and waking fairly refreshed. For the rest of the day I could hardly concentrate on what I was doing. On the way home I passed Will mowing the second cut silage at Hazelwood for the clamp at Home Farm. Harold's voice on the radio crackled with enthusiasm, he had just inspected the clamp at Quincey's, 'No waste at all,' he said. 'Marvellous, it's marvellous.'

*24 June*

I woke at 4.00 am to hear it raining solidly. I thought of the silage grass which had just been cut, and the hay crop lying in soft swathes. The worst summer job I have yet done was at Owlnest. Up in the cake loft over the parlour was a thick layer of debris, dust, cake dust, and rat and mouse droppings. Roger and I cleaned this area together: I shovelled and he used a commercial vacuum cleaner. My throat and nose were choked with the unclean atmosphere and the stuffy, disgusting smell.

A violent storm in the afternoon cut out the motor of the milking machines at Owlnest and Honeybed. The field called Pigeon's Close was bathed in warm sunshine when I rounded up the cows. Long streamers of rain trailed from an indigo sky over the distant hills, and vivid flashes of lightning lit up the livid clouds. The cows began to hurry up the hill and the darkness swiftly overtook us as the sun went in and I was chilled by the rushing wind. Looking back over my shoulder the whole of the Marford valley fell under the shadow of the approaching storm. The first raindrops splashed on the concrete as I put the tractor away in the shed. I had a vision of being struck by lightning on the tractor and of it careering out of control across the fields.

Despite the weight of my depression, and a continuing sense of separation from everyone else, I donned ordinary clothes as soon as I reached home and went to a parents' evening to play the role of the dutiful parent. There was very little inspired work on the walls, and hardly anything of a 'going on' or experimental nature. The paint work on the walls and ceiling was dreary and dark, and sitting in the old school classrooms, with their high ceilings and high-up windows, was like sitting at the bottom of a well. The classes are large for the size of the rooms, the teachers were pleasant and caring – apart from the headmaster – and I was cheered to be told that both my children were intelligent and extremely mature (no wonder), and that Elizabeth is the best in her class at everything, including sport with the boys. Daniel's teacher said she wished she had a class full of Daniels.

*25 June*

This morning I woke at 6.30 am to the sun streaming in to my little, white bedroom, with its pretty, blue, flowery curtains and prints of Cotehele pinned to the wall. In the corner, my clothes hang on the overhead beam because I have no wardrobe.

Last night my behaviour alarmed John: I was so strange, dull and unresponsive, but without any positive signs of illness. My eyes would not focus properly and I thought that if I could keep going until my day off, I could sleep all day. I withdrew from everyone, distanced from the needs of the family. John rang Philip and asked him to milk for me at Quincey's. I worried that Philip would think I was shirking. I stayed in bed for the morning and, feeling somewhat better, went back to work for the afternoon. Philip helped to get the cows in, and another thunderstorm rattled on the roof and nearly drowned the noise of the radio. In case the motor cut out, Philip set up the tractor and generator, but the milking passed without incident.

I had to go to Riverton to the solicitors' to sign the contract for the selling of Causeway House. Under the trapdoor of my surface life, there is a great well of sorrow, a mourning pit of experience that is being shoved underground, but will one day rise, with insistence, to the light, inescapable and inexorable.

Roger did two hours of roguing[1] the wild oats today. He was paid

---

[1] Roguing is the process of uprooting or destroying the plants in a field that are not of the type planted or do not conform to the desired specifications.

*90p* an hour. Harold makes up a small gang of people and they work across a field in line.

*26 June*

Philip told me that yesterday a woman getting in her cows near Marford was killed by lightning which struck her umbrella. John told me that Vic has had the same symptoms as I have had and Vic thinks it must be the fly killer. This seems plausible, as I was three days at Honeybed and the apparatus was fuming and vaporising right over my head throughout all the milkings. I must have been absorbing it into my body and brain. John is certain that it is not operating properly and has sent it back to the manufacturers. I shall take care to switch it off before I milk anywhere in the future.

I ate my breakfast in the rhododendrons after an easy milking at Home Farm, I sat in the sun in a mossy glade. Most of the blossom has faded, and on every rosette of green leaves the stamens and seed pods perch like large, crumpled spiders.

Margaret rang last night to say that her brother had been killed in a road accident. It is quite appalling that I am not able to offer anything but profound sympathy, but the waves are almost over my own head most of the time.

*29 June*

The weather is strange – periods of heavy rain, followed by warm sunshine; or just cold and dull – the worst possible combination for hay-making, and makes it impossible to sit out, or achieve a tan.

A party of foreign journalists of mixed nationalities visited Lyndon on Saturday afternoon. John hired a mini-bus to take them and their interpreters round the estate. On the principal of the worst first, (Honeybed is never visited on these occasions, and is too far away in any case) he brought them to Home Farm where I was milking. I put on a beaming smile to have my photo taken, and managed to tell John, without anyone else hearing, that I had found another aborted calf in Deermead. It was perfectly formed, though completely hairless, and the size of a small spaniel. It had a few hairs on its muzzle, and the skin pigmentation was a darker colour than the deep-red of its body.

I drove a cow away from it, presuming she was its mother, until I saw another cow trailing the afterbirth. I left the tractor in the field to mark the place and changed the gates to prevent the cows returning to Deermead. The journalists toured the other farms and the exhibition rooms, and had tea with scones and cream and strawberry jam in the restaurant.

I threw away the abortive cow's milk, and put her in a box to be examined by the vet. I carried a bucket of disinfectant and an empty fertiliser bag out to the calf, which I then put it in the bag. I wore my rubber gloves in case it was contaminated by the highly infectious brucellosis bacteria. I gathered up the bits of membrane and scattered the disinfectant, somewhat ineffectually, on the patch of ground and drove the tractor back to the dairy. Later on, John went round the field and discovered another dead calf. This depressed him because cows which have aborted do not milk well, and usually dry up early. It also means that another cow is wandering around and possibly spreading the infection. It is often surprisingly difficult to tell when some cows have calved, whereas with others it is very obvious. I inspected the rear of each cow as they went through the parlour, but did not find her.

The cow that was hanging round the dead calf was the one which aborted several days ago. John thought the cow I had put in the box might have had twins, as the dead calves were of similar size and development.

I am very tired again tonight. When do I not feel tired? I must save the remnants of my energy for clearing Causeway House later next month.

Graham and his wife have gone to the South of France for their holidays.

# JULY

*1 July*

Now the early barley turns from green to gold, and the laden ears hang down meekly, the long, soft awns pointing to the earth. A Piper Comanche aeroplane waits on the airstrip for the weather to improve, and the wind to die down, so that it can spray the mildew on the wheat at Stock Street. The potatoes are in flower, the blobs of white blossom held clear of the foliage on slender stalks. In the cornfields, the patches of wild oats veil the colour of the growing crop.

Roger earns £6.50 a day for seven hours work pulling them up. Wheat which is contracted for seed would not be accepted by the merchants if any wild oat grains were found in it. Wild oats ripen before the cultivated corn and some has already dropped to the ground by the time the corn is harvested, ready to perpetuate itself next year.

The grazing fields have been topped, the appearance of the fields is tidied and new growth encouraged. Owlnest Park has turned a dull, dead ochre colour. The turf is rotovated and shallowly torn to shreds. Tom, the tractor driver, backed his huge machine up to the dairy to hose down one of the bearings which was smoking. A piece of electric-fencing wire had wrapped itself round the implement. I asked him what the machine was, not recognising it.

'Ancient,' he replied, 'it's probably the only one left in the country.'

All the men, apart from the dairy men, are going to the Royal Show tomorrow on an annual outing paid for by the farm.

Colin was severely shaken when the trailer he was tipping up came away from the tractor, and the towbar, released from the weight of the trailer full of silage, flicked up and crashed through the back window of the cab, stopping a few inches from his head.

The vet said the aborted calves could be twins, but the cow must be isolated for ten days. She hates the confinement of the box and has refused to eat, an effective way of drying herself off. She will have to go to the butcher as the alternative is to keep her for eighteen months without any production. What a waste of all that careful breeding and rearing. Fat number '409' from Honeybed fetched over £400, and poor number '14' from Home Farm a mere £120.

There is no end to the dismal weather. A small farmer in Marford has been trying to get his hay in, and I have watched his progress with almost as much anxiety as he must feel.

The raspberries are ripening at Causeway House. I picked some for the freezer, and sorted out the books, some of which I packed in boxes and brought to Hazelwood. I have had no time to read them, but I am happy to have my books with me again.

*14 July*

The cow which aborted was cleared by the vet and returned to the herd. She has lost weight and is giving scarcely any milk. The herd was unsettled, and fought and raced about, and she had to fight for her place within the herd.

Bert came to tell me that he had recently topped the field that I put the herd in last night. He had left a message that there was a lot of ragwort in there, but I had not got it. Dead ragwort is more poisonous than ragwort growing. Alarmed, John and I tramped round the field measuring the amount of mangled ragwort. There was enough to give us good reason to be alarmed. John told me not to put the herd in the field for a week, but as they had spent one night in there already, there was little point moving them quickly.

'If they die, they bloody well die,' he said wearily. I silently agreed. In the event, no cows died from the ragwort.

Kevin found a cow dead of bloat in Pond Ground the week before.

I am not looking forward to that experience.

I go to Quincey's with a vague apprehension. David's notes are terse and to the point, but he came into the parlour for a chat which I appreciated. He and his family are going on holiday to a cottage in Wales, where he has been going for twenty-five years. Philip is going to France in his caravan for three weeks, and Bob is returning the hospitality of friends he visited in South Africa, he is treating them to a week in Jersey at a good hotel. John and I went to the Lake District for my long weekend. We chose a small guest house farm in the Northern Fells, and, although the outside paintwork was a bright blue, the inside furnished *a la* Woolworth, and everything in our room a differing shade of pink, we were made welcome and comfortable.

John feared he was developing another hernia, so the mountains remained unclimbed, but in our explorations we came across a small wooden house for sale. With the knowledge of the money I shall receive from the sale of Causeway House, and the fact that we are living in a 'tied' house, I made an offer for it. It was an impulsive decision, but either I am good at these, or there is simply no time to hesitate or deliberate. Events rise like bubbles to the surface of existence and must be dealt with before they either go, or overwhelm one. We travelled home in a calmer, more secure frame of mind, which was just as well as I am now going over to Causeway House almost every day to pack up all the portable possessions to cut down on removal expenses, and simplify the dividing up of our belongings.

Edward has made an offer for a small cottage a mile away from here, which I pass on the way to Honeybed.

One of the heifers has calved in the group John and I inspected recently. The calf is too early to be wanted by Lyndon so it has been sold to a smallholder and the heifer is at Quincey's.

Kevin and Geoff are now relief milking during the holidays, and Vic is an odd-job man as Rodney has taken over at Honeybed. Rodney and his wife have moved into the adjoining house to Jim, ugly in itself but with a magnificent view. Rodney has caused some aggravation already by letting his dog run over Jim's well-kept garden, and he has been bumptious with the builder. John had to go and see him about this. He is a talker and delayed me for half an hour when he fetched his milk, with lurid tales of farms he had visited when he was an inseminator. He said he had seen a man beating a cow on its belly while it lay on its back with its legs in the air; and that when a slurry pit on one farm was cleared out, eight dead cows were discovered in it.

I am not sure if I believe everything he says. He is cheerful and enthusiastic, a great bouncing puppy of a man. Vic has not found a job and is still in his house in the village, and regretting his decision to leave. He is suffering from the effects of the fly killer, or worry, or both, and has migraines and a lump on his neck.

The dairy discussion group met at Honeybed for their summer evening meeting, and as a project they were invited to look over the unit very thoroughly and to discuss how the buildings could be improved, the number of cows increased, how they could be accommodated, and all within the budget as an economical proposition.

I invited the group back to my house, where I made a cheerful fire, filled the house with flowers, and the Lyndon restaurant provided platters of sandwiches, sausage rolls, portions of chicken and cans of ale. A rough map of Honeybed hung on the wall and each member said what he would like to do there and how much he thought it would cost. John wrote down all the suggestions and hopes to put some of them into practice. Vic, Rodney and I were able to say what we thought should be done to make the parlour safer.

A welder is on the farm this week. Bob kept him busy at Owlnest for three days, welding gates, hurdles and parts on the tractor. The welder will go to all the other farms in turn, mending and putting right all the things that have been broken in the past months, or anything in need of changing.

Hen pheasants are emerging from the woods with their chicks, and squirrels undulate across the road in front of the van in the park. The sprayed edges of the fields are an earthy, unobtrusive brown and the dead foliage has melted into nothing under the weight of the constant drizzling rain. Silage making has been held up, hay-making has not even started, and the harvest should have begun.

John has contracted out some wheat which he must deliver to the buyers by 13 August. It is not beginning to ripen yet and if he cannot harvest it he will lose £24 a ton. If he fulfils the contract he will get a higher price for it, but if he cannot fulfil it he will lose more than £4,000. Wheat is selling at £120 a ton at the moment. The wheat at Hazelwood is cleared of wild oats and the field of green ears stretches to the horizon, level and solid with straight stalks, and tightly packed upright heads. Right across the field a new oil pipe-line is being inserted. The oil company pays compensation for damage done and crops destroyed. A roller has flattened a wide swathe through the massed corn to mark the path of the pipe.

The Piper Comanche aeroplane sprayed the weedy wheat successfully, zooming, swooping and swerving under the telegraph wires in a display of aerobatics that alarmed the nearby school who rang John to ask if it was really safe.

Lord Elroy has complained that some of the crops are 'dirty' – that is, weedy. He called in an agent to give his opinion and the agent said they were not too bad, that it had been a difficult year and that they could only be controlled with greater use of sprays and further expense, thus cutting into the profit margins.

The rides [1] on the estate are being cut, and all the long grass and nettles smoothed out. The field at Owlnest has been re-seeded and rolled and should germinate rapidly in this damp weather. There is so much grass this year that the silage camps are nearly full, and there are still a thousand tons of maize to cut and clamp before the winter. To assess the quantity and weight of silage produced, the first loads are taken to a weighbridge in Marford, and the driver of the Sambron makes a note of the number of loads delivered to him at the clamp.

The kitten from Honeybed, now half grown, has dislocated his hip and it is strapped up to his body to keep the joint in place. He is unperturbed by his disability.

Roger has transferred his interest to an amateur dramatics company which is putting on an open-air production of a Shakespeare play. He says he is helping with the lighting. Edward is also in the play.

The remaining hens at Causeway House have been fetched here, or despatched if they were not in lay. John killed them for me; I would

---

[1] Rides are the path or track across an area of countryside reserved for horseback riding.

have killed them but I hate doing it. We brought home the bodies and plucked and gutted them – crudely, but we were both tired – before bed. Only one week to go before the sale is completed.

One of the long hedges at Hazelwood has been earmarked for a demonstration by conservationists. They will show a group of farmers how to lay a hedge in different ways so as to conserve wildlife, but without encouraging damage to crops. John has fenced off a corner of that field and planted trees and allowed the group to study the flora and fauna. The banks of the lanes are gentle with the powder-blue petals' of cranesbill and the feathery plumes of meadowsweet.

*17 July*

The undergrowth round the plantations of trees in the park has been hacked and savaged by the foresters and their machines. The ground is so boggy that in places the earth is gouged and scarred. There were orchids growing in the grass at Five-ways and John picked me a handful before they were all cut down.

Rodney has had trouble with the compressor on the bulk tank at Honeybed: the compressor is responsible for the cooling of the milk, and the tanker driver will refuse to take the milk if the temperature has not been reduced to a minimum level. The long weekend there was relatively simple and I had finished milking by 7.20 am – a vast difference to the winter routine. I washed down, scraped the yards, and inspected the dry cows and was home by 10.00 am. Malcolm called to tell me he had put the calves out in the field, in case I thought they had escaped; Edward called with some clothes; Philip called with antibiotics to deliver to Quincey's; Simon called with some council officials; and John called to tell me about an interview he had just had with Lord Elroy. The day before there had been the usual monthly meeting, and Lord Elroy had asked John to come and see him on the following day in his study. For some time John has felt that the good relationship they have had for years had deteriorated, that Lord Elroy was fussing too much over small things, and did not appear to be satisfied with what John was doing, nor appreciative of his efforts. He went in some trepidation, and I waited anxiously at home. From what John told me afterwards Lord Elroy handled the interview with great diplomacy, disarming John's aggressive side and appealing to his sympathies. At the same time he was frank and made it clear that he was the boss. Lord Elroy acknowledged that they had both been under considerable strain and pressures in the past months – we now know that Lord Elroy has had his own marital problems, and that the financial side of the estate is a perpetual and increasing worry. Lord Elroy said he thought John had become more arrogant – I think that this is a defence mechanism against further hurt – and aggressive. He explained that his passion for tidiness arose from the fact that, as he takes nothing out of the estate for himself, and all the profits go straight back into it, he takes pleasure in seeing it looking as well-cared for as possible. The farms support all the other departments at the moment. It is on John's head that the responsibility of the continuation of the estate falls, and the clash comes when John, trying desperately hard to make money for Lord Elroy, sees his labour force deployed on 'inessential' operations. Although, in my opinion, he has insufficient labour for even the absolute essentials. When he is told, (not asked) to move a pile of stones, or cut a bank because it can be seen from the house, when he knows his men are utterly stretched getting in silage for the cows, or milking until they can hardly see straight for weariness, such details seem irrelevant.

Lord Elroy then asked John what his plans were regarding me. John felt that the interview had cleared the air. It is a pleasure to work for someone who cares as passionately for his property as does Lord Elroy, whatever one's politics. There is no litter anywhere, no abandoned machinery, no plastic bags flapping in the dust. Many times I have seen John pick up a piece of baler twine, or wire or paper. The gates may be tied with string in places, and there may be broken fences on parts of the farm, but always there is a sense of constant improvement. New gates appear, wooden fences replace wire ones, and the improvements that are made to barns, such as the Yorkshire boarding are neat, functional, and well done. Wood is always used in preference to corrugated iron.

I lit a fire in the small front room in the evening and we lay in each other's arms on the sofa and listened to Elgar's *Dream of Gerontius*, carefully taking the telephone off the hook so there would be no disturbance. There was no sound but the music and the flickering of the flames in the grate.

The word 'harvest' forms on everyone's lips in every conversation. I stopped to talk to Bert. His honest handsome face showed genuine concern at the fickle weather. He knew what it would mean to lose the contract for the wheat. His fine, broad hands clenched as if he could not wait to get started. Harold has been to Yorkshire for a fortnight and is generating steam to get the last of the hay and lucerne silage in before all hands are wanted for the harvest. The weather remains cool when it is dry, and cold when it is wet.

My job of the week at Owlnest was to replace the old milk tubes between the jars and the clusters with new ones, and to push an accumulated pile of week-old, and very smelly, slurry into the lagoon. There is no spare grass at Owlnest, whereas at Honeybed there is a surplus. The soil conditions are quite different at each farm and different weather suits the different soils. The approach verges to Owlnest are green again, despite the sprays; the vigour of nature, and the life of the earth, is strong and it gives one a tremendous optimism.

A baby rabbit hopped up to my feet while I was talking to Bob in the afternoon about cows in general and how to treat cows that have summer mastitis.

'There isn't much that I don't know about cows,' he said confidently. I have learned much from Bob. I told him his parlour is a pleasure to work in, which is true. Norman was putting nitrogen on Merchant's Close and Hanging around. He worked all day on the fields, replenishing the fertiliser from a trailer piled high with the cobalt blue bags. Heaving them off the trailer onto the spreader, he balanced on the trailer holding a large, sharp knife in one hand and slitting the bags as if he were cutting the throats of some helpless animals. He put the bags in a tidy pile on the side of the trailer.

Norman had been to a Pontin's holiday camp in Somerset. It cost him and his wife £70 for a self-catering chalet for the week, and he was going to start saving up for a holiday at the same place next year. He had enjoyed the night club show every night and the colour television in the chalet. He says that all the men on the farm are going to help to turn the workshop into a disco and will decorate it. One hundred and fifty tickets have been sold and Harold is the organiser.

Norman was fertilising at Quincey's the next day, and Alan, unfamiliar without his coating of JCB, was turning the hay. There was a beautiful, flaming, angry sunrise, and it was a hot, sultry and uncomfortable milking in the afternoon. The new heifer kicked a bit, but was not too bad. A big hare sprang up from the grass in the cows' field and the form it left was warm and dry.

I booked tickets long ago for all of us to see *The Winter's Tale,* the Shakespeare play in which Edward is acting. I invited friends to come with us and share our picnic in the grounds before the play, as is the custom. The ancient manor house, in the grounds of which the play is to be performed, is hidden from the world in the dull, flat countryside beyond Riverton. We spread the picnic on the damp grass by a huge fallen elm trunk in the old-fashioned garden, and afterwards, replete with food and wine, watched the play from tiered seating under an awning. Across a stone-edged swimming pool, and against a backcloth of formally cut hedge arches, the play proceeded.

The cast's voices did not carry well – if at all – but the costumes, casting and lighting made it visually memorable. As dusk fell, moths and bats were caught in the rays of the lights, and shone briefly like fireflies, and the colours illuminated were rich and lovely. After the interval the rain fell steadily, drenching the players who continued stoically, some with bare feet and only flimsy drapery covering them. Not one appeared to shiver. The last scene was of the bear pushing the clown into the water. He may have been colder, but he could not have been wetter than before.

Every other day I have been to Causeway House to clear and clean the house for the clearance on Monday. Surely everything will at long, long last be easier when the roots of the past are severed and transplanted.

*25 July*

Roger lost his jacket while roguing in the cornfield, and a new one cost £30. The one he lost was slightly too small for him but would have done for Daniel. For the whole of my day off, and all the time between milkings, I packed, cleaned and sorted, aided by a good neighbour and friend.

Her mother said to her, 'You're not going to help that dreadful woman, are you?' which stung through all the layers of deadened feeling.

Parts of the move contained elements of comedy and tragedy, and much of it was bizarre. John was in charge of the young stock at the weekend for Jim, and so that he could help me too he got up at 5.00 am because it takes three hours to do the rounds, checking and feeding. He asked for the use of a tractor and trailer on Sunday and drove it to Causeway House. Roger rode in the cab and Elizabeth bounced about on a bale of straw in the trailer. He manoeuvred the huge vehicle into the orchard and Edward, a neighbour, and John struggled to load the hen house onto the trailer. John then helped Edward take the freezer to a friend's house. When the trailer was fully loaded with wire netting, hurdles and other useful smallholder's items, Edward said all it needed was a cardboard cut-out of the Queen at the window of the hen house, waving her cardboard cut-out hand, as the procession passed through Riverton.

The removal men began to load at 9.30 am on Monday morning, and finished at 4.00 pm. They completed the unloading at Hazelwood at 6.30 pm, depositing all but the most basic furniture I need into the large downstairs room – now a storeroom for Edward's share of the furniture until he moves into his own house.

The saddest part of the move was saying farewell to the garden. In the quiet of the evening I slipped back to the house to sweep the empty rooms and bid goodbye to the past. I thought of the hopes we had, and of my delirious happiness on the first days after taking possession of the house and its orchard, gardens and outbuildings. I embraced it and loved it with a passion. Edward and I gave all of ourselves to the place – to the detriment of our marriage. The house itself, when empty, regained its dignity and spaciousness, which for me it lost when I abandoned it and it became an empty, dusty, soulless shell. I picked a rose from each generously flowering bush and, weeping, carried these fragrant symbols of love back to my other home. I cried in bed and through most of that night, but the children were cheerful and gay.

During that day the lucerne silaging was completed at Owlnest, and at 8.00 am they came to sheet it over with the massive black, plastic sheets weighed down with hundreds of tyres to cut out the air. Later in the week they covered it with bales of hay, stacked high.

I was talking to John in the dairy when Lord Elroy came in. He had heard the long range weather forecast predicting only a fortnight's good weather. Anxious that the harvest should be successful, he thought John should get in a local contractor to speed it up. Though he did not say so, John thought that it was too early to make this decision. The roguers have finished and all the corn is cleared of wild oats. Now one thousand acres of corn has to be cut.

Roger has been taken on for baling, that is unloading the trailers stacked with hay or straw into the barns. On the first day of work he did not realise he would not be home for lunch and did not take anything to eat. No one offered him any of theirs, neither food nor drink. He wore his new jacket and his best shirt and came home filthy, much to his surprise. The next day he took half a loaf of sandwiches and wore his oldest clothes.

All the hay-making is done by machine. It is not necessary to leave the tractor's seat, except for opening or shutting the field gates, or when something breaks down. That day, when the dew was off the grass, the combine harvesters began to breast the barley, great, red paddle steamers flailing the corn before them, and leaving a wide wake of broken stalks spread out behind them. I could not resist driving to see them and was gripped by tense excitement. When the combines flash a red light, the tractors and trailers move into position beside them and, as they move along, the combines unload the heavy mass of honey-coloured kernels in a thick stream, pouring from the outstretched arms into the trailer alongside. The men will work from 7.30 am to 8.00 pm without any days off, unless it rains on a Sunday. All their efforts are concentrated on the harvest. Fred is in charge of one combine and Will of the other. When harvesting is over the machines are serviced and put carefully away. All broken or damaged parts are mended or replaced so that there will be no delays the following year. Up to several thousand pounds may be spent on them, but as a new one could cost £25,000 it is worth looking after them.

My forty-first birthday began with a shining, golden sunrise at Home Farm. The sun's rays shimmered through the leaves of the proud oak in the little paddock in front of the dairy and I stood in the doorway and shed tears of joy and happiness. Spread before my gaze, the countryside was translucent in the calm light of the summer sun. The milking went smoothly and soothingly, and convinced me that the cows' were a really lovely herd. This opinion changed in the afternoon, but it was good while it lasted.

Lord Elroy, in track suit and running shoes, with boyishly tousled hair, ran in to see Jim. He seemed surprised to see me there.

It was the first glorious summer day we had had for weeks, and with the help of the children, I began to sort out the muddle in the house. I demolished the piles of washing, most of which was curtains and bedclothes that I wanted to wash before packing them away. Daniel ironed and Elizabeth washed up, and they swept and cleaned until I went milking. They fetched the cows in for me and then went to play in the adventure playground recently created in the park.

Tom's wife brought me a drink of ice-cold homemade lemonade at 4.00 pm and, while I sipped it, she told me of their holiday in a caravan in Devon, on a site with a swimming pool and riding school. They had enjoyed it so much that they booked it for next year. They have three children, small-boned like her, with appealing faery faces. They play on their bikes around the farm and on the estate. Their proximity to the main drive through the estate, with the tractors and trailers continually passing their door, must be a worry. The corn barn is adjacent to their house and during harvest time there is the roaring of the driers, sometimes nearly all day and most of the night, the noise and fumes of the tractors backing within a few feet of their door, and the choking dust smothering every surface as the chaff and light seeds are separated from the grains. In the open space where the fertiliser sacks are stacked in towering piles, worth £80,000, the ground is already covered with a thick layer of sand-like chaff. Imprinted on it, as if on sand, are the marks of the tyres of the trailer parked underneath the snout of the blower, which pokes out of the wall of the barn. At intervals they bear away the chaff and seed to the woods for the pheasants.

My children returned to the farm at 5.00 pm and I had not finished milking. I told them to go and look for John who was mowing Golden Gate for hay. The nineteen acres took him five hours to mow. When I went to collect the children Daniel was riding in the cab of the big, green Deutz tractor. While I waited for Elizabeth to have her turn I lay on the still-damp grass and was warmed all through by the sun.

The summer evening, blended with the sweet smell of cut grass, the parallel curves of the green and gold lines crossing the undulating pasture, and the distant, drowsy roar of the tractor driven by the person I love, so clearly encapsulated the idea of life and living.

Then it was my turn and we circled the last patch of standing grass, thick and soft and tracked through by pheasants. In the long grass three hen pheasants and their chicks hid and scuttled. Each time we approached their area, John slowed down and waited until the tiny bobbing heads, and little, downy, scrambling bodies were clear of the huge, hard, powerful, shining discs and knives of the nine-foot-wide mower.

Once at Hazelwood, the children and I sprang into activity and we laid the table, swept the floor, picked flowers, had baths, and, when I had placed the long unpolished candlesticks on the table, I went out to buy a celebratory Chinese take-away. John brought Roger home at 7.30 pm and brought with him a bottle of champagne. In the glow of candlelight, and sharing the champagne with the children, I opened presents and cards with laughter and tears.

Edward's mother sent a card, but enclosed a letter saying 'I will not be sending you a card or letter again, as in taking a new husband, I will no longer be part of you, or you of me.' The more we care, the more we have the power to hurt and be hurt. I had loved – and do love – her deeply.

I have never received such thoughtful and meaningful presents, and the love surrounding me overcame my sadness. We ate, drank and were happy. It was a beautiful, satisfying day.

*26 July*

John wanted to show me how one can tell when the corn is ripe enough to harvest. He drove to a field of barley on one of the hills near Marford. Stopping on a triangle of grass at the road's junction, we walked into a field, the long awns scratching bare legs, thigh-high in a sea of gold. The grains of barley, instead of being uniformly hard, were soft and milky in some places, and firm and cheesy in others. John was disappointed by it. From there we drove to the land at the foot of the downs, where Roger had been baling hay into a Dutch barn. He had gone home, but Tom, naked to the waist and a golden brown, and Geoff and Ralph had stayed on. The only sound was the cricket commentary from the radio in the cab of the tractor. A breeze sighed faintly over the long, pale yellow fields stretching to the downs.

The heavy green of the hedges in full summer panoply divided the irregular field shapes, and stiff hogweed grew among the thick, dry grass of the old, deserted yards and tumbling buildings of what had been a thriving farm, now taken over and swallowed up as part of a larger enterprise. John contacted Harold on the radio and asked him for his opinion on the fitness of the corn in Marquis Leaze, Round Pond and Hollyditch. Deciding that none would be ready to harvest over the weekend, John told Harold to clean off the combines and put them away.

The field of wheat which had mildew on it earlier this year is undersown with lucerne. The pretty, slender heads of wheat are still blue-green with growth and the lucerne is growing so well it threatens to overtake the wheat, which will not be ready for harvesting until September. Then the combines will cut the wheat very high, taking only the ears. The lucerne will be cut for silage and include the stalks of the wheat chopped up in it.

John showed me his plans and explained how he estimates the yield of straw and hay from the fields, and the amount of hay and straw needed by each farm for the winter. He has to know the amount each barn will hold, and which barn will be used for what. The winter is estimated at one hundred and eighty days.

A mile away from Home Farm the roar of the drier and the dust from the chaff were audible and visible. The corn is tipped from the trailers onto what looks like an enormous cattle grid with a pit beneath it. From there it is sucked up into the first cleaning process. Free of the husk, straw and dirt, it falls in a steady stream into a weighing machine which automatically registers the metric equivalent of two hundredweight. Every half hour samples are taken to discover the moisture content, if it is too high, then the corn must be artificially dried before passing into the storage bins. The corn is drawn up to the top by an enclosed conveyor belt and zigzags its way down through hot air which is pulled through a percolated belt. On the last layer it is cooled before it is once more sucked up a chute and onto a twenty-two-yard long elevator running high in the roof of the barn and over the top of the twenty-two metal bins, each one of which holds forty to fifty tons of corn. A slatted catwalk at the top of a steep ladder gives access to the elevator and the exit chute, from which the corn is shot into the bins. The full bins that I saw will be sold and gone within a week. There is a constant turnover until the harvest is finished and then the remaining corn is held and sold off at intervals during the winter to maintain cash flow.

Every load, and the field from which it was harvested, is written down so that every harvest can be retrospectively examined. I was awed, impressed and excited by the scale and efficiency of the operation.

Norman spends most of his day here in the summer, he is in charge of the drier and someone has to be there all the time in case the machinery gets blocked, or anything goes wrong. He was nowhere in sight when we arrived. On the table by the moisture meter, and on the armchair, were several magazines including *Farmers' Weekly*. On top was a copy of *Penthouse*. When we came down the ladder from the catwalk, Norman was assiduously brushing the yard clear of dust and debris, and the copy of *Penthouse* was turned upside down. John pulled his leg about that, and he laughed and so did I.

Further up the road outside the dairy, Fred and Will were vacuuming the combine harvesters, preparing for a new field and a new variety of corn on Monday. It was after 8.00 pm. They found the remains of Roger's jacket in the combine: I burnt it.

The makers of the fly killer say that it was faulty and was not switching itself off and on automatically. A new one has been fitted, but I have not used any of them since I was ill. The flies have not been troublesome because the summer has been wet and cold. At Honeybed Rodney told Jim that Kevin had not milked the cows out on his days there. Jim told Kevin. Kevin, upset, told John. John went to see Rodney. Kevin is particularly sensitive to criticism as he is new to milking, and John does not want him to be discouraged. Rodney does not realise that everything is passed on and everyone is a potential source of gossip. Kevin is a proved hard-worker and I am beginning to suspect that Rodney is not.

The manager of the neighbouring estate rang up, ostensibly to ask John about some matter, and he asked me if I were interested in joining their cheese enterprise. I am not, but my ego was boosted!

*30 July*

The Lyndon barbecue and disco was held for the first time this Saturday. It was such a success that it is hoped Lord Elroy will give his permission for it to be held again. The workshop was emptied of all the equipment, and great sheets of camouflage netting and a parachute hired from the RAF station, were draped on the walls and hung down the centre to form a division between the dancing and sitting areas. Branches of trees were interlaced in the netting and bales of straw arranged as seating around the edges. A mobile disco flashed its lights and blared its music from the top of the porch entrance. The barbecue, under an awning outside, issued hot dogs and hamburgers beside the two diesel stoves from the potato shed, and these cast a warm glow into the dark vastness of the park.

It was the first time John and I have appeared together at Lyndon out of our normal 'boss and worker' roles and it was strange. Most of the men were there, with wives, girlfriends, and sons and daughters if they were old enough. John danced with various people as well as with me. Nobody asked me to dance, so I asked Harold and then Norman. It was just possible to talk above the racket of the music.

'He's a good bloke is Mr Peregrine,' said Norman (he never calls him John). 'He works with me a lot in the summer and we do the grain drier together. When he comes it always goes *clickety click*. He can always put it right. Of course,' he said as we jogged in a tight circle, 'we think he's a hard bugger sometimes. I expect you do, too.'

I nodded agreement. I said, 'He expects you to give everything you've got, and more.'

Norman nodded his agreement.

'But,' I said, 'he expects a lot from himself, too, so you don't mind.'

Norman nodded again and said, 'I expect he expects a lot from you too.'

I nodded vigorously, being by then too hoarse to speak at all.

Lord Elroy stayed for a time, and circulated, but told John he was not in the mood for dancing.

Only the stockmen worked on Sunday, and it happened to be my day off, so I luxuriated in bed until lunchtime. We had a proper Sunday lunch of roast lamb (one of our own) with mint sauce and new potatoes. John and I rolled up the carpets as the removal men had dumped them in creased heaps. I arranged the books in some sort of order on the shelves, and Daniel, desperate to earn money for a book on cricket that he wanted, cleaned both the cars, polished the brass, washed the floors, cut the privet bushes and clipped the lawn edges. Elizabeth took the dogs out. It was warm, dry and summery.

A really beautiful milking at Honeybed increased my happiness and air of well-being on the Monday. Elizabeth is attending a music school at a market town seven miles away each day this week. Every year a few pupils from her school are selected and this year she is one of them. I am on a rota with the other parents to get them there.

One of the little girls lives on a farm on an estate on the side of the escarpment overlooking the plain of Riverton. This estate is barely farmed at all, and is a complete contrast to Lyndon. The winding drive is pitted with pot-holes and, although the verges were cut, they were roughly and infrequently chopped, rather than mown. The beautiful trees among the banks of bracken were evidence of its former prosperity, but now it is overgrown and neglected. The verge opened out suddenly into an open, sunny clearing and a pack of hounds, in the charge of two men, sat, stood and lay in the sunshine. Further on, the drive wound beside a lake where a thousand young mallards basked and quacked on the banks and on the road. The blue bar on their wings shone iridescent in the bright light.

Fog muffled the house when I emerged into the dawn the next morning. Hazelwood always lies low in the mists, but I was surprised to find the same heavy blanket of fog at Owlnest on the hill. Underneath this layer, a warm, continuous wind ruffled the leaves on all the trees. Until 7.00 am I milked in a haze of content, knowing that I would not wish to be, or do, anything else. Then the bull got out.

On leaving the parlour the cows had to pass down the race beside the paddock where the two bulls are segregated for the summer. One cow was bulling strongly and I could see her circling round on the path, ridden by other cows and nosed over by the bulls, who in rivalry began pushing each other, heads together, straining their muscular bodies in antipathetic force. One of them then tried to jump the fence and, failing, straddled the barbed wire and was stuck. Nobody responded to my calls on the radio, and I began to hunt for an implement to cut the wire. The bull struggled and I feared he would rip himself to pieces on the barbs. I could not find any wire cutters. Bob is on holiday and all his tools are locked in his garage. Somehow, the bull scrambled over the wire and set off at a run down the track after the cow, apparently unhurt. I finished the milking as the main priority and inspected him when I went to the dry cows. He had one encrusted cut on his side and that was all. The next problem was to get him back. I waited until the afternoon to do this.

In the lunch hour I signed away £3,400 as a deposit on the house in the Lake District. The fog grew worse in the afternoon. The gloom in the collecting yard was almost impenetrable. The cows stood in a solid mass under an oak tree, tails switching rapidly and ears continuously twitching. The heat smothered the animals and the looming buildings.

Thunder rumbled and a few drops of rain fell and dried as they touched the ground. The smell of wet earth seeped under the blanket of fog. The bull walked straight through the electrified rods across the drive and walked over to the other bull who was restlessly treading the fence line. I blocked the exit to the drive with the tractor and shut all the cows up in the yard. I opened the gate to the paddock and hoped that the other bull would not come out. With a little encouragement he walked into his field with docility and they rubbed their heads together without aggression and with obvious pleasure.

Bob's garden is blazing with colour. Philip is watering Bob's tomatoes. Kevin also likes working at Owlnest 'because everything works.'

The barns at Honeybed are filling up with straw. The stubble gleams as gold as a Van Gogh painting against the border of fir trees beyond the field. The maize is waist high and the broad-bladed leaves blot out the red earth under the avenues of sturdy stalks. In the stubble the pheasants search – too successfully – in one field where the combine went too fast and the grains spilled out with the straw, to John's great annoyance. John and Harold travelled to Wales yesterday to look at an unmanned potato harvester at work. This means that, apart from the driver, it is completely automated. If John decides to buy one, the four women who sit at the back of the present machine sorting out the stones and clods of earth from the potatoes will not be needed. The new machine is expensive, but we would save on wages.

Today John is at an NFU meeting at the local market town. A wild, mild day at Quincey's: the grass rippled and glistened, and the distances over the downs were tempered by the pale, cloud-flying sky. The cows udders took on a creamy-yellow shade as if the grass was full of buttercups reflecting their light upwards; only there are no buttercups, herbs, weeds, or flowers. The branches of the trees dipped and swayed and the leaves fluttered in the wind. Golden Gate is being baled today, although the bales of hay are damp from the rain yesterday. The urgency of harvest is overtaking other activities.

The Hereford bull.

# AUGUST

*6 August*

Roger has been laid off for a few days because the weather, though warm, has been cloudy and windy with intermittent showers. The combine harvesters are parked in the wheat field, waiting for the weather to improve. The deadline for the contracted wheat draws near. I do not understand why John is not haggard with worry, but he is calm and cheerful. The manager of the neighbouring estate confided that he could not sleep at night for worrying about the state of the corn and the fact that so much of it was green when cut. John told him that he had put some corn in the bins that would have to be re-circulated and re-dried through the drier in three weeks time to prevent it going mouldy. The hay-making has been difficult and not successful. The hay from Golden Gate, which should have been so good, steamed and smelt as if it was cooking (which it was) in the barns at Hazelwood. Heating destroys the nutrients in the hay and turns it mouldy. So damp were the bales cut in the heavy thunderstorm that the stack was built with a chimney to draw out the heat and let it escape. I climbed to the top of the stack and put my arm in this deep hole. The invisible heat rose and mushroomed under the roof of the barn. If the hay had not been baled, it would have been made useless by the rain, so there was not much choice.

John was minding the grain drier on Sunday. The furnace was roaring and glowing like a mad animal chained in a dark corner. Last year the spontaneous combustion from the dust in the corn piling up within the drier itself caused a fire.

I explored an area of the woods near the forestry buildings, where a big pheasant pen lies, surrounded by high wire netting and a low electric fence to deter foxes. The young pheasants, in plain, dull-brown plumage, ran nervously in and out of the trees and bracken. Hanging on the branch of a larch were the bodies of squirrels, a jay and a stoat. There was no sound in the woods but the ticking of the electric fence and the occasional chirp of a bird. It has been a bad year for the pheasants. Many have died of a disease which is a source of great worry to the keepers. Dead birds have been sent away for analysis, and the keepers do not know if it will be safe to let the penned birds into the woods in case they infect the free healthy birds, or if they will be edible when shot.

Myxamatosis has attacked the rabbits and they crawl about the fields with blind and swollen heads, still nibbling the grass, unaware of dawn, dusk or danger.

A huge straw rick stands beside the dairy at Quincey's. Roger was part of the gang that built it. Colin said that Roger was 'doing all right'. I had wondered, as Roger is not an obviously physical type of boy. He is saving up for a computer and that motivates him.

The discharging sore on the end of the backbone of number '21' is healing at last. David told me that the cause of it was her violent bulling last year, when so many other cows rode her, that her spine was damaged and bits of it broke off under the skin. These pieces have worked their way out of the suppurating sore, and nothing could have be done to heal it. Last week I saw the jagged edge of another bit of bone sticking out of the pus and matter, and this week the sticky stream has dried up and the lump on her back is smaller. Her paralysed tail dangles uselessly, befouled with urine. Strangely, she never has dung on her and is always clean.

The hard lump in the udder of another animal has developed into a huge abscess, the disgusting mouth of which gapes between the teats. The cow never flinches or shows any signs of discomfort. Kevin, milking at Owlnest while Bob is away, got up one morning, had his breakfast and then fell asleep in the chair. His wife woke him at 6.30 am. Oversleeping is the milker's nightmare.

Kevin found summer mastitis in one of the dry cows. This is a really bad infection that can cause the loss of part of the udder, the whole of it, or even death. The cow, when I saw her, looked ill and miserable. Her udder was small and shrunken because she had no milk, but one quarter was as hard as if a block of wood had been inserted into it. Nothing but a few watery drops of clear, yellow liquid came out.

On the blackboard at Honeybed I wrote, 'A smashing weekend at Honeybed,' and meant it. The cows were clean and quiet, the gate only opened once, and the milkings seemed to be over before they had begun. Only seventy-seven cows are in milk. There were no problems whatever. Rodney collected his milk on the Sunday morning and we discussed the winter system and the possible ways of improving it. He said he did not get a petrol allowance and it took him ten minutes to walk home, and when he was toing and froing it took quite a bit out of his day. I could not raise much sympathy, because I know his meals are waiting for him when he does get home, and the house is just across two fields and up a gentle slope. Coming down to the dairy he has the view of the vale and the downs to admire.

In contrast to Honeybed, Home Farm was a seething frustration. The tractor would not start, the scraper blade was broken, there was no hot water, and the top of the hose came off in my hand. I had to leave everything in a mess to get the girls to the music school, and then had to go back later to finish the job. The dung stuck to the walls like superglue in the warm, sultry weather.

Roger, with John and Jim, drove some of the young stock to Stock Street from Owlnest and loaded them into the lorry in batches for transporting to the fields at Honeybed.

The stiff and scratchy stubble at Loxwell was ploughed up the day after the straw was baled, and rape and turnips have been sown. If they are not sown by now they will not germinate in time to produce a winter feed for the out-wintered cattle.

John had a bad week emotionally and I am a perfect barometer to his moods, reflecting in every degree his happiness or his misery. I wish I were not so easily affected. Memories of the past, and fears for the future stab and sear with agonising relentlessness. We comfort each other with gentleness and patience, humbly grateful that we at least have someone who understands, and upon whom we can lean.

The insurance for the new house in the Lake District and my car is concluded at last. The house is of wood and is therefore an insurance problem. I have had to raise more money for it, and see my bank manager. I have bought the car from Edward, as he is to be provided with one by his firm. John's car went to his wife.

I went to the concert given by the music school at the end of the week. I have slowly sorted out the house; the piles of boxes and homeless belongings are dwindling. I have dealt with all kinds of little restless pressures.

With more time at home, I have spent more time in the garden. The Californian poppies are unfurling their fragile, tissue paper petals on their wire-straight, hairy stalks. The stocks and antirrhinums [snapdragons] are in flower, and the jolly nasturtiums are flaming and pouting from under their sturdy, round leaves. The pots of geraniums flaunt their scarlet in otherwise dowdy corners.

*9 August*

A bony, rough-coated, sunken-eyed, and scouring calf is in the pen at Hazelwood yard. John decided to try and save it rather than send it to Barkers. Dung samples show that it has worms and coccidiosis, although it had been dosed for worms – just as children are dosed for measles.

Jim asked the vet if the livestock could pick up the recently diagnosed salmonella from the pheasants. The vet who has been advising the keepers has told them that the birds can be released providing every one of them is shot! One thousand, five hundred birds are carrying the germ out of a total of six thousand, and there cannot be any guarantee that all those carrying the bug will be killed in the shoot. Our vet said the calves might be affected, but he did not think the older cattle would be.

John passed a badger on the road a few days ago. It had been run over and was half dead. He killed it with his hammer, put it in a sack and took it to the Ministry of Agriculture for testing for TB.

My day at Home Farm was pleasant and easy. I always look forward to going there despite the frustrations that usually occur. Everyone likes Graham and so do I. I fret against the muddle but I am at ease within it.

Combining began in Round Pond. While the men go home, John drives the combine in the lunch hour, Harold drives the other machine, and one of the men drives the trailer. Thus there is no hold up throughout the day.

I planned to take a picnic with the children and eat it in the field. On approaching the field a cloudburst saturated the corn and brought all harvesting to a halt. Harold and John curbed their frustration and their tempers, and John drove the trailer of corn to Home Farm to unload it. I drove Harold back to his van, and he hit his head severely on the roof of my van and went off cursing. I picked John up from Home Farm and we carried on with the picnic. The rain had stopped, so we drove down to the lakeside opposite the house, and sat on a rug on the wet grass, ninety-three acres of uninterrupted wheat behind us. A skein of Canada geese flew overhead, honking and piping. A heron flapped slowly to the heronry in the trees on the far side of the lake, and ducks arrowed through the water. A whirling mass of rooks filled the sky over the beech trees in front of the house.

Elizabeth went to play in the gardens and Daniel went to the sports centre. I forgot to pick him up as arranged at 6.00 pm, and went to see John set up a bird-scaring gun in one of the cornfields. I remembered Daniel at 7.15 pm.

I was up early on my day off and packed a picnic for an expedition to Wales to see Andrea. The views of the mountains were non-existent, and the clouds hung low and dreary all day. The grass and thistles were too thickly beaded with moisture to sit anywhere but in the car.

Andrea was hoarse from shouting instructions at the children she is teaching to ride. She is paid £12 a week, her keep, and she shares a room with two other girls. Despite this exploitation, she is enjoying herself.

Elizabeth dislikes travelling in the car and, although she did not dare to grumble, the expression on her face was one of total martyrdom. All day Daniel was obsessed with a loose tooth, which came out as we reached home.

That evening Roger presented his time sheet to John, who thought he had overestimated the hours worked, and he was very angry. Roger denied the accusation and stood firm. Caught between the two, I tried to discover the misunderstanding and be fair. John said he was with Roger at a time when he claimed he was working, and, in fact, the lorry had broken down and they had had to wait for assistance. But as Roger had also had to wait, and was not free to do anything else, what else should he have said? John Collis, in his book *The Worm Forgives the Plough,* puts it succinctly that one's time is owned by one's employer. The problem exposes the difficulties of being paid by the hour. My sympathies mostly lay with Roger.

All the men worked all weekend, finishing at 8.30 on Saturday night and starting at 8.30 on Sunday morning. The combines shake into life as soon as the dew is off the wheat. The winter barley has been cut, and the contracted wheat is ripe enough to be harvested. A breakdown in the drier itself, when a pulley broke and the spare pulley provided was the wrong size, necessitated a ten-mile dash to the agricultural engineer's before they shut. The loads of corn coming in had to be temporarily dumped on the Home Farm barn floor in golden pyramids, like sculpted, edible sand dunes.

Norman passed me in the dairy as I was clearing up. He was on his way to his vigil in the drier, where he has imported a more comfortable armchair. He keeps his magazines under the cushion of the seat. His wife has acute anaemia and every day he takes her to the hospital for iron injections. His face is preoccupied with the worry of her illness.

Swooping down the hill to Hazelwood and supper, I could see the combines like large, red beetles creeping over the cream-coloured fields beyond my house. Straight after we had eaten John drove over to them. The track passed the dilapidated house which used to be the lock keeper's on the old canal, now tangled with trees, weeds and brambles. The field next to the old towpath is known as Wharf Field. The car bumped along the dry, dusty path into the heart of the cornfields, while the dogs loped ahead. Fred and Will were driving the combines, following each other's concentric circles. As Fred drew level to us, John leapt on to the ladder and hauled himself up into the cab, shouting to me to follow him. John had a quick consultation with Fred on how it was going, and Fred said he would take a break. Without halting the combine he swung himself out of the cab and down the steps. John told me to sit in the seat and steer, and he instructed me on how to drive the machine. The combine was slow to react, and it is similar to steering a large ship, the back wheels act like a rudder, affecting the turning of the combine. At the corners I drove out into the stubble, stopped, reversed and moved forward into the sea of ears. From inside the covered cab, which is air-conditioned to stop the driver breathing in the black dust, we looked down on the revolving flails gently positioning the heads of corn for guillotining upon the steel roller. A row of metal spears, held above the surface of the ground, lift the corn up, which is particularly necessary where it has been flattened. The flails keep the heads of corn upright, and a continually turning auger, running from each side to a central mouth, presses the ears and stalks together so that they enter head first. The stalks are then severed by a row of knives, which slide back and forth so swiftly that they make a silver blur. Through a darkened glass window behind the driver's seat, I could see the interior of the combine where the corn was piling up. Colin, who was driving the tractor and trailer, was already moving parallel to us, adjusting his speed and position to ours. At the press of a button, the stream of wheat flowed out in an arc into the trailer. The dry, rustling straw poured evenly out of the back in a long, light shawl. The straw on these fields is to be burnt, so the ground will not be ploughed and the root system destroyed. The next crop will be direct-drilled into it. The combine, when halted and in gear, pants, shudders, and reverberates with suppressed energy, a weird mechanical animal.

We made a last visit to the drier to see that all was well. The sandy, golden ochre of the rounded wheat grains slithered in tawny heaps off the trailer and in flowing waterfalls over the grid. The grains of barley are long, pointed and a light fawn colour.

The next day, John took Roger with him in the cab during the lunch hour. Each trailer holds approximately three combine loads, and three trailers carry the wheat to Home Farm. Each trailer load is approximately seven tons, or £600 worth of wheat. Each acre is estimated to yield two and a half tons of corn, and there are a thousand acres of corn on the estate. One of these fields has been infested with couch grass. That field has been sprayed with a total weed killer while the corn is standing, which is supposed to be safe if the corn is not cut for a week afterwards. No wonder health food addicts are suspicious of the food we eat.

*17 August*

The calf in the yard is improving, his eyes are brighter, though his hindquarters are still plastered with dung. Harvesting is progressing in jerks in between the heavy rain, brief showers, humid heat, fog and dull cloud. Twice only has the sun been hot on my back.

John started up the drier at 5.00 am on Monday and Norman took over at 7.30. There was no combining as heavy rain had fallen, so Marquis Leaze was ploughed and the men were set to work on other tasks. John has a list of wet weather jobs and Harold decides which men should do which jobs. Alan, working in the JCB and digging in Owlnest Park, cut through the water pipe, thus cutting off the supply to the houses, farm and cottages there; he spent the rest of the day re-connecting them. By the end of evening milking, rusty water was coming through the pipes.

I enjoyed another good day at Honeybed. A plague of slugs is invading the dairy and Rodney is trying to kill them off. Around the doorway lay more than a hundred fat, slimy, pale bodies – some five inches long. The collecting yard at Honeybed drains well, and the cows straight, strong legs were smooth and white. Philip, back from his first visit to France, was brown and relaxed.

Daniel is going to the local comprehensive school in September, so this morning I chose to buy his new uniform. In the evening, Linda and Tony, whose wedding I went to, came for supper and met John. They are in farming themselves and were interested to see the dairies. In the dusk, driving across the airstrip to Home Farm, a rabbit sprang up in front of the car and, instead of darting into the shelter of the potatoes, it ran in the light of the headlights. John increased his speed and would have killed it, but I pleaded for its life, and he let it go. I was not logical – we had eaten rabbit stew for supper that very night.

The nights are closing in, I have to switch the lights on in the dairy in the mornings again, and I carry my torch with me once more. I wonder how I will drive the tractor in the fields when it is dark. A beautiful, rosy sunrise at Owlnest streamed over the fields and flushed the tiny clouds a delicate pink. I hastened home afterwards to meet John's stepmother who had come to see him. The three of us had lunch at a local inn and then accompanied her round the galleries at Lyndon.

I was rather late for milking. John had to collect my niece, who is staying for a week, from the station. It rained again at tea time and continued all evening. There is enough of the contracted wheat to satisfy the buyers, so the deadline has been met and the money earned.

I exchanged my day off with David. He wanted to go to a wedding in Manchester. A day off midweek is useful and I spent it writing letters, sewing name tapes on, taking the children and my niece to ride on the pony, and preparing a supper in the evening for Simon, Catherine and the new secretary at Lyndon. We discovered that Simon's salary is considerably below mine, and that Catherine, a teacher in London, is earning £4,500, whereas I am now earning £5,700. We all agreed that Simon should be earning at least £6,000 because of his responsibilities.

Thursday was a depressing day, humid, damp and dark. No combining was possible. The milkings at Home Farm were quick and easy. One of the stone pillars at the lodge entrance was demolished by an unknown tractor and trailer, seen from afar by Harold. Suspicion fell on a neighbouring farmer, whose tractor driver has denied all knowledge of it, but whose tractor and trailer fit the description. John has been involved in the ensuing discussion with the farmer, tractor driver and Lord Elroy.

The children rode on the pony again, ate lunch, and went swimming in the afternoon. John received a letter containing the proposed financial settlement from his wife's solicitors.

All went well at Quincey's until Geoff came to tell me that he had found a slipped[1] calf in the field he was topping. I went out to find it. The calf was very tiny and I could not discover the mother.

I had to cut down all the nettles, thistles and docks on the artificially

---

[1] A slipped calf is a calf which has been born prematurely.

made bank which screens the dairy and is planted with trees. The ground was saturated with the recent rain and so slippery that the van nearly got stuck in the mud.

The dry cows have been moved to the large silage field at the other end of the farm, the hedge surrounding it is full of gaps and the whole field has been electrically fenced by Jim and Vic. Vic is still job-hunting and Lord Elroy is worried that he will not move from his house – Vic must be rather more worried. Without overtime he only earns the minimum wage, less than £60 a week. After the harvest, the jobs which can be found on the farm for him at the moment, will dwindle. He applied for a job last week. John knew the farmer who had advertised the job, and thought he might be able to help, so he rang him. The farmer looked at the one hundred and forty letters he had received and said that Vic's had been eliminated because he had said that his reason for leaving was trouble with his neighbours.

The long track at Quincey's was sticky, and clogged with red mud, but in the distance the hills and wooded slopes were enticing under the sultry, sulking sky.

The children had friends to lunch and played in the Lyndon gardens all afternoon. Edward collected his belongings from the storeroom in my house in the evening. I was tired, miserable, tense and muddled, and so was John. Happily, my weekend off coincided with this dreariness and doubt, and a long talk enabled us to resurrect our normal optimism.

The wheat was too wet for combining, so we packed the car with children and dogs and went for a walk on the downs. The sun blazed out, and we doffed our shirts as we followed the old Roman road through the chalky soil beside the banks of wiry grass and wild flowers, pollinated by a few remaining butterflies. A kestrel surfed the air currents and the dogs ran and ran, panting and slobbering with exertion on their return. We ate an apple and a biscuit each lying on the top of the curving slopes high above the plain.

John was anxious to get back to Lyndon before the combines started again, but the moisture content was too high until the afternoon. When we got back, he took the two girls to ride in the combine, and see the grain drier and the office. I showed Catherine the exhibition rooms, and there we met Lord Elroy. He stopped to speak to us and introduced us to his guest, a man whose nephew is to work at Lyndon for a year before he goes to Cirencester College of Agriculture. As the nephew is to take over a large estate and is heir to a fortune, he is obliged to learn how to farm and manage the estate. John told me that although he will receive £20 a week in wages, he has to pay Philip and his wife, with whom he will be lodging, £25; he is not short of money and, in effect, he is paying Lyndon to train him.

I wanted to see the straw burning and at 3.30 pm the children, my niece, Catherine and I assembled at Rumsey Field. We stood at the topmost edge, overlooking the road and the view to the downs. By our feet we found a sick hedgehog, its little, plump hands and feet were folded neatly into its stomach and its little, bright, black eyes and snout poked out of the bristles – through which I could see the fleas running. I put it down in the maize field and while we waited for John and Harold, we each picked a cob of unripened maize and ate the sweet, juicy kernels.

The men parked their vehicles at the foot of the hill and lit a small pile of straw. Then, carrying a bundle of the lighted straw on a long-handled fork, each began to run along the rim of the field in opposite directions. The straw shed little, orange, flickering flames in a line and, when the bundle was used up, they gathered up another and ran again. The tiny, vicious, dancing flames grew, and spread, and began to move, blown by the wind away from the road and up the hill towards us. The noise of the fire grew like the rushing of a mighty waterfall and the air grew thick with the smoke which billowed over us. The flames, leaping high in pitiless, brilliant beauty, roared over the field, encroaching on our territory until we retreated to the safe band of ploughed land around the field. The crackling of the stubble, and the snapping of the fallen grain as it burst in the heat like popcorn, was like gunfire. Harold, with more bravado than sense, drove his van over the blackened, shrivelled stubble where a few flames flickered lazily, to make sure it had been a 'good burn' and had not left any patches untouched.

When the men had gone home for the night, John and I went out for dinner with some friends.

*18 August*

The fields behind Hazelwood are cleared of corn. Harold voluntarily worked on his own on Sunday evening to finish them. On Sunday afternoon John and I took the children down to Littlecote House for a picnic and a happy afternoon. We ate our sandwiches in a field where a family were languidly stacking sodden bales of straw on their ends in an effort to dry them. Beech trees laden with mast [beechnuts] arched overhead and the dark-green, berry-heavy hedges dipped into the valleys from the rounded hillsides.

Littlecote House, with its solemn, secret, exterior, and its lovely lawns and flowers, lay under the summer sun. A red flag, lions rampant, fluttered from the flag pole against the blue sky. The crowds here have no feelings of awe – which Lyndon tends to inspire, but Lyndon has not the friendly informality which draws the masses and the money. A Wild West frontier show at Littlecote sucked people in and ejected them in ten-gallon hats and spurs – which would make Lyndon shudder.

My niece went home today (Monday), and Tom began to rotovate all the headlands[1] round the fields and Ralph spread the straw with a hay tedder in preparation for it to be fired.

*22 August*

Roger has passed all his o-levels – to my immense relief, not only because I have not seen him doing any work and have been too involved in my own survival to be of any help to him, but because it has been such a disturbing year for all the children. We have lived in such a hugger-mugger way that concentrating must have been very nearly impossible. He is fanatical about his computing and took a train to London on Saturday to spend all his bale money on a computer. He was home by 2.00 pm, and setting it up and programming it in conjunction with the television.

The sky was just lightening when I drove the van into Merchant's

---

[1] A headland is a strip of unplowed land at the ends of furrows or near a fence or border.

Close at Owlnest. A thin, knee-high layer of mist floated on the glistening, dewy grass; from the field below the cows moving slowly into the yard were silhouetted against the east, where the rising sun was tipping the long, light streamers of cloud with every shade of rose and yellow. The mist removes all the sharp edges and the cows appeared to be wading through a dream-like, silent sea.

My weekly task was completing the changing of the rubber pipes in the milking system, which was so difficult I had to ask for help. It must be a job that Bob hates doing. I shifted the stinking heap of slurry that has built up at the end of the collecting yard and scrubbed one half of the parlour, ready for Bob to continue his painting. The upper half of the wall is a clean, bright white.

Bob brought me a large and juicy cucumber and told me he was hoping to go to Canada next. He had been asked to give a lecture tour in New Zealand, but could not find a sponsor. I asked him how he managed to get his cows to come into the parlour so easily and he said 'Kindness and firmness and routine. Cows love habit. If you stuck a pin into them every day they'd get used to it. It's up to you to get them used to anything. Start as you mean to go on. What would you do with a naughty child? Smack it. Well, it's the same with cows. When the heifers come in, if they are very bad, I put the kick bar on and if necessary I tie their legs so they can't move. After a fortnight or so they're all right. I haven't had to beat a cow very often, but I can remember getting one down in the parlour and giving it a really good walloping. My cows are very docile and quiet, and I can do anything with them. There's no such thing as a slow milker unless there's a physical reason for it.'

Daniel and Elizabeth set off on their adventure holiday. We had to meet the coach in Bristol and, as we neared the centre of the city, they fell silent and looked apprehensive. They had had to do all of their own packing and Elizabeth had forgotten her wellies, and Daniel his comb and hairbrush. I promised to send them on. This morning a card came from Daniel, 'Everything is all right,' was its brief message.

I had lunch with Margaret on the way home from Bristol. She had been washing her dead brother's clothes. Because he was killed in an accident, it has meant many complications and unnecessary pain. I know she is suffering and I am doing nothing to help.

The wheel had almost come off the tractor at Quincey's and I used the van to get the cows in from Poole's Night. They were widely scattered and, not being used to the van, were not co-operative. Philip drove Bob's tractor over and scraped for me.

The in-calf heifers had been taken to Stock Street Farm the previous day to be freeze-branded and then separated into groups and taken in the lorry to the different dairies. Each dairy sends a list of the vacant numbers in the herd and each heifer is allotted one of these numbers. This is stamped on it with a branding iron, frozen so cold by immersion in alcohol and carbon dioxide that it literally freezes the hair and blisters the skin painlessly. When the scab heals and the hair grows again, it grows white, an indelible mark on their black hide.

One of the heifers had calved while she was at Stock Street. She was taken up to Owlnest in the morning with twenty-nine others in the lorry. In the night she broke through the fence and returned to Stock Street in search of her calf. The distance was well over a mile. I was sitting in the van and looking at the heifers on my way home, when David came over. We discussed the heifers, whose slender legs and long, twirling tails were still filthy from the excitement and fear of the day before. David's herd is such a comparatively new one that it will be another year before he gets his own replacements. The heifers in the field are a mixture formed from the surplus from all the dairies, and of variable sizes.

David said that he would like his drive to be planted with trees, partly for aesthetic reasons and partly as a shelter for his house, which is exposed. He feels that being provided with a house is not really part of his salary, as if he were paid enough to buy a house, that house would have appreciated enormously over the years, therefore he would have been worth far more than he is now.

He had just bought some Rhode Island Red cockerels to fatten up for Christmas and the freezer. As we talked in the bright, windy sunshine, a grey vapour spread over the land, so thin that the sun shone hazily through, and so low that it grazed the tree tops and one could see the sky beyond it. It was rapidly blown around by the wind and did not seem to threaten rain. All through the park the vapour flew along, thickening slowly until it blotted out the distances and, by the time I went down the hill to Hazelwood, the whole plain was covered.

John drove his eldest daughter to Devon to start her job there for a year before she goes to university.

Protruding from the vagina of one of the first cows to come into the parlour at Home Farm was a withered afterbirth. Puzzled by this, I walked over to the drier to fetch John to see it. He told me to keep her back for the vet to inspect her. She was due to calve in November, so somewhere there must be a large calf lying dead in the fields. I searched in vain. When the vet arrived he declared that her calf had mummified inside her at about four months. Sometimes, when the calf dies, a protective layer is formed around it preventing infection. Eventually, the cow starts bulling again, and disturbs the womb which tries to eject the foetus. The calf was lying just inside her, very small, and very dead. The vet pulled it out and did not think there was any need to isolate the cow.

There are blackberries in the hedges and on my cultivated bush, and mushrooms in the fields. I picked corn cobs and ate them for breakfast. The rape and turnips have germinated and the grass in Owlnest Park is thick and silky. The weeds that grew in the grass were sprayed and are now withering up. The field at Hazelwood, where the calves grazed, and which was causing the worm infestation, has been sprayed with a total herbicide and is now a hard, brittle, dead orange colour. It has to be cultivated and reseeded. The oil line has been dug, sunk and refilled and the damaged land drains re-done. The empty, golden fields behind my house are fired and blackened, charred and ugly. The single ash tree on the skyline was singed by the flames.

John was angry. 'The men fired that field,' he said, 'and that is why I like to do it myself.'

Paul, the builder, is filling in the holes in the yard at Hazelwood with the help of a young lad on a government scheme. He borrowed a stiff brush and when he brought it back he stayed to talk. He is afraid of being made redundant as he reckons he is the most vulnerable because he came to Lyndon last. One of the gardeners has been dismissed recently and this has caused unease and despondency. Paul's wife works in the house and she cleans all the exhibition rooms. Every exhibit has to be taken out from the showcase, cleaned and replaced exactly. All the silver is cleaned regularly and every room swept, cleaned and dusted. She works in the restaurant too.

Paul said, 'You must have seen her.'

I replied that I had only managed to go there twice since I began work. Paul has been married before and has a child, but said that, in the interests of the little boy, he forced his wife to have him and would not see him any more. Originally, his wife had said she did not want the child, but the visits he made had upset the boy so much that Paul thought it was better for only one parent to have him, and so he renounced his son. His present wife has two children from her previous marriage and her husband never sees them. Paul's views on the state of the country are definite. He thinks that decline and war are inevitable, and that England should get out of the arms race and become neutral. Any blacks not satisfied with living here should be sent home, '. . . then see whether they preferred it here under any conditions,' and that if everyone was a communist there would be no more trouble, because everyone would believe in the same. If all dissenters were shot then, at some point, there wouldn't be any left and so it would all be okay.

*29 August*

The calf at Hazelwood ceased to make progress and Barkers were told to collect it. In the pen with it was a much larger calf that was lame. Barkers were told to leave that one. When Malcolm went down to feed it, the pen was empty. In their defence, Barkers said it had a 'discolated [sic] hip' and would not have been any good anyway. Jim thought it could have been fattened; I thought Barkers were right.

I caught up on housework on my day off and in the evening John and I fired the stubble in one of the big fields near to Quincey's. He collected the tractor from Bob and three old tyres from the silage clamp. Gathering a pile of straw together, he made a bonfire of it and then threw the tyres on until they were blazing fiercely. Towing one of the tyres on a long wire he drove off round the edges of the field. The tractor disappeared over the brow of the hill and I could follow its progress by the little puffs of smoke which were soon obliterated by the increasing clouds rising into the air and blowing towards the downs in a rolling, spiralling mass, billowing white at the edges and an angry dirty, brown at the centre. I spread the fire in the opposite direction with the fork, as I had seen John and Harold do. When the field had been burnt and the fire was exhausted, tiny streamers of pure white smoke blew from the embers like some primeval scene when the world was in the making. We walked the field to make sure it had been a good burn and that all the stalks and weeds had gone, and the ground showed clean and crumbly under the flakes of dusty, black ash.

Milking took exactly an hour in the morning at Honeybed, not counting the washing down, and three-quarters of an hour in the afternoon.

An apricot sunrise spread in loveliness over the vale and warmly tinted the uncompromising colouring of the cows in the collecting yard. I began to paint the range of calving boxes during the weekend, scrubbing the flaking, rusty metal and all the doors with a metal brush and then painting them black. The concrete walls are to be painted white. The sun warmed my back and the sloping concrete yard glared white. I had the radio on low for company, and thought of all the occasions when I had despised people who could not do without the radio – especially Radio Two.

The heifers are 'springing', their bodies are preparing for calving, and their udders are enlarging. It is interesting to see how different each udder is and to recognise the types or strains passed on by the cows and bulls. When they are very near to calving their udders are as tight as drums and the skin is taught and smooth. One of the heifers at Owlnest has the ugliest teats I have ever seen: they are so thickly covered with warts that the teats are twice the normal size, rough, scaly, and repulsive.

John's sister, Sarah, came for the weekend. Her son had just failed all his o-levels and she had been appointed to a new and challenging job, so we had much to discuss.

Ron, the sprayer, invited us to a party that evening. John was very tired and so was Sarah, but I felt we had been honoured with the invitation and must go, or it might be taken that we – particularly me – were setting ourselves apart from the men.

Almost all the farm workers from the estate were there, the atmosphere was relaxed and happy, and it was an excellent party. We reluctantly left about midnight, both because we were exhausted, and because both John and I had to be up early the next morning. Ron said he never went out for an evening if he was working the next day, Norman was not at the party – his wife is still ill and he is incarcerated in the drier most of the time, sometimes until midnight.

One of the combines broke down on the Sunday and John was away all day, either driving round, or in the workshop. A laden trailer burst a tyre in the afternoon, and John had to find a spare vehicle, remove a tyre and put it on the trailer.

Sarah sunbathed in the garden and cooked a magnificent supper of roast beef, Yorkshire pudding, potatoes, vegetables and gravy, something we have not enjoyed for months. Roger has been staying for a few days with Edward and then went up to London for two days on his own. He spent his time in the museums.

On the bank holiday weekend the men had either the Sunday or the Monday off.

Rodney strolled into the yard at Honeybed with his dog, a border terrier. He is proud of this dog. 'She'll fight anything,' he boasted. 'She absolutely routed a big Labrador by dashing under his nose, through his legs and biting his marbles.'

I looked, without admiration, at the small whiskery face and coarse brown-haired body.

Rodney believes in calving his heifers and *then* bringing them into the parlour as the shock is so great that they are stunned into behaving. The farm policy is to run them through the parlour for about a week before they calve, to get them used to the sights, sounds and smells, and having their udders handled. This is kinder to the animals and easier in the end to the milkers. I knew that John would insist on Rodney using our methods so I did not argue.

The herdsmen have been told that the heifer beef calves are to be sent to market this year instead of rearing them, so they will be kept on the cow at the dairies until market day. This is more trouble for the herdsmen, but is more profitable for the farm.

John drove out to fire the Gallows field in the Quincey's tractor; the very next day he sent the agricultural engineers out to see to it. The reason for the stiffness and awkwardness off the clutch was found to be the fitting of an entirely wrong part, and of negligence on the part of the tractor repairers, which has made many hours of extra and unpleasant work for all the dairymen.

Bob cannot improve his cubicles this year, which is a disappointment. As soon as I finished milking at Owlnest, Philip came to run the dry cows through the parlour to check their udders and spray them for flies. I am not usually involved in this routine, because the dairymen prefer to know exactly how their cows are doing. Philip ran them through swiftly, feeling each quarter for lumps, or unusual heat, and then used a knapsack sprayer and a long-handled nozzle to spray them until the parlour reeked with the smell. One cow had mastitis and I hand milked that quarter, tubed her and put her in with the milking herd until she is better.

Geoff is hedging the fields at Hazelwood. From a distance they look very neat, close-up they are hideously mangled and hacked by the powerful hedge cutter which chops into tiny bits the cut shoots and branches, leaving a mulch of debris to rot away. Geoff does the job well, and carefully.

I gave all my white furniture a coat of paint at lunchtime and sat in the sun with Caroline who came for lunch. Elizabeth and Daniel wrote long letters, mainly about how many people had been sick and where: a bug is doing the rounds of the holiday centre.

A rich, orange harvest moon shone in the early morning sky before the sun rose, and all day a heat haze covered the fields at Quincey's. A tractor droned monotonously, cultivating the field we had fired. Around the edges of the fields, and along the hedgerows and verges, the weeds, flowers and grasses are seeding. The docks are shedding their rust-red seeds, and the thistles their soft, white thistledown. Clumps of nettles stand dusty and dry beside the pink sprays of rosebay willow herb. On the estate's drives the gawky, tailless, young pheasants run in anxious, speckled groups. A few are developing their winter plumage and shedding their infant camouflage in untidy patches. Fewer rabbits are seen and the keepers patrol the last wedges of standing corn, guns cocked to shoot any possible lurking foxes as the combines shave away the last hiding places.

One of the dry cows at Home Farm had mastitis. I drove the whole group of cows in from Greenmoor, the field under the wood. Each farm has three separate herds now: the milkers; the dries; and the heifers and near calvers. They must all be seen every day. Philip helped me and sprayed them as they went through the parlour, we separated the ones nearest to calving and put them in with the milkers.

Bumping gently over Cathill One on the tractor in the afternoon sunshine, I contrasted my life with those of the solicitor and the accountant who I had had to visit in my lunch hour: I had no doubt that mine was preferable. Ahead of me the herd walked placidly. Far out in the field, and away from the other cows, I could see a heifer and a little black and white blob on the ground beside her. I stopped the tractor a few yards from her and walked slowly to her. The calf was already on its feet and went wobbling off towards the copse. The worried heifer, her udder smeared with blood, tenderly mooed at its side. I left them there and drove the herd in for milking. In the yard was the first casualty of the season, a dead Friesian calf, which lay waiting all day for the knacker to collect it.

# SEPTEMBER

*3 September*

The fourth quarter of the year began on Monday and my day off is now Wednesday, so I worked one day less this week because of the changeover. Now that it is dark in the mornings it is not easy getting the cows in. At Home Farm I held the torch in one hand and steered the tractor with the other, barely able to see in the streaming rain, I prayed that I would not drive into one of the craters the cows had dug in the sandy ground. In Cathill Two another calf was born with its back hooves bent over, it managed to hobble in on its hocks. If it does not improve naturally, the vet will have to sever the tendons which are holding the feet in this position. Today I was happy and contented, inwardly convinced that I was managing the cows and heifers competently and well.

Roger and John and I had coffee on Sunday with Catherine. She is looking after her father for a few weeks in the large and beautiful family home, an eighteenth century mansion. She showed us the gardens; the smooth lawns; the gracious herbaceous borders; and the walled vegetable garden, most of which is a wild, warm wilderness. The plums, damsons, peaches and pears were ripening fast and little, sweet, scrunchy, apples were soaking up the sun. We climbed to the top of the church tower, past the huge bells, up-ended in silence, and on to the leaded roof. The mellow landscape stretched across the plain to the foothills of the downs. Despite the ravages of Dutch elm disease in this area – which is famous for its tall, lovely trees – the village beneath us was indiscernible within the shelter of the remaining species.

The children were due to return from their holiday, so we did not linger and afternoon milking started right on time. Even so, I was too late home for their arrival at Hazelwood and was not there to welcome them. I was very disappointed. Andrea is home today as well. That night Daniel was sick; he had brought the bug home with him. He should have started at his new school this morning and had to stay in bed – an unfortunate beginning. I went home at breakfast time to see him, but I had to go back to Quincey's to paint the parlour an eggshell-blue until midday.

A calving cow delayed me that night, it needed the combined skill of John and Philip to pull it out. I soaped my arm and plunged it into the cows vagina, trying to ascertain the position of the calf. It was normal, but stuck. John and I heaved and strained on the ropes and the calf's head appeared, blue tongue lolling out between its jaws. Philip stretched the cow's skin around the calf's head, sliding it back to facilitate movement. Just as the head was crowning and the cow was groaning with pain and effort, there was a sharp splitting, cracking sound which made us all exclaim in horror. We had to keep on pulling and the calf slithered out and flopped heavily onto the floor, completely inert and a dull-yellow colour from the fluid in the womb. John rubbed its ribs vigorously, Philip put a few drops of calf reviver on its tongue and it gasped and wheezed, while I released the cow from the halter and she began to lick it enthusiastically.

In the evening I went back to make sure she was not haemorrhaging. That morning, with my brain muzzy from lack of sleep, and the fog as thick as a traditional pea-souper, for a while I thought that I was in the wrong field altogether, searching for non-existent cows. David's tractor *does* have lights (some didn't) and, eventually, they beamed through the fog and picked out the indistinct shapes of the cows. It would have been easy to miss one.

The self satisfaction I had had at Home Farm deflated at Owlnest when I muddled through the day, bungling my way to the end. Bob had rung me up the evening before I went there, he told me there were two heifers due to calve that night in the little paddock. On my arrival I went to see if they had calved. Both heifers were murmuring over a small, unsteady calf. I shone the torch over the surrounding area and, lying stiffly in the grass, partly shrouded in its membrane, was another calf – dead. Later on, I towed the pathetic body up to the dairy by fastening a length of the ubiquitous baler string round its hind legs. Philip helped me to remove both of the heifers from the paddock. He put one of the heifers in a box with its own calf and another that had been born in the herd that night, and which I had not noticed in the morning – very bad herdsmanship.

I let the milk from a cow with mastitis into the tank by mistake, and a heifer with mastitis leapt about so madly with the kickbar on that she burst the gate open and careered into the field, bucking and leaping. Her antics were so extravagant that the kickbar fell off. Another heifer refused to go back into the box to feed its calf and I had to improvise a gate to guide it in; I opened one of the field gates to do this and forgot to shut it. Some of the milkers went into the wrong field and I had to fetch them out. One group of dry cows was at the furthest end of the furthest field, the other was in the lush new ley of Owlnest Park and had to be moved to reduce the danger of bloat. John wanted the tractor as he was going to fire another field of straw, so I had to walk to get the cows in.

In the afternoon Philip, Jim and Kevin moved a group of heifers up and one jumped over the fence into the plantation on the hillside. It took much sweating effort from us all to dislodge her from the undergrowth.

I slept at lunchtime, again in the evening, and went to bed early to shake off a slight, persistent headache.

Harvesting ceased over the weekend because of the rain. John says he has already sold two hundred and twenty tons of corn more than he budgeted for. The yields have been higher than anticipated and they are running out of storage space. John showed the children the wonders of the corn store. Roger was vastly impressed at the enormous quantities of wheat and barley, the height of the piles of grain in the open store, and the depth of the bins. He simply said, 'Good grief,' rather repetitively. Roger is growing rapidly and is now more than six feet tall.

The rain has freshened my garden and the asters, petunias,

geraniums, nasturtiums, antirrhinums and roses make cheerful splashes of colour.

John is giving all those working on the harvest an extra two days off, which, with the weekend they could not work, gives them a four-day break. It is the first time he has ever done this and he had to tell them he was not setting a precedent!

*9 September*

John and I quarrelled fiercely over the question of my days off. I had been told that going to the Dairy Event at Stoneleigh was one of the dairyman's perks, because we do not go to the Royal Show. The event fell on a Wednesday and Thursday, so I assumed it was a bonus day off. Four people go on each day and I was allotted the Wednesday.

I said innocently, 'Oh good, and I'm off on the Thursday,' thankful to have the Thursday at home to catch up on the housework as usual.

John said immediately and forcefully, 'You can't have *two* days off – going to the Dairy Event is your day off.' He was amazed at my indignation.

'I'd rather not go if that's the case,' I said abruptly. I have come to feel militantly about some things. While I was digesting these antagonistic feelings Philip arrived and said that, as it was Rodney's day off on Wednesday, he would get a day off some other time, and I would have to milk for Graham on the Thursday, but I could also have a day off in lieu.

John and I clashed again in planning our visit to the 300 Cow Club conference in October. We shall be away for two nights and I am to go as John's guest. The two nights adjoin my day off and I said again, 'Oh good, I'll take them as two days holiday.

John said sharply, 'You can't do that. You'll have to swap day's off.' I remembered that people are not encouraged to have holidays in the winter because that is the busiest time for the dairymen. However, I had been invited by John and it could be called a 'busman's holiday'. I have had only four days holiday this year and I experienced an intense resentment and revolt. My time off is so limited that I can barely cope as it is, and to have that curtailed further is a disaster.

John accused me of living only for my days off instead of for work and that sword thrust really hurt. These are the occasions that I foresaw and dreaded when John and I enmeshed each other in our emotions. The delicate balance between boss and worker is easily upset and all problems are exaggerated. We overcame this problem by talking it out, but for a while it shattered my confidence in all directions.

On 1 September the head gamekeeper discovered the body of a calf next to the wood in Greenmoor, so riddled with maggots it had to be burnt where it lay under a bale of straw. It was the calf of the cow I had brought in with mastitis at Home Farm. Philip, Graham, John and I saw her that day at close quarters, and we could not tell that she had calved. From Thursday to Monday she was not milked, but now she seems none the worse, although her lactation is bound to be affected.

Another heavenly sunrise and a hot day made the painting at Honeybed a pleasure. I put on shorts and made a band of clothing out of my shirt to keep myself decent.

It is an unwritten rule that one should leave the parlours completely ready to switch on in the morning so that milking commences promptly. Rodney does not heed this common sense and I start off irritated by his lack of consideration. Rubbish lay about that I had to clear, the gates were not 'set' and various things were left undone. This would never happen at the other dairies. I leave it as I would wish to find it, but the hint does not sink in.

Margaret and Christopher came for a meal and John and I took them to see the corn store. I want everyone to see it, it is so amazing.

John's daughter is working at Nettlecombe Court in north Somerset, and we went down to see her, taking Andrea with us. Anna showed us the red stone house, a centre for geological studies, and the church nestling in a hollow at the end of a long drive. We picnicked on the hills under a grey, cloud-laden sky and then drove to Blue Anchor Bay, where the sea front is a neat, but lengthy, caravan site. Far past the end of the promenade is a jumble of gigantic, fallen rocks, whose strata lay at all angles to the sea and the sky. The dogs padded about, enjoying the smells which were singularly of sewage.

Some of the men use their days off to go wooding round Hazelwood, felling the remaining dead elms that linger in the hedges.

John and Philip have come to the conclusion that Rodney has certain gaps in his knowledge of cows, which could be disastrous in such a thing as milk fever. John decided to circumnavigate this problem as tactfully as possible and tell him that he must get help until he is more sure of himself. Rodney took umbrage at this suggestion and told John that he knew most things about cows, which I know from my own observation is patently not true. If he admitted ignorance or uncertainty, John and Philip would think no less of him, and be very willing to help.

With the onset of the heifers calving I am suddenly much busier and home much later. The milking heifers at Home Farm were docile and calm. One due to calve kept kicking her belly and fidgeting in the parlour. I boxed her and after supper John went to look at her. I was in bed feeling sick and extremely queasy with the bug. He came back and said he would need help and asked Andrea to go back with him. But the cow was my responsibility, so I got up and dressed with Andrea.

We entered the box at 10.00 pm, with torches, ropes, a bucket of disinfectant and the HK calving aid. The calf was so tightly wedged inside the heifer that we has difficulty slipping the ropes over its feet. The presentation was normal and we pulled slowly when the heifer strained. I was soon convinced that the heifer would split and that we ought to be calling the vet, but John refused to panic and pulled steadily while I stretched the skin of the vulva back over the head. With the tongue of the calf protruding purple from its mouth it came flopping out onto the straw, quite limp and apparently lifeless. The usual pummelling and straw up its nose had no effect, so I went on my knees in the damp, warm straw and gave it the kiss of life, willing it to live. My breath gargled down to its lungs, again, and again, and again, and then there was the faintest movement

Brock, my dog.

in the gaping mouth, so small I was unsure I had seen it, then another, unmistakeable, and the staring eyes flickered as if to blink, and its heart began to beat. The calf laboured to breathe, gurgling and rasping until I had cleared, and kept clearing, the mucus in its throat and lungs. I pumped its legs up and down to inflate the lungs, and rubbed its body to stimulate the circulation. At last we left it, propped up slightly on a bale of straw. The mother, still in a state of shock, refused to look at it. I rang Graham in the morning, fearing to hear that he had found it cold and stiff, but it was alive and well and feeding. That was a moment of real happiness and joy.

Vic is still searching for a job and spends much of his time travelling in his old car seeing prospective employers. He works well with the men on the estate and they think he is a good stockman. He turned down one job last week because it was milking only, and he would have had to pay for his house and milk.

It has been proposed that Kevin should have a flat at Hazelwood, by creating one out of the barn adjoining my house. But to save the cost of this it has been suggested that when I move out of here, Jim will move in to my house, Rodney will move into Jim's half of the cottages, (the larger half), and then Kevin will move into Rodney's half. Geoff is getting married in September and a thatched cottage is being renovated for him. Status has a significant part to play in these delicate manoeuvrings. Lord Elroy said to John, 'With respect to Alison, Hazelwood is too good a house for the relief milker.'

Lord Elroy has been to Iceland for a holiday and during his absence Lady Elroy moved out of Lyndon. I caught the germ that Daniel brought home, but was not sick, only nauseated all week. I was afraid that it would spoil the weekend that John and I had planned. We were leaving Andrea in charge, and going to the south coast for a night. We set off on Saturday afternoon, after the men had finished work, and ambled, in a leisurely way, across country in the direction of Winchester. Children were flying kites on Danesbury Ring, an ancient hill fort overlooking Pewsey Vale.

We stopped for bed and breakfast in a private house in Boldre. In the morning we took the ferry to Studland, and swam in the sea and dried ourselves by the sun on the hot, white sand. We walked on the

Purbeck Hills on the short, wiry grass, and climbed up to the hill fort, which has half-slipped away down the steep, chalky cliff. For a brief interlude we were as free as the soaring seagulls, and consciously appreciative of each moment of happiness.

A heifer began to calve in the box at Quincey's. All morning, while I painted the parlour eggshell blue, I heard her groaning occasionally, but when nothing happened I called John on the radio and we haltered her, tied her parallel to the box sides and pulled the calf out with great effort. The poor beast made a lot of noise, grunting and moaning, and afterwards refused to get up. The longer a cow is down, the harder it is for them to get up. We allowed her a little while to recover and then encouraged her on to her feet. The calf had a huge head and a swollen eye like a boxer. Two cows in the next box watched us with interest. David is starving them to make them dry off, to give them a rest before they calve again. It was after 1.00 pm before I was home.

Now I drive right round the edges of the fields to get the cows in each morning. Cows will hide away to give birth. In one corner of Merchant's Close, a heifer had calved so recently that the calf was flat on the ground, the membrane which covered its body and head glistening in the lights of the van. I sprang out of the van and pulled the membrane off its head, just in time to stop it suffocating. The calf shook its head feebly and flapped its limp, black ears. I drove cautiously on into the blackness, now lightening with the dawn, flashing my torch into the edges and corners of the field, but still I failed to notice one heifer, she was standing with her calf in the middle of the field. I left them and drove the rest of the herd in.

Straight after milking I inspected the dry cows in Owlnest Park, put straw in their rack and observed a cow of enormous girth standing apart from the rest. Being short of time I used the tractor to look at the bunch of dry cows on Longhill. I scrubbed the pit of the parlour as instructed so that Bob can continue his painting. This was a hands and knees job, and not pleasant. I was not sure how I ought to get the calves and heifers into the boxes on my own, but there was no one to see my mistakes, so I walked out into the field. I attempted to steer the first calf in the direction of the dairy, hoping that the heifer would follow, but the distance was too great for the calf which crumpled up and would not cooperate. I walked all the way back to the dairy and drove the van to the calf, lifted it in the back and drove away, making imitation calf noises. The mother followed anxiously, and I shut them up without difficulty in the boxes opening onto the yard. The next heifer would not follow the van, so I put her calf in with the first heifer, but she butted it away and would not accept it. I removed the calf to the next box and walked to get the heifer in. She could not understand where her calf had gone and was not happy to leave the field. The last one came in without problems.

The calving cow in Owlnest Park showed no signs of imminent birth and I went home for lunch, both weary and hungry. When I returned I went to look at her, I saw that her water bag was hanging out, but she looked unconcerned. I started milking. Philip came, looked at her and went off to calve a cow at Quincey's. When he came back she had one live calf and one dead calf. We could not tell if it had been born alive and suffocated, or if it would have survived had someone been present. John said that it is impossible for the herdsman to be there at each birth when they are looking after one hundred and fifty cows virtually single-handed, and it is unreasonable to expect them to do so. Nevertheless I was saddened.

Combining recommenced in the morning, but rain stopped it in the afternoon, so the men baled the straw in Rockhouse and Combe Grove. Wedged in the ditch at the side of Tower One at Honeybed was a cow, completely immobilised.

Two heifers had calved in the night and one calf was dead. Two other heifers had broken through the electric fence in search of their calves which had been taken to the calf rearing unit. I left the heifer with the live calf in the field, and when the rest of the herd came down to the yard she brought it with her, so I was able to easily shut her up. I radioed Philip, who haltered the cow in the ditch and pulled her out with the tractor. He dosed her with calcium for milk fever, but she did not respond so the vet was called. He diagnosed phosphorus deficiency and dosed her for that. I gave her hay and water and we propped her up on bales of straw.

Two newly calved heifers came through the parlour instead of the expected one and Philip and I searched in vain for the missing calf.

The cows sometimes hide them away, as deer will, and the calf lies unmoving until the mother returns to it. Unfortunately, if the cows are moved to a different field, and if the calf was feeble to start with, it will die from lack of nourishment.

The scraper had been damaged again and the tractor brakes are as bad as they ever were.

Walter, the builder, and a lad were working on the alterations that we hope will improve Honeybed. Walter offered his congratulations to me and said he had been through it all himself. 'My second marriage is pretty well perfect, though I couldn't honestly say I love my wife. You don't need to love someone to live with them. I did with love after my first marriage.'

Rodney hovered on the farm in the afternoon. From the way he talked one would think that all the alterations had been done at his suggestion, and no one else had originated any of the ideas. Very irritating.

A hot wind gusted fiercely at the same moment as I drove the cows past the Dutch barn and a black polythene sheet, that was protecting the hay, almost ripped in half. It sprang out at them, cracking and snapping like a cowboys' whip. I feared the cows might refuse to pass it, but in contrariness they filed past stolidly, ignoring it.

I stayed in bed for all of my lunch hour, affected by nausea and a bad headache from the bug, but milking in the afternoon cleared my head a little. Jane came to stay again and Andrea made a delicious stew from the old hens from Causeway House.

*15 September*

Elizabeth was sick all over her carpet in the night and stayed off school.

A football match has been organised for the Lyndon men, the over thirty-fives against the under thirty-fives. At 6.30 pm twenty-two men met on Lyndon's sports ground under a lowering grey sky, supported by wives and children. Roger was asked to referee, but only blew the whistle twice, once at half time and once at the end. John was one of the few in shorts. There were several rough and tumbles, but it was a cheerful event. Mick played vigorously, egged on by his wife who in between shouting for him, shouted at her children. The next day, Philip said that he would never play again, he could not move, and John could hardly walk.

Andrea and Jane have taught themselves to knit, they sit hunched over their needles and balls of wool like two old grannies by the fire. Three heifers due to calve were in the small paddock at Home Farm, calmly chewing the cud in the torchlight at 5.00 am. Straight after milking I checked on them again. One, hidden in the holly bushes, had calved and was lying helpless on her side. The calf, its head up and legs tucked under it, was still attached by the umbilical cord. I could not get her up and, in thrashing around, she caught me a painful blow on my chin with her head. I was planning to run for help when I saw Norman strolling in the distance in his non-working clothes, he was taking his wife to the hospital for more tests. Together we pushed the heifer on to her belly and she scrambled to her feet and began to lick the calf

It was Roger's seventeenth birthday and we celebrated with a take away Indian meal by candle and firelight, and the children were allowed to stay up late. John and I went back to Home Farm to see a cow; she had calved on her own. I was quietly grateful to her.

Walking noiselessly up the field at Honeybed in the dark the next morning, I was slightly alarmed to see a light flashing in the far corner. It is so unlikely that I am not alone, that I am never afraid that I might not be so.

I approached the light and at the same moment shouted, 'Hello there.'

A voice hailed me, 'Who's there?' It was Rodney, forgetting it was his weekend off – I cannot imagine anyone else on Lyndon forgetting their day off. Unlike anyone else, he did not return to bed, but tagged along and would not be put off.

The milking was dirty and muddling as a consequence and I could not concentrate. Number '410', a nice old cow, grizzled grey with age, was in the box for calving; hating the confinement, she thrust her way out of the sliding doors and burst out of the box.

I painted the window frames, but was home early enough to have a sleep, and we went to the theatre that night.

My small vegetable garden has yielded cucumbers, courgettes and broad beans.

John has drawn up the cropping plan for all the fields and drilling will start shortly. Lyndon does not use its own seed because it would have to be dressed[1] for disease and pests and this would make the operation much more complicated. For a thousand acres of corn about twenty-seven hundredweight of seed corn is needed.

On Sunday we went wooding at Green Lane, near the old canal. John used the new Ford tractor and an old trailer. He chainsawed the felled dead elms into pieces and the children, Jane and I picked them up. I drove the tractor from trunk to trunk across the newly cultivated earth. Elizabeth and Daniel were grizzly and quarrelsome at first, but when I lost my temper with them they became much more cheerful. They enjoyed making a bonfire to clear the sticks, and riding on the trailer. A large log dislodged itself and hit Elizabeth on the head. There is now a pile of logs outside my gate at Hazelwood, which is gratifying and will save me a great deal of time this winter. When the logs had been tipped out, John went up to Owlnest to collect his children and I took mine to an inn where we met as a combined party for a drink in the garden. This was a momentous occasion and something of an ordeal, though it passed off very pleasantly with everybody apparently relaxed.

All over the weekend I tended to the cow which had been in the ditch. She was not eating much, but did not seem distressed. I covered her with straw and she was propped up with bales. Andrea and Jane came to look at the kittens in the barn, and John said we must move the cow because of her circulation. With a concerted effort we rolled her completely over. A terrible smell arose from the flattened ground and her legs, smeared grey with wet and mud from the ditch, stuck stiffly out. She could not move and her limbs were numb. Her udder had milk in it, but on it was an ominous dead-white streak. We rolled her into a normal lying position and drenched her with another dose

---

[1] Dressing is a chemical seed treatment, typically antimicrobial or fungicidal, applied to the seeds before planting. It is usual to also add colouring so that the seeds are less attractive to birds and are easier to see if spilt.

of phosphorous, but it was clear to me that she would not recover. John rang Barkers this morning and I hoped fervently that they would shoot her first and drag her into the lorry afterwards, and not vice versa.

Harold has asked for time off; his wife is ill and he is worried about her. She was at the football match, looking pale and wan. Harold says she keeps having blackouts and she is afraid of being alone.

Susan is back, for her final year at the technical college.

The specialist veterinary report on the pheasants' disease has arrived. Swabs were taken from the affected birds to determine whether there were any salmonella bacteria in them which could have led to serious contamination and the threat of widespread food poisoning. Not one bird was affected – a relief to the game-keepers.

*19 September*

Barkers reported that the cow at Honeybed had a broken back and leg which they thought must have happened when it was pulled out of the ditch. Its liver was bad, one reason why it did not respond to the calcium, and gangrene had set in in the leg. Two vets had visited it on three separate occasions, proving that no one is infallible. Poor beast.

Barkers told John they had been to some of the New Forest ponies that are being sold for human consumption. There are too many ponies, and too little grazing, and a glut of acorns on which the starving ponies are poisoning themselves. Seeing the crowds and the TV cameras at the sales, Barkers had retreated. At the next sale they had got a farmer to buy some of the ponies for them. The crowds were not deceived and followed the truck home and were still pestering Barkers, the hyenas of the farming world.

My Angus heifer has gone to slaughter. I bought her in Riverton market for £10, a tiny, black teddy bear of a calf. I reared her at Causeway House and finished her in the paddock at Hazelwood. My stomach churns on the last day of living for all my animals. It is a sickening end to a pleasant and peaceful existence. Handled from birth and unaware of violence, she was too tame and unafraid, and would not be driven into the lorry. At last she became as wild as an unbroken pony. It was necessary to lasso her and lift her bodily into the lorry (with the help of John, Jim, Malcolm and the lorry driver) She was a great, sleek seal of a beast, whose curly, black poll[1] I had scratched, and into whose liquid, brown eyes I had gazed in times of sorrow and happiness. I am the Judas and I must bury my emotion of betrayal fathoms deep, or give up farming.

The entrance to the abattoir at Barkers is narrow and awkward, and it was blocked by a lorry lifting heavy metal tubs with a hydraulic arm. In the tubs were the intestines of slaughtered animals, tainting the air with their stench. One man was busy emptying all the cut-off lower legs and hooves into a tub, and another was slitting the lengths of gut and stomachs and tipping the half-digested contents into a slurry tanker. In a corner a man was dragging a pile of sheepskins, recently occupied and still trailing the ears and empty heads. Blood trickled out from under the slaughter house door and, through the half-shut doors, one glimpsed carcases hanging.

The butcher said he could not kill my heifer until the next day as they were unexpectedly busy, so we unloaded her – who had been so kindly and gently treated all her life – and left her surrounded by the smells of fear and death. It is necessary to stop thinking altogether on such occasions, but the tears rose to my eyes as I bade her a secret farewell. Next week I shall eat her meat and be grateful.

Vic has found a job starting at the end of the month. His wife is on the verge of a nervous breakdown. She is worried about moving the children from the school where they have settled down and now like it. Vic is, himself, in a nervous state and his hands tremble perpetually.

Jim does not want to move into Hazelwood when we move out so there is an impasse. The house will not be offered to the others in the chain. Harold would like to move away from his house as his wife is isolated and depressed there. She is on drugs which have given her hallucinations, and tranquillisers to counteract the effects of the hallucinations. She is going to a specialist on Tuesday.

John had a long talk with Harold, and I went to see her – she is very afraid of being alone. She was sitting before an unlit fire, pale and sad. She looked dopey with the drugs. Harold came in from work, cleaned out the fire and lit it for her. I stayed for an hour and her daughter came

---

[1] The poll is the top of an animal's head between the ears.

home from school to be with her for the rest of the day. Harold has organised the children's party, the skittles evenings, the discos, and he wants a youth club and a social place where wives can meet for coffee, or events can be held. He is particularly keen to do something for the wives, whom he knows are lonely and isolated, and without the daily contact that all the men have with other people.

I had to take the tyres off the silage sheet at Owlnest in preparation for the opening of the clamp this week. The second cut of lucerne is proceeding. The milkers and steamers are getting hay and straw to provide roughage because they are still 'loose' on the new ley.

One of the milking cows has a badly torn teat, probably trodden on as she was rising. It was no use trying to milk it as it was so grossly swollen. It will dry up eventually after forming an abscess.

John, Bob, Rodney and I travelled to the Dairy Event in John's car on Wednesday and Philip, David, Graham and the new student went on Thursday. I made sandwiches, but John and I received a salad lunch in one of the marquees, whisky at the Breeding Centre and cups of tea and coffee from other stands, so I shared my sandwiches out on the way home. My pleasure in the day had been frostbitten by our quarrel, although that was over. It was unfortunate that there was a Dairy Discussion Group meeting that evening, which made the day a long one and the night extremely short.

Three calves lay dead in a heap at Home Farm when I arrived for my long weekend there, in fact, four consecutive days altogether. Graham helped me to pull another dead calf straight after milking. A depressing start to the day.

I lost myself in Cathill One earlier, which would hardly seem possible. I could not face driving in the dark on a tractor without lights and I used the van to get in the cows. I drove down the slope by the central, circular copse to collect some cows sheltering there by the far hedge and then could not get the van up the slope on the wet grass. I reversed and drove round the copse and up the other side, but instead of striking out towards the distant dairy, which was invisible in the murky drizzle, I completely lost my sense of direction, and then could not tell at which point to break away. I could see no cows, or lights, and a sensation close to panic seized me, which I knew was absurd, but did not feel so.

*25 September*

The first day off at home for a fortnight. I am obsessed with my days off and justifiably so. Simon invited John and I to his cottage last night and we took a Chinese take away with us and had a very enjoyable and convivial evening. I was so tired that I slept badly and my eyes are puffed, and my cheeks burn as if a dry, hot wind is passing over them. I woke at 5.00 am from habit and dozed fitfully until the alarm clock rang, the dog barked, the cistern flushed, and the children entered the bedroom demanding notes for school and forms for teachers. Elizabeth has not recovered from the sickness and she is still not happy at the school. She came to lie on the bed to tell me about it and cry. I must do something, I cannot bear her to be miserable. John and I discussed future plans for our wedding, the reception, and the move, and the evening was a cheerful hopeful one.

The calf at Home Farm, that I bottle fed for the four days that I was there, died suddenly on the last day, and was stiffening and cold in the box when I took the bottle in. I put two cows in the boxes for the night and both had calved by morning. Later, I saw another leg sticking out of one and, on examination, felt that the calf was a breech, with one hind leg bent back. When it was pulled it was dead.

Heavy rain fell frequently at the weekend, drenching the cut lucerne and preventing the harvesting of the last field of wheat. The weather is so warm and humid that there is a danger of the corn sprouting where it stands. On wet, foggy morning the fields are vast and lonely. The oaks loom eerily out of the mist, their crowns lost in vapour; I have visions of their branches crashing onto the van. The cows bring clouds of midges into the parlour with them and they are indiscriminate in their biting. A heifer at Home Farm suffered a broken hip and, until she was found to be in calf, was destined for slaughter. Now she has calved, her calf has been taken away to the unit and nothing will keep her in the fields. She haunted the farm buildings, breaking out of Cathill One and Two and the paddock in succession and bawling all night. Her pelvis is lopsided and one back leg is shorter than the other. Her udder is a bad shape, but she is a 'character'.

The dry cows have eaten all the grass in the park so, on Sunday morning, with the hot, brilliant sunshine alternating with grey cloud piled high in the sky, I moved the electric gates to extend their grazing.

Elizabeth's friend came to play in the afternoon. Her father, the gamekeeper, collected her, his face bristly with unshaven beard. He looked disgruntled. He has had a hard and worrying summer. He had been tidying the pheasant pens and the kennels, since which time he has received a complaint about their untidiness!

On Monday I had a distinct foreboding of unpleasantness about to happen at Quincey's. The note in the office telling me where to find the cows was not clear. The message was in David's writing, but partly crossed off. I set off to Nine Acres, down the muddy, squelching, slippery track, the tractor sliding sideways in the mire. No cows there. Back to Poole's Night. No cows. Alongside Eleven Acres. Not a glimmer of a black and white body anywhere, nor anything to be seen on all the flat plain of Quincey's fields lit by the efficient headlamps on the back and front of the Quincey's tractor. I must have looked like a meteor in the dark. I returned to the dairy to puzzle over the note. With rage beginning to burn inside me I decided to try Lower Quincey's and was churning down the track once more when I saw one cow standing in Twenty-Two Acres. I backed the tractor and drove into the field and there, in the farthest corner, and not responding in any way to the noise of the tractor, were the cows, lying in a tight group. Why should Graham's cows get up and start moving in the direction of the dairy, when David's cows have to be individually pushed, lingering over every bite of grass they can snatch and stopping as soon as I chase up another group. One heifer tried to jump out of the parlour and another tried to jump in, both straddling the gate and bar and suspended in mid-air. With much kicking and struggling and clattering they got back to *terra firma* undamaged.

I painted the parlour in the morning and on my way home noticed a calf born in the field. I looked at it after the afternoon milking and decided it would be better to leave it. I presumed that David would get it in the following morning, and milk the cow the following afternoon. It was the wrong decision. David rang up in a rage and told me to get it in. I was in a meeting with John. Fortunately, I had told John of my decision to leave it out and he had approved. John said I must not go and get it in, compounding the predicament. I rang David to explain why I had not. He had cooled down by then and said it was not worth getting it in in the dark, but in the future I must get in any calf that had been born in the day. I said would. I was upset, but not as much as last time. I am hardening up, but because I genuinely thought I was acting for the best, and not shirking, the germs of anger and injustice writhed. David and John carefully avoided mentioning the calf, and Philip fetched them in in time for the cow to be milked in the morning.

Bob's parlour is a model, as he says himself. It is completely painted in Atlantic-green and white, immaculate in every corner, pencils hung on strings for instant jottings, racks for rolls of tail tapes and scissors on strategic hooks, it is really 'up together'. The milking was soothing, the cows hurry into the parlour, the heifers are quiet. Peaceful though it is, it is still hard work. A heifer supposed to be in a box and calving overnight was missing in the morning. Philip found her in Blackthorns, but never found her calf, although he searched all day.

The silage clamp was open and the sweet, rich smell lay in the humid air. My task of the week was to put clean sand in the cubicles. From a heap in the backyard I loaded it onto a loader, carried on the back of the tractor, and made by Bob for this purpose. He is good at these inventions and spends hours in the workshop creating them. Then I had to shovel the sand to the far end of each cubicle. Most of the day Ralph, Bert and Colin were bringing the lucerne silage up for the inside clamp and, when they had finished, I had to bring the cows up and make sure they ate some (the grass has less and less nourishment in it at this time of year). Coming up to the yard was out of their routine and they wandered back along the filthy track to Moat Ground, and lay there in a solid mass for the rest of the afternoon.

A cow in the paddock began to calve. She chose her place near the gateway and I could watch her while I was milking. When the feet were sticking out and I could see the muzzle between them, the convulsive movements stopped altogether. I thought I had better help. I grasped the feet and pulled and the head came out easily – and then stuck. The feet were too slippery to hold; I tore off my apron and used the strings as loops but they were not strong enough. Again, I pulled feverishly. The calf's eyes opened, and blinked calmly at me. I rolled back under the fence and rushed to the office. No calving ropes. I ran to the dairy. Ropes on a hook. I snatched them off the peg. The cow stood quietly while I walked slowly to her and slipped the ropes over the knobbly joints and began to pull. I pulled with all my strength while those large, long-lashed eyes gazed tranquilly at me. As I pulled and the body was squeezed by the pelvic bones, they began to close and the calf slid out limply and I was afraid it had died. But in a moment it had lifted its head, shaken its ears, sneezed the mucus out of its nose and was obviously healthy. On its feet it was a huge, gangling, beautiful heifer calf, one of the replacements for the dairy.

Another cow moved restlessly over the grass, a tiny dribble of mucus trailing from her shining backside. At 8.45 pm I drove back the four miles to see her. Nothing had changed. At 11.00 pm John went back to see her. Nothing had happened. In the morning she had calved and the calf was dead. An error of judgement. We should have put her in the box, examined her, and probably pulled the calf. We both felt bad.

As Bob says, 'You have to struggle with human nature sometimes.' In this case human nature, or exhaustion, won.

Autumn is turning the beech trees brown and yellow, and there are blackberries in the hedges and rose hips and elderberries. The farms are creeping with pheasants. Few rabbits have survived the myxamatosis. The colour of the woods are changing, and in the gardens the apple trees are bearing a heavy burden. Convolvulus spreads its twining heart-shaped leaves and white flowers among the old man's beard and the hawthorn hedges.

Rodney has painted the calf boxes white. The welder has welded the broken bars, and the gates run on little wheels, or swing smoothly on their hinges. The new scraper gleams primrose yellow and the tractor, serviced and oiled, sits snugly in the hay barn. Even the blackboard is new, like virgin snow – but black. But the cows were reluctant to come into the parlour, some of the heifers were wild, the milk pump would not work, and Rodney had forgotten to fill up the hoppers. The silage clamp has been opened and with the change of diet the cows' dung streams out in liquid waterfalls once more. Concentration is demanded for every minute of milking.

Vic was at Honeybed, fixing up a wind shield on the barn to shelter the cows, which are to calve there this winter, and reduce the pressure on the box. He has asked if he could stay at Lyndon. He says his wife is not fit to move. She is on valium and is 'up and down at present'. The children seemed all right, but sometimes could do no right. He was having to do the packing, and they were moving on Friday.

John was sorry to have to tell him that there is no job anywhere on the farm, and no hope of getting my job as I will carry on after the wedding.

*26 September*

My long-awaited day off was unsatisfying. One day off is not enough. It takes one day to unwind and the next to relax and enjoy the time off, and this only happens every three weeks. A dairy meeting broke into the morning. The meeting itself was a good one: no messing, useful discussion and a friendly atmosphere. John told the men of our plans to marry on the 20 December, and that we should be away for Christmas. It is a bad time for me to be away, but a good time for him. Owen, my predecessor, is staying with Graham and offered to milk for me over Christmas – an ideal solution.

A warm, bland sun shone on Lyndon all day. My geraniums and asters, blooming so cheerfully, did not match my mood. I collected the Angus meat from the butcher and packed it for the freezer, and today we had our first meal of roast beef: delicious.

The silage clamp at Home Farm has been opened and Ralph and Fred said it was the best silage they had ever seen, completely uniform in quality. The cows ate it eagerly.

The dry cows were clustered on the sloping grass in front of Lyndon House. The air was still and soft and warm and the lake reflected the trees and the picturesque cottage opposite. A large iron-grey heron flapped slowly up the lake, and the beautiful trees stood motionless and calm. It was peaceful and idyllic.

My van got a puncture on the way home and I tried to mend it, but the wheel nuts were immovable. Hazelwood was in sight so I walked home and Malcolm and Kevin brought it back for me, mended, which was kind of them.

Norman and Bert were drilling wheat in a field where the soil changes half-way across, exactly following the contours of the field. One half is a rusty red, the other a chocolate brown. Norman layered the seed with slug pellets. Will and Alan were power-harrowing in another field, breaking down the soil after ploughing. Tom and Colin were ploughing. All of them were working into the dark.

Harold went home to his wife. She had had a bad day with thoughts of suicide. Fortunately, she had rung the doctor instead. Norman's wife has been told to prepare herself for the possibility of going into hospital for an operation after she has seen a specialist in October. Vic moved out today. Lord Elroy is going to see Jim to ask him to move to Hazelwood. Geoff is getting married tomorrow. Last night he had a stag party at the inn and today he had to go home from work with a bad head. John was not amused.

# OCTOBER

*4 October*

I staked the goat out in the grassy yard the day after the wedding, and found the yard bedraggled with bits of sodden paper, an old shoe, tin cans, and a fish, with confetti, wet with rain, sprinkling the gravel. Andrea came with me to the county town where my *decree nisi* was announced and Edward and I came before the judge to settle the agreement on the children. The stifling, smoke-choking atmosphere in the old Victorian building, where couples struggled to keep smiling, and pinstripe-suited solicitors, hovering round their queuing clients, made a dismal and sordid ending our marriage. The judge sat up high in the empty court room. My solicitor had not sent a vital letter to Edward's solicitor, who was present with him; mine had not thought it necessary to be there at all, and so we had to settle the amount of money the children would receive, then and there.

Andrea and I went shopping and were home in time for tea. Roger drove the car to Marford to pick up Daniel from swimming, as practice for his driving lessons. One is swept on by life and emotions are obliterated by the most trivial necessities.

A day of mess at Owlnest. A cow had calved in the yard the previous night and was still down, her legs splayed out on either side of her. The ligaments stretch to allow the pelvic girdle bones to open so the calf can be born. Until they tighten again in a few days, the cow is vulnerable on slippery surfaces, she has not got the normal control over her legs, which are, at that time, only loosely jointed in their sockets.

Further damage is done if the cow falls down. If the ligaments tear, the cow has then no control over her legs and cannot use them to rise. Normally, she uses her hind legs as a lever. Watching a cow striving to get on her feet, nearly achieving it, and then crashing down on her belly and udder, is painful to behold. Philip, Ralph, John and the new student, William, came to get her into the field with the aid of the Sambron. The Sambron backed up, pushing a pallet [a flat wooden board] towards her. Carefully tucking one hind leg under her, we rolled her over onto the pallet and held her upside down while Ralph raised the pallet in the air and drove, cautiously, into the paddock. He lowered the pallet and we rolled her off it and left her in a comfortable position to recover. The rough surface of the field would give her a better grip than the smooth surface of the concrete.

The system has changed again now the silage clamp is open, and I floundered in unfamiliarity. The numbers of cows in the herd, which Bob had written on the blackboard, did not tally with the number of cows that came into the parlour. While we were moving them into the paddock, two heifers appeared at Owlnest Park, missed when I was getting them in.

The next morning, Bob discovered another that had calved and that I had not seen at all: this was bad. Two cows in the paddock showed signs of calving. The normal procedure at this time of year, is to let them calve outside, but so many calves have died this year that a mineral deficiency is suspected. The policy now is to put all cows in boxes for closer supervision. I had not been told this then, and I left the two cows in the paddock. This was another mistake. John said he would look at them on his way home from a meeting this evening. At 11 o'clock he came to tell me that the cows needed help.

I dressed rapidly and we were there in fifteen minutes, but it was already too late to put one of them in the box. She was lying head down on a slope, on her side, her feet extended rigidly and the calf's feet sticking out, equally rigidly, from under her tail. Without pausing we pulled the calf out, but the cow would not, or could not, get up, and at each attempt she slid a little nearer the very deep ditch at the far end of the paddock near to which she was lying. It had only a shallow, puddle of water at the bottom, and we did not fear she would drown, but the difficulties of pulling her out once she was in, were immense. The night was dark and clear. The calf lay curled up, safely out of the way of her thrashings.

We drove the remaining cow into a box and I brought a bottle of calcium to the recumbent cow and inserted it under her skin. I was in an utterly black mood and very tired. The needle of the tube was blocked at first, and we could not find a halter to tie the cow in the box. John was soon in a similar frame of mind. Starting up the tractor, John drove into the field with a good length of rope. I shone the torch ahead of him. The cow's head was in among the brambles, and in another minute she would have slid on the mud into the ditch. I tied the rope to her hind legs and John pulled her on to the level ground as gently as possible, expecting to hear the crack of her bones each second. We left the tractor parked between her and the ditch and propped her up with bales of straw. We carried the calf to the boxes where the other cow, 'a flighty bitch' was careening round, proving perilous to halter. By the time we had calved her, cleared and cleaned up, put both calves on her, and driven home, it was 2.00 am. John set his alarm for 3.00 and went all the way back to see the cow in the field. She was on her feet and great was the triumph.

I was numb with tiredness in the morning, and all my old hatred of Honeybed rushed back as I scraped and scrubbed there. John said I must go to see Bob about the disasters of the day at Owlnest. I went apprehensively, and so miserable about everything that I almost did not care. I hoped fervently that I would not cry.

The first person I saw was Philip in the backyard. He called cheerily, 'Here she is!' and gave me a smile.

Bob walked out of the boxes, looking frayed. I said humbly, 'I seem to have made a mess of things here.'

To which Bob replied, 'You certainly have.'

We stood in a group and Bob let off some steam, then he took me into the office to show me how to make sure I would not muddle the numbers again. Philip made a little speech on how we can all make mistakes, and how it was the most difficult time of the year. He said that if he ever got bad-tempered to be sure and get back at him. This was kind of him because I cannot even imagine him being really unpleasant. He went, leaving me to Bob. Bob was in a temper, but as he was trying to show me on his charts just how he works his methods out, it became plain that he himself could not quite remember, and a tiny flicker of amusement began to spread inside me. He was much more annoyed with John because John had reproved him about the condition of the needle and on not having a halter. 'I haven't had a halter here in seven years,' he exploded. In between these bouts of anger he was kind and understanding. We parted amicably and I left the dairy in a cheerful mood, the last reaction I had expected. I hastened home, and not stopping to eat lunch, I changed and went to my appointment with Elizabeth's teacher.

The interview was inconclusive and her loyalties impregnable, but she is now aware of Elizabeth's feelings and of our problems. Calling at the village shop to stock up the groceries I met Malcolm's wife. I knew they were having marital troubles, and she looked distraught and unhappy. Many of the things she told me as we stood by the cans of soup and meat reminded me of how I had felt at one time. After I had listened to her she said she felt much better. I told her to come and see me at Hazelwood if she ever needed someone to talk to. I know from experience that to be able to talk is an inexpressible relief.

The afternoon milking at Honeybed flowed, and no cows needed attention and none appeared to be about to calve. By 6.45 pm John and I were driving out of the yard on the way to the Lake District to officially take over the possession of our house. We were suffering from a dire shortage of sleep, from the pressures of work, and I drove the first half of the long journey in a state of rigidity despite the loveliness of the breathtaking sunset into which we were heading. The excitement and anticipation that had trembled within me earlier in the week had dulled to a sensation of mere dogged determination. At midnight we were there and the soft, sweet air enveloped us, and the sense of the unseen mountains surrounded us. We lit the wood-burning stove, ate pork pies and coffee and blew up the inflatable camp bed. The furniture consists of carpets, curtains, lampshades and a fridge. With the windows black holes in the wall, we fell asleep.

Our awakening was to the most beautiful morning and we sat enraptured at the play of the sunrise and shadows on the mountains and woods. On the craggy hillside opposite, a stag and hind walked across a bluff, in slow, unperturbed procession, and a buzzard wheeled in leisurely circles high in the sky above the valley. The birds of the house made themselves known to us, especially one known as Cheeky, a great tit who perched on our hands to take peanuts. Much later, we opened the gate from the garden which leads to the fell, and wandered, drunk with the pleasure of this paradise, to the top of the fell to survey this new world. The house was so warm that, like Adam and Eve in the Garden of Eden, we walked about naked. The next day we shopped, cut

Cows in the collecting yard.

the lawns and painted the bedroom. After two more days of walking and painting, we were home again and on the next morning, Monday, I was back at Quincey's.

Roger has got himself a Saturday job in Woolworths.

### 16 October

Winter has come to the farms. The silage clamps are open, the milking cows are in at night, and the systems have changed. As it was in the spring, the changeover time – when the systems overlap

– is the most tiring period. The cubicles have to be scraped, but the fields have to be walked. The dry cows, out day and night, have to be inspected, and newborn calves have to be brought in. The cows in boxes have to be attended and fed, the milking takes longer and longer as more cows calve, and more heifers come in to be milked, or to become accustomed to the parlour. The heifers need careful and patient handling, and the old cows are prone to milk fever and mastitis. A few cows will not feed their calves and these must be hand fed, or suckled on a more maternal animal.

Daniel stays after school on Mondays to play football, and I pick him up when I have finished. On Monday he walked to Quincey's in drenching rain, two miles on a main road without a footpath, in the dusk, because he thought I had forgotten him. I was delayed by a calving cow (the calf was upside down). My guilt at my disruption of their lives and security, and the feeling that I was an abominable mother rose and choked me as I looked at his tear stained, weary face.

For the whole of September Andrea has been in charge of the house, a great help to me, but with adverse effects on the children. Daniel has been awkward and difficult about the jobs he has to do, and this annoys Susan. Roger has been hectoring the younger children and bullying them verbally. At last the atmosphere boiled up into a 'scene', which I began by talking to them about 'pulling together, helping each other and co-operating'. It ended with my hitting Roger (to my shame) and this sent him into a paroxysm of weeping, and me into gloomy despair. Since then, Andrea has returned to university and I have taken charge again, and I am establishing a winter routine. Daniel is coping better with the pressures from his new school, unaccustomed homework, scouts and too much rugby. In addition to the external pressures on the farm, there were eleven people staying in the house for a few days. Andrea, two of her friends from university, a friend of Susan's, and my parents on their way home from a holiday in France. This was stimulating and enjoyable, but the housework and the state of the house passed completely out of my control – very disagreeable to me. For the first time, I was not able to put flowers in my parents room to greet them. A little thing, but it mattered to me.

The weather has been as stormy as our lives, heavy rain alternating with brilliant rainbows, angry sunrises and lowering humidity. Deceptively cold mornings have crept in, and give me goose pimples up my back when I have not put sufficient clothing on, and the dawn wind sighs through the parlour. The fire in the kitchen burns day and night now, welcoming to come down to, and warming to come home to.

With the children sitting round the table yesterday evening, or later, when they were in and out while I was ironing, or when we were amicably chatting over breakfast today – another rescued kitten playing on the floor, and the kitchen bright with geraniums – I am reassured once more. John is under pressures of his own, and vented his rage at Home Farm one day when the cows broke through a fence at the back of the barn and created a mess among the bales of hay. The strands of barbed wire, curled in hazardous loops, threatened to tear their legs and udders. He was not at all pleased when I let the rinsing water into the milk through sheer tiredness and lack of concentration.

Since Rodney took over at Honeybed, the electric fencing has not worked efficiently; the cows have ceased to respect it and go where they please. I spent an hour trudging through the fields getting them in one morning. There have been disappointments too. A monster calf was born at Home Farm and it died the day I was there, although it had survived three days under Graham's care. Nobody knew why it had died. Moments of elation and satisfaction in the job, and evenings of happiness and cheerfulness with family and friends, compensate for the black times.

Undercurrents on the estate are contributing to a general atmosphere of unease and may lead anywhere.

Rodney and I went on a calving course together at the agricultural college. It took place on his day off, and so that we could get away in time he came to help me at Honeybed. He arrived at 7.00 am, a big, bouncing boy of a man, cheery, enthusiastic, boastful and naive. He has a smooth, handsome face and beautiful, even white teeth. He even tells schoolboy jokes. He helped me to calve a cow before we left, and could not understand why another calf and cow were in a field where they should not have been, and seemed no more in charge of the place than I was.

The demonstration calves had been in a freezer and were insufficiently thawed out. One was bundled into a tub of warm water, while the other lay on the floor in a grotesque position until it was needed, at which point its limbs were wrenched round with gruesome, ice-shattering sounds. Their sunken eyes and protruding tongues made grisly accompaniments to the lecture and discussion.

On the journey home, Rodney said he had something to tell me that he thought I ought to know. He said someone on the estate was making a dossier of my days off and was saying that I had already taken three weeks holiday, and was planning to take more for my proposed trip to New Zealand with John in the early spring. He kept saying, 'To be forewarned is to be forearmed.' I had been described to him as a 'marriage breaker' and that I was 'the only relief that has a relief', meaning, of course, that John is always helping me.

Rodney said that he and his wife had decided to not go to any of the estate functions, or join any of the activities, as so many misunderstandings and accusations seem to be being made. He said he owed a lot to John because John had given him the job when he was fairly desperate. 'I can see what John feels about you,' he said, 'and I hope, sincerely, you will be happy.'

'I've had five days holiday since I came to Lyndon,' I said, 'and I have never asked John to help me, except in circumstances when anyone else might be expected to need help, and receive it.'

I did not bother explaining that there have been times when I have refused the help he wanted to give, and I would have been glad to accept, because I knew it would cause resentment. But the pleasure John and I have had at working together on something we care deeply about has, probably outweighed our sensibilities on some occasions. This may have been to the benefit of the farm, but it has been to the detriment of the human relationships on it. I know I am a source of gossip, and the whole situation is difficult, precarious and unsatisfactory, a penalty for the happiness I have had. If this person (I did not want to know who it was, nor did Rodney want to tell me) should go to Lord Elroy, my conscience is clear.

I went into the house and sat rather drearily by the fire, alternating between a strange elation – for I am not surprised by the revelations – and acute depression, wondering if everyone who appears amiable and friendly on the surface, is full of anger and resentment underneath. I was saddened to think the person might be Philip, and I thought it might have been better if Rodney had not told me. I pondered on whether to tell John. I knew his reaction would be instant and uncomplicated anger. Not being good at suppressing deep emotions, I told him that night. We decided that, psychologically, the person must be Bob.

It so happened that I worked two consecutive days at Owlnest after this, and the first one was the hardest day I have had for some time. From 5.20 am to 12.30 pm I did not stop working, and from 2.30 pm until 7.00 pm likewise. Bob gave me the first cubicle-cleaning demonstration of the winter, and asked me to put more sand in the cubicles. I was not able to do this on the first day and planned to do it on the second. I jammed the tractor in the cubicle passage and had to radio for someone with more expertise to come and manoeuvre it out, nearly crying with vexation.

On my way home, Graham radioed that a cow was calving at Home Farm, and asked someone to come and look at her, as he was on his way to the airport with Owen. I said I would. I tried to get the cow out of the paddock and into a box. She went round and round the holly bush in the paddock, just like the nursery rhyme, and was so wild that it took John, Jim, Kevin and myself to finally get her in. The house, when I did get home, was full of people that I wanted to look after and could not.

The next day at Owlnest was slightly easier. I scrubbed more of the parlour than my officially designated area, and I scraped out immaculately. I did not put in the sand as I thought I had worked long enough, but I left a note saying I would do it next week. I left thinking that I had done everything well. John did not appear at Honeybed the next morning until 9.00 am and he said I had upset Bob again, and that in the end he had had 'a flaming row' with him, worse than the annual row he has always had with Bob in the past. I stared at John, aghast, filled with a sick, sinking apprehension. John forbade me to go and apologise, and, indeed, I had no intention of doing so, not feeling that I had anything for which to apologise this time. John thinks that Bob is exploiting me. My parents, with whom I talked over the problems, thought that the anonymous person with the dossier on me has, in fact, a grudge against John.

I was unwilling to drive through the estate after that, not wishing to see, or be seen, knowing full well that news will have spread about the row. I had to call Philip out in the afternoon to help with a heifer, and he was as kind as usual. Without him saying anything, I detected a feeling of sympathy that, whether intended or not, warmed me.

*23 October*

My day off immediately after the last entry ended the tensions and frictions within the family, and restored us to a calmer, more normal, era. I cooked the children a proper breakfast, and took Roger, Susan, and her friend to college, because the rain was hissing on the roads. I shopped, cooked, cleaned and pottered, and regained control of myself and the house.

I had one enjoyable day at Home Farm and then it was my weekend off. Friends came for a meal in the evening and adopted the latest Honeybed kitten, now restored to health and gaiety. I stayed late in bed on Sunday morning, Daniel went to the rugby club in Riverton, and in the afternoon I pulled up the dead flowers and vegetables, and tidied the garden. I lit a fire in the small front sitting room and we played games with Daniel and Elizabeth. Family life, for a brief period, was consolidated.

Norman has been away from work for a fortnight with gastroenteritis. Stuart, the building foreman, has been offered Hazelwood farm house and has accepted. Jim refused to move. Kevin is to move into Stuart's house at Golden Gates and he is pleased, so the problem of who should move where is solved.

The maize is being harvested. We put a box of cobs in the freezer. The other fields, so golden and fawn in the summer, and brown under the plough and harrow, are sheened over with the tiny green spears of winter wheat. The cycle has begun again. The trees have turned and the cherry in the front garden blazes in a spectrum of glowing colours. If the sun would shine, the countryside would light up with the splendour of the trees and hedges. In the park there is a young, red oak shaking its scarlet leaves in solitary flamboyance. Conkers, beech mast and sycamore keys litter the lawns, and twining ropes of bryony trail in the hedgerows.

I opened the big doors to let the cows out of the cubicles at Quincey's on Monday morning and a movement caught my eye. At the edge of the circle of light cast on the concrete yard, a new-born calf was toppling over the edge of the slurry lagoon, under the rails which guard it. He fell on a solid pile of dung, and by grasping his tail and one hind leg I pulled him out. In another minute he would have plunged deeper into the muck and probably disappeared out of sight. He had been born in the cubicles in the night, rolled or crawled under the eighteen-inch-high gap under the doors, wandered across the open yard, and so under the rails. His mother mooed anxiously from behind the doors. I moved them both into a box before I scraped. My elation at saving the calf turned to horror when I wrenched the passage door clean off its hinges by catching it with the pusher on the tractor. The door lay undamaged, but inert, too heavy for me to attempt to get it back on.

Lurking at the back of my mind all week was the thought of meeting Bob again. John went to a Cow Club conference for a night and two days. I chose not to go because of the possible ill feeling it might cause. John spoke to Bob on his usual round of the dairies and told me that nothing had been said on either side about the row. Bob rang up as usual the evening before my day at Owlnest to give me his list of instructions. The tone of his voice differed very slightly. Not exactly apologetic – but a hint of it – and concerned that I had been overworked, but puzzled as to how.

'John told me you had been here until one o'clock, but what were you doing in that time? I know I work there until 1 o'clock sometimes, but I don't expect you to.' He mentioned the sand and told me not to bother if it was too much.

I said, 'I will if I can.'

He said, 'I know you will. And you mustn't clean more of the parlour than your share.'

The day at Owlnest passed peacefully. A lovely golden sunrise preceded a fresh autumn day. No calves were born and the milkings were uneventful. Bob came to see me when I was scrubbing the parlour at 6.30 pm, in the gloaming.

'You ought to be going home,' he said.

I explained that I had not managed to do it in the morning, so I was doing it now. He was the same as before and we were both cheerful. He had a little rant about John, the lights in the big barn had gone out again and the cows would be treading on each other's teats in the dark. But the episode appears to be over: to my relief.

John told Philip he had had a row with Bob, and Philip said, 'I know!'

John, on his way home from the Cow Club meeting, came straight to see me at Honeybed, and we shared the gladness of our reunion in the dank, smelly parlour for a brief, but happy, moment.

*30 October*

I picked walnuts from the ground beneath a gnarled tree at Honeybed, blackberries from the sun-warmed hedges, and apples from the few remaining ancient trees in the old orchard: tiny, joyous compensations for the long hours of work, and weariness in the bones. There cannot be many jobs that are harder, or demand more endurance. Once or twice this week, I sincerely felt I could not, and would not, stick this job another week. The real problem is the length of the working hours, which I believe be too many for anybody, and totally unreasonable in comparison with most other jobs. Though conditions have improved dramatically in farming, and are continuing to improve, farm workers are still underpaid and overworked.

I thought all the remaining kittens at Honeybed had been disposed of, or died, but I found two more cuddled up on a bale at the back of the barn. They were mere puffs of hair and bone, and nervous. As. I write, they are purring on my knee in front of the kitchen fire, completely at home and at ease with the other cats. Already they have lost their look of extreme starvation and malnutrition. The sun is shining with a white brilliance on the sharp frost of the night.

The Hazelwood silage clamp is solid with five hundred and fifty tons of maize, and the constant procession of tractors and trailers splashing through the mud and puddles of the yard has ceased. The calf barn is thickly strawed in preparation for the first batches of weaned calves from the calf unit. The potatoes in the fields lie un-dug and unapproachable in the saturated earth.

Twin Charolais calves have been born to a cow at Home Farm. They are a pale milk chocolate colour and have dark eyes and noses. Despite their prettiness, they refused to suck the cow. I had to hand milk their mother and then bottle feed them. At the end of the day I repeated the performance, practically force feeding them. No sooner had I put the last empty bottle down, than the perverse creatures moved over to the cow and started sucking vigorously.

It was fine enough for the cows to go out for the morning. I had to fetch them in at lunchtime. In the empty adjoining field, a black and white lump lay bulked on the ground, quite still. I approached on foot, fearing to find a dead body, but it was a cow with a yellow tape on its tail: a dry cow, but near to calving.

It scrambled to its feet awkwardly, its gross udder bulging and tight. I did not know how, or why, it was in the field on its own. I moved her in with the herd and, when she came through the parlour, I asked Graham for his opinion on whether she had calved and therefore should be milked.

'Your guess is as good as mine,' he said cheerfully.

Later, I drove the tractor out into the field and along the boundaries. By a sheltering hedge, a freshly trampled patch of grass and a mangled afterbirth told me that the calf was somewhere in the field. In the ditch, a few paces away, the calf lay curled up. I thought I would heave it onto my knee and then on to the tractor, but the calf – which must have been born the day before, and was lively and strong – had other ideas. As I bent down to lift it up, it started up to run, and kept running. I headed off in the direction of Home Farm and went to get help. Graham caught it, but it struggled so hard he let it go. It ran down the race to Queenwood, back up to Home Farm, down into Cathill Two and catapulted through the fencing into Cathill One. Graham shouted to me to bring the van to put it in, and I drove madly through fields, muddy gateways, and up and down the slopes and hollows. Graham disappeared, running round the circular copse in Cathill One and I found him sitting on the calf on the edge of the copse. I had to rope its legs together before he would get off, and even then it kicked and struggled and bleated like a sheep. We were lifting it bodily into the van, and laughing at the absurdity of our efforts to catch one small calf, when Lord Elroy walked round the copse and asked us what we were doing. He had seen us in the dusk, thought he had heard a sheep and could not understand our antics. Both Graham and I were plastered with muck and mud, exhausted and exhilarated.

We reunited the calf – which was still struggling – with its mother and darkness had fallen before I was home.

The weekend at Honeybed began ominously. A cow in the cubicles had milk fever, and I gave her a bottle of calcium. John helped me to calve a cow in the morning. The calf was a breech and died inhaling fluid before we could get it out.

The cow with milk fever did not respond, and in her attempts to rise, wedged herself under the bars of the cubicles. Graham came over to help ease her into a better position. The scraping was delayed and the normal timetable upset. The vet came and warned that she might be dead in the morning: she was. She lay where she had been all the day before, only instead of panting quickly, she was quite still. Pity swelled in my heart. She died of pleurisy and pneumonia. The other cows ignored her, neither interested nor upset. When they had been shut out in the yard, I scraped out the cubicles and John and Philip came to pull her out, not an easy task in the confined space. We had to prevent her legs jamming in the bars. The tractor pulled slowly, the chains tightened, there was a horrible crack of some bone breaking, and she slid clear of the cubicle and into the slippery passage, from there she was pulled into the yard, down the ramp to the lower yard, through a heap of slurry and into the barn. I sluiced the dirt off with a hose, and left her waiting for the knacker man, a pathetic and ungainly lump. He brought a small lorry with an automatic winch and this pulled her up the ramp. The dead calf joined her and the man, his face impassive, drove off up the drive in a roaring lorry. Soon after he had gone, a cow calved normally, and soon after that another. This calf was a breech and had twisted in the womb so that its legs stuck out, upside down. I worked as swiftly as I could, desperately anxious to get the calf out alive, but this one also drowned as it was born. I gave both the breech calves the kiss of life, and my failure to save them depressed me. They were so very near to life, and were strong and otherwise healthy calves.

Without any calving, and no extra jobs, and working steadily and continuously, my day at Quincey's was ten hours long. Now I have to load the wheelbarrow *twice* a day and distribute the cake on either side of the forage passage in a long line. This is the straw that broke the camel's back. Although, alas, it is not straw, but four hundredweight of cake. My shoulder muscles bulge and ripple. The clocks went back at the weekend and it is dark again when driving home at night, and dark in the mornings. The trees in the park are in an ecstasy of flame-like lightness and a vivid airiness. The bracken in the woodland is changing shades from rust to apple green, and even the dullness of the skies and the dripping rain does not deaden the loveliness.

Me scraping slurry in a barn.

# NOVEMBER

*13 November*

This morning I received notification that my first marriage was dissolved on 11 November. At times I feel I am no more than a leaf borne on a swift-flowing current, hastening without pause over shallows, rapids and dangerously deep pools.

The decision to marry John at Christmas was dominated by the fact that it was a good time for him to take a few days away from work. Also, I have a long weekend off in that period, plus Christmas Day itself, because I worked last Christmas. Lord Elroy does not wish the house at Owlnest to be unoccupied for longer than is necessary, so the move to Owlnest is planned for the beginning of December, exactly one year from my arrival at Lyndon. This time the changeover of the rota will be in my favour; I will have the Thursday, Saturday, Sunday and Monday off. Over these four days I hope to create order out of chaos.

In spare moments we are making arrangements for our wedding and the reception, and a farm party to be held in the new year. Our honeymoon will be spent at our house in the Lake District. The accommodation there is cramped and we are taking my four children and three dogs with us. There is a small double-bedded bedroom, a lean-to big enough to squeeze in two bunk beds, a garage serving as a spare bedroom, and enough room for one person on the sofa.

I have made the Christmas cake and the puddings, though homemade cakes are a normally a thing of the past, and convenience foods fill my larder.

When we move, both Daniel and Elizabeth will have to cycle to school. The comprehensive is two miles away for Daniel, and Elizabeth will have to bicycle through the park, a four-mile journey each way: it is safer than the main road, but lonely. I suppress my fears. Their Christmas presents this year are brand new bicycles with drop handlebars, without which they would rather walk.

The long weekend at Home Farm was all pleasure. Every morning began with a sharp frost, followed by a crisp and sunny day. I enjoyed simply breathing: inhaling the clean, exhilarating air.

I am afraid of the Devon bull who is in with the dry cows at Home Farm. I walk circumspectly round the cows, peering at udders and eyes, and the bull stands motionless, but for his head turning to follow every movement, his sharp, straight, bone-white horns poised in delicate menace. His build, unlike the ponderous amiability of the Herefords, is similar to the fighting bulls of Spain. I do not doubt that he can run faster than I.

The pleasure grounds of Lyndon close for the winter in November, so after Sunday lunch and before milking, John, Elizabeth and I visited the gardens for the last time this year. The lake was a glassy calm, reflecting the banks and slopes on the other side. The poplar leaves shimmered, and the sweet chestnuts lay thick on the ground under the broadsword leaves of the chestnut trees. The lovely, aromatic smells of damp earth and the woods arose and mingled with the scents of summer, lingering on the lawns where the grass had been cut in the last mowing.

John and Elizabeth fetched the cows in for me. The Home Farm herd is now the only one able to go out in the daytime. The land is free-draining and does not poach so easily.[1] Blue sparks and puffs of smoke spurted from the tractor at Quincey's like an angry dragon. I abandoned it and Philip brought the Owlnest tractor down and scraped out for me, this made the day easier. I am getting used to the discipline of the wheelbarrow – I must be stronger and fitter this year. The physical work does not drain me as it did.

[1] Free-draining land is land which does not hold the water on the surface, poaching is caused by cattle trampling wet soil and churning it up.

John's wife and family moved out of Owlnest today. It was a bad day for him.

Two cows waited in the calving box at Owlnest, peacefully chewing the cud. I looked at them intermittently and was surprised to see one go straight into heavy labour, with no preliminary symptoms. Lifting her tail I saw a hoof nail hanging out of her, detached from the leg. A thoroughly unpleasant smell erupted from her. I called Philip and in ten minutes he was there. He plunged his hand and arm inside her and pronounced the calf a breech, and dead. When he withdrew his hand it was covered in black and white hairs and red with blood.

'It's a vet's job,' he said, and went to call the vet.

The vet arrived when I was packing up. Philip said I could go, but I chose to stay. The examination confirmed Philip's diagnosis.

'You can send her to the knacker's now, or I can try to get it out, but the cervix is almost closed so there is very little room. I can't do a Caesarian because the uterus is so infected she would die anyway.'

Philip, unwilling to lose a good cow without trying, asked her to try and get it out. With difficulty the vet roped the calf's legs. The legs appeared, the hooves swollen and distorted, and the hair coming away from the skin. The vet used handfuls of lubricant to ease the passage and worked patiently to pull it out, little by little, an inch at a time. Philip worked the calving aid, and the calf was gradually dragged out, taut along the metal bar. The cow stood patiently, alert and well. A dreadful stench bubbled out of her and disgusting sludge dripped and oozed from her. The hindquarters came out, but the bulk of the rib cage and the shoulders stuck; slowly the muscles of the calf began to stretch and tear, the skin split and the calf disintegrated. Its bowels burst with a stinking dispersal of gas. There was nothing more we could do. The cow now lay on her side, her distended belly bulging. We stood and looked, our hands and arms red and reeking.

'Have you any suggestions?' asked the vet.

'No,' we said.

So she cut the remaining bits of calf away from the cow and Philip put them in a sack. I went off to get John's permission to send her to Barkers. Philip managed to get her on her feet and she walked into the lorry when it came.

Barkers reported that cutting her up was one of the worst jobs they had ever had: they had to keep walking away, the smell was so bad. Philip was sick when he buried the calf.

Barkers are busy at Lyndon. From Owlnest they went on to Home Farm. One of the dry cows had split herself, slipping on the concrete when coming in for a routine inspection. She was due to calve in two weeks. She had been lifted off the concrete into the paddock and lay on her belly with her back legs at right angles to her body. Both legs were broken. I thought she should be shot before she was dragged into the lorry, but that is not the way they do it. Perhaps they would try and get the calf out alive when she was dead.

David found a dead cow in the cubicles. She had calved in the night and the uterus had come out with the calf. The cow had died of shock. The calf had survived. A cow at Honeybed slipped her calf and looked very sick, so she went too. Calving, despite modern medicines, must resemble human parturition in the last century, when it was a time of great risk and only the fittest survived.

A good old cow at Honeybed has had mastitis in one quarter for several weeks. She has been dry and it was hoped that, if she were treated, she would be clear of it when she calved. Her calf is four days old and the pus pours out like custard. She is a source of infection in the cubicles and is to go to market on Friday.

A freezing east wind blew into the parlour all day at Honeybed. I do not usually mind working alone, but when darkness fell and the wind keened over the valley and through the collecting yard, the lights of Marford, twinkling in the distance, emphasised my loneliness. The tenant of the farmhouse came to ask if I would like a cup of coffee. She wore a fur hat from China that so enclosed her head and face that I did not know who it was until she spoke. The coffee, in a little flask, was scalding, strong and genuine.

There is no midday feed or sugar beet to put out this winter, and the system has been improved and is not such hard work. John is having to put pressure on Rodney to keep the place clean. He leaves the parlour dirty, he does not wash the tractor and scraper, and he does not tidy things away. I get discouraged and do not feel like scrubbing and tidying there either. Even Philip has muttered a few words about Rodney and his 'muddle'.

The potatoes are gathered in at last, tucked behind an eiderdown of straw bales in a pinky-brown mountain at Home Farm. Now they will be sorted and bagged, and the scenes that I remember on first coming to Lyndon will be re-enacted. John collects the 'potato women' every morning at 9.00 am from a nearby village, the rattling sorting machine jerks into life, and the roaring stove casts its warmth on the little group of busy women bundled into coats, gloves and head scarves, chattering like starlings.

In a field at Redhill, a clamp of pale, creamy maize silage looks like a child's sandpit, strewn with the dinky toys of tractors, trailers and the Sambron.

To furnish the house in the Lake District before Christmas we hired a thirty-five-hundredweight van in Riverton. While I worked at Home Farm on Friday afternoon, John and Roger loaded it with spare beds, chairs, tables, bedding and crockery. At 8.30 pm John and I were on the road. The children, absorbed in the TV, hardly noticed our departure. Rufus, the Red Setter, squeezed into the cab and finished the journey on my knee, keeping me warm. At 1.30 am we ate fish and chips in a motorway cafe. The road on the last stretch is uphill and winding. There was nothing on the rood but crackling leaves.

We climbed stiffly out of the van at 3.00 am to a still silence and the pure, dry air. I lit the fire and we took out the mattress, strategically placed last, then not wanting to wait until the morning, unloaded everything else. At 5.00 am we flung ourselves on the bed, *just* twenty-four hours after I had left my bed the day before. By 8.00 pm on Sunday we were home again, rested, refreshed, and spiritually and physically satisfied. The house, simply but adequately furnished, awaits the arrival and approval of the family.

A blind calf was born at Quincey's, its eyes mere slits. It can feed and will go for veal.

Bob has had another row with John. This time it is over the silage at Owlnest. He did not mention it in his phone call on Monday evening. On Tuesday morning I stood and looked at the wall of black silage overhanging the good layer of first cut, and wondered what I was supposed to do about it. The cows will not eat it, and John hopes it is only the outer layer that is bad. Apart from the waste, it blocks up the lagoon if it is scraped into it. I had forked down a part of it when I glimpsed Bob crossing the yard for his milk. He was still furious and did not see why he should spend an hour a day forking it down when it is not his fault that it is rotten. In spite of his attitude, and his feelings towards John, and vice versa, and his feelings towards me (and goodness knows what they *really* are), I do like him. I certainly sympathise with him this time. The milk tanker had come early so I gave him some of my milk.

I met Simon and the builder at Owlnest after work to discuss the alterations and decorations to be done prior to our moving there. It is all unreal. The date of the move from Hazelwood is fixed and the removal van is booked.

*27 November*

Each year all the men on the farm are treated to a free supper and drinks at a local pub, the modern equivalent to trestle tables in a barn flowing with beer and pies *à la* Bruegel.

Last year, and for the first time, wives were invited. John and I arrived at the pub together. The wives, carefully dressed for the occasion, grouped together. I joined them while John moved round each group of people. Work seems to be a taboo subject at the social gatherings, except in the most general way, when it is permissible to mention an enormous calf, or a field that was a real problem to harvest. Behaviour is controlled and I have never seen anyone flirting. We played darts after the supper and the student was teased about his diet. He is a good-humoured lad and liked by everyone.

Edward sold me the tickets to a concert he could not go to. John and I went. The music reminded me so vividly and painfully of the first months of my first marriage (one of our first records) and of my happiness then, that I cried all the way through the performance.

Rain at Honeybed and the tractor brakes not working. Rodney, on being asked how he managed on the slopes, said he hadn't noticed. Harold was disgusted by the state of the tractor when he had to mend it. John was in a rage with Rodney as he had written off the back wheel tyre of the large, loaned tractor by driving over a bolt when he was scraping.

I took the children to see Owlnest for the first time – without John – and I tried to explain to them how strange he would find it and why. I had friends to lunch and showed them the estate. Then I wrapped up a few Christmas presents, found a carpet layer to move and lay our carpets, and packed up and delivered the china and breakable articles. Finally, I went to a school play.

The day at Quincey's was totally wearying. The lagoon full and pushing slurry into it is a hopeless task. What went in came splurging silently out. Anger underlay my exhaustion as I pushed the heavy wheelbarrow up the forage passage last thing at night. I reached home, told the children I didn't want to speak to anyone, took a whisky up to bed, and cried and cried with sheer exhaustion.

I talked it over with John and we pondered on how the system could be changed. I feel that John must not help me. David is a perfectionist and I want to keep up his standards, but they are beyond my capacity. John talked to Philip about the problem, which I did not want him to do, and the next time I was there, Philip came to push the forage back and do the wheelbarrowing. David is intelligent enough to have thought out the simplest system, but a new, purpose-built unit ought to be easier to run than an old, patched up and added onto place like Home Farm.

John's eldest daughter is looking after her family while her mother is on holiday. We invited her, her boyfriend, and the rest of John's children to Hazelwood for the evening. John collected a Chinese meal for eleven on his way home, and the families mingled in an easy, happy, jolly evening. I thought it would be a good idea for them to see me in *my* home before we move into Owlnest, which has been *their* home for so long. They can have nothing but memories and conflicting emotions about the place when we move in. I am full of the deepest admiration for them and the way that they are coping with the whole situation.

Colin and Geoff remove some of the bad silage from Owlnest every day, with the tractor grab.

Colin said to me, 'I suppose you'll be getting married soon. Are you getting married at Riverton?'

'Yes,' I said.

'I was married there,' he said. 'In and out in ten minutes. The room's quite nice though and, anyway, so long as you loves the person, it doesn't matter where you get married does it?'

The invitations have been written, Andrea is to come home and help us move and she will make the wedding cake. I have completed my Christmas shopping, transported the new bikes to Owlnest and have had no lunchtime sleep for a week. My life is a speeded up film. Underneath there is a calmness and a surging happiness, but there is no time to savour it. But there will be.

The dairy meeting was more of an ordeal this month. John ran through the usual items, costings, silage problems, etc., and then he brought out the rota of the Christmas holidays. David's day off falls on Christmas day and New Year's day this year and he wanted to know if he got any time off in lieu. He was fairly belligerent about it.

I thought he should, but I kept quiet.

Graham said, 'Nobody has in the past, it's just tough luck.'

By slight nods and eye glances, we made it plain that we all felt that he should get the time off, and it was decided he could take it in the summer. Then Bob, who had been getting very white and pinched-looking challenged the fact that I was away in the winter when no one had been allowed to have holidays in the winter before.

John said, 'Well, Bob, when you get married, perhaps it might be different.' Everyone laughed. John continued, 'I believe I gave you a whole month off in February to go to South Africa. And now that we have raised the subject, let us look at the holiday chart and find out how much holiday people have left.'

David had one day left, Graham was about to start a week's holiday (in winter), Bob had had all of his, and Rodney had not taken any of his. I stated that I had had five and a half days off since joining Lyndon and I would be taking one day when I moved house from Hazelwood to Owlnest. The rest of this year's holiday I wanted to put onto next year for our visit to New Zealand.

The situation having been diffused, the meeting ended early.

Bob came over to me and assured me that, 'It is nothing personal,

Alison, I just felt it was the principle of the thing, saying one thing and doing another.'

I wondered what I really thought; what anyone really thought, and what they would go home and tell their wives. Since the row with Bob, Graham seems more sympathetic, Rodney more aggressive, and David more affable, but it may all be in my imagination.

The children went north with Edward to visit their grandparents, John and I made our wills and I saw the first Caesarian at Lyndon for eleven years.

The cow at Home Farm had been standing in her box all day. According to her records she should have calved two days ago. In the afternoon a streak of blood ran down her udder. When milking was over I haltered and examined her. The hoof of the calf had caught on the lip of her vagina, but when I put the ropes on the feet they locked inside. John came and felt and pulled, but with no result. The vet tried to pull it out and the huge forefeet and nose emerged. The calf was dead. The cow's pelvis was too small. The vet went off to get help.

John and I fetched bales of straw, stronger lights on extension leads, and buckets of hot water and soap. The vets stuck needles full of anaesthetic along the cow's spine to deaden the nerves which spread out over the sides of the animal. One of the men scraped the hair off the hide in a long line down the left side of the belly. The cow lay on her side in the straw, looking lively and kicking occasionally. John held her legs still and I held the lamp above the area to be cut. The scalpel raised a thin red line on her flank. Another stroke, and another, and the hide parted, exposing red flesh, muscles, and fat. The knife stroked again and again down the long red line. A thin spray of blood rose into the air and was immediately clamped by a colleague. Concentration was intense. The cow heaved once, and was quiet. I began to be afraid I was going to faint. Waves of nausea engulfed me, my cheeks ached with the draining of my blood, and a red mist blotted out the faces around me, voices became distant and meaningless. I leaned on the wall behind me and concentrated on holding the lamp still and bright over the steaming gash. John smiled up at me. Both vets started plunging their arms into the gurgling, swelling, bubbling, cauldron of the cow's belly. One was trying to find the womb, the other was trying to prevent the intestines from spilling out. I began to feel better. When the vet found the calf, he cut into the womb and a leg thrust up, wrapped in its membranes. Another leg poked up and the vets strained and pulled with intense effort, their hands sliding on the slippery limbs. The calf slid out, huge hindquarters smoking in the light.

'Christ, what a whopper!'

They dragged it on to the straw at the side of the box.

Rapidly, they began to shove the intestines back into the flaccid hole left in the cow. Needles and sutures were unwrapped from sterilized cases, and quickly and carefully, taking turns to ease their bent backs, they stitched her up, layer after layer, knitting her sides together, and squirting antibiotics between the stitches and injecting her rump with penicillins. The cow, on whose head I was by then sitting because of her struggles, threatened to dislodge us and our ministrations. By 10.30 pm it was finished, fresh bedding had been laid, a bucket of water left beside her, and a light left on for the night. We were then able to go to bed. She was on her feet before milking next morning.

The next day, I put two calves on her, and on the following day she went through the parlour. When the scar is healed she can go back with the herd. Harold has a new van and I have inherited his. Mine, with a hole in the floor I could put my feet through, has gone to a local farmer for £200. He seems to be keeping his hens in it.

Eight and a half tons of potatoes have been returned to Lyndon from the buyers because some are frosted inside. The riddling machine cannot distinguish between the good and the bad. The sorters have re-sorted them and sent them off again. They were returned again. John is trying to solve the problem.

The first batch of calves is down at Hazelwood in the barn.

A group of Germans is shooting at Lyndon this week. They kill an average of fifty birds a day each, and they are allowed to take away one brace. The rest are sold at £2.50 a brace – this is not a good price – to outlets such as hotels and London stores. Harold is one of the people loading for the guns. One of the high-sided trailers is set up for transporting the dead birds: it has racks to hang them on. Norman and Fred stand by the trailer, where the rows of bodies hang by the neck, their beautiful plumage is a discordant, jarring splendour amidst the carnage. The beaters stride the woods, banging the trees to drive the birds to their death.

Rumour has it that we are not to receive a bonus this year, and that there will not be the usual reception for the staff. Perhaps I saw the last.

# EPILOGUE

The wedding went ahead as planned, and we spent our brief honeymoon in the little wooden house in the Lake District, with our four children and three dogs. We have now been married for over thirty years.

Just before the following Christmas, John received six months notice to leave Lyndon. He had been there longer than any previous farm manger. The staff and John's men were shocked, and extremely supportive of us. We are still in touch with several of them. I felt I could not stay on for several reasons, so we left Lyndon together in June, having worked as hard as we ever did right up to the end of the six months.

John did get some money for unfair dismissal, and was offered similar jobs, but we decided to start a new life in the Lake District, beginning it in the little wooden house, and as we were unemployed, we spent our first months there enlarging it to house our family and friends. Our two youngest children came to live with us. Roger went to live with Edward, and Andrea went to university and then worked in journalism.

We started our own gardening business, and were then fortunate to become tenants of a small National Trust farm near Morecame Bay, which we ran organically. But all that is another story . . .

And what happened to Lyndon? The next farm manger stayed for five years, and gradually the farms changed completely. The farm house at Owlnest was let and the dairy herd moved to Quincey's; all the cow buildings were demolished. At Home Farm, the big tractor barn was taken down to be re-erected at one of the other farms. The farm house was converted into a hotel, and the corn drier and storage were dismantled. The land became a golf course. The Home Farm cottage was knocked down, and all of these cow buildings were also demolished. As for Honeybed, Steve, my predecessor, became herdsman there, but whether Honeybed was let or sold, I don't know.

The central parkland area was put down to grass, and sheep introduced for a while.

Quincey's dairy was doubled in size with three hundred cows, and was then let to a local farmer who already had a large herd elsewhere.

All the land and units outside the park, were let to individuals, so the estate was no longer managed as a whole, and ceased to make a profit after John left.